ALMOST A HUNDRED YEARS

Also by Hulda Hoover McLean:

Uncle Bert: A Biographical Portrait of Herbert Hoover

Hulda's World: A Chronicle of Hulda Minthorn Hoover, 1848–1884

Tide-drift Shells of the Waddell Beaches

Tide-drift Shells of the Monterey Bay Region

Tomorrow Is the First Day

Life at Rancho del Oso: Ranch Recollections

Painting Around the World

Paintings of Rancho del Oso

ALMOST A HUNDRED YEARS

Hulda Hoover McLean

Waddell Creek Association

Santa Cruz, California

2002

Copyright © 2002 by the Waddell Creek Association
ISBN 0-9721270-0-3
Rancho del Oso Nature and History Center
3600 Highway One, Davenport, CA 95017
Telephone 831 427-2288

First printing

Printed by DeHart's Printing Services Corporation
3265 Scott Boulevard, Santa Clara, CA 95054

Edited by Judy Steen

Designed by Stephen Pollard

Index by Jean Middleton, www.IndexEmpire.com

Cover photo by Diane West-Bourke

Foreword

by Sandy Lydon
Historian Emeritus, Cabrillo College
Aptos, California

If Hulda Hoover McLean had been born in 1956 instead of 1906, she would presently be forty-five years old and the governor of California. Or President of the United States. But, she was born in 1906, long before American women could even vote for their own president, and lived through a century that saw their horizons widen to include the highest positions of power. When she was asked at the end of the twentieth century to name the century's single most important development, she responded that it was the "growth of freedom, acceptance and encouragement of women to use their capabilities in fields of their choice."

As you read this remarkable autobiography, you will learn that Hulda never felt constrained by much of anything. And everything she chose to do she did extremely well. Artist, naturalist, writer, farmer, politician, businesswoman, wife, and mother are all titles that she has worn, and when you travel along through her incredible life, you can feel the energy that bursts forth when she focuses on a new challenge. Hulda Hoover McLean is no run-of-the-mill woman, and this is no run-of-the-mill memoir. Hulda is a savvy, tough, perceptive, smart lady.

I first met Hulda in 1976 when she and her husband Chuck began attending an Asian History class that I was teaching in preparation for a trip to Asia the following summer. She and Chuck sat toward the back of the classroom, and she didn't say much, but her brilliant essays suggested that she knew a lot more about things than I. She has a penetrating gaze, and when she looked up and raised an eyebrow or tilted her head, I knew that I was on shaky ground and had better scramble. She probably didn't know it, but she became my bellwether, and I would test and push ideas and decorum until I got a disapproving frown from Hulda, and then I would stop.

Most residents of Santa Cruz County know Hulda as "that-woman-up-the-North-Coast-who's-related-somehow-to-Herbert-Hoover." And, from that springs the notion that she was a woman born into privilege who deigned to live among the commoners of the North Coast. Even now you can hear the echoes of a British drawing room in the way she pronounces words and carefully parses her sentences. Yet, by her own admission, she was anything but a little lady when growing up. Full of mischief, she was probably labeled as "high-spirited" by those responsible for her upbringing. From the beginning she tested the boundaries that others had laid out around her.

Her autobiography is like a multi-faceted jewel, each polished surface reflecting a particular element of the times through which she traveled. The earliest is her Hoover family patrimony and the international stage upon which it played. Her father, Theodore Hoover (always "Daddy" to Hulda) was a Stanford-educated gold-mining engineer who eventually settled into the position of Dean of Stanford's Department of Engineering. During his student days he discovered the wild and beautiful Waddell Valley, and when his international mining efforts allowed, in 1913 he bought the valley. The Waddell became Theodore Hoover's touchstone and Hulda's by extension. The North Coast captured her heart during her childhood summers, and she eventually returned to spend more than half her life there.

Hulda's uncle, Herbert Hoover ("Uncle Bert"), was the thirty-first President of the United States, and when she ventured into Santa Cruz County politics in the late 1950s, she often wrote to him for advice. His counsel was sometimes very direct. During the first Christmas that she was a member of the county Board of Supervisors, she was troubled by all the gifts she received from those seeking her support. When she asked Uncle Bert how to handle these gifts, he responded tersely, "Take no gifts from anyone." When she took that suggestion to her fellow board members, they finally settled on a policy of only accepting gifts that could be consumed within twenty-four hours. That would make cigars, whiskey and fruitcake permissible, but not a chinchilla coat.

Her father's international business interests and her uncle's political career give this autobiography an international theme, from the pre-World War I submarine attacks on trans-Atlantic shipping through the attack on Pearl Harbor, to the Vietnam War, Hulda was always aware of the bigger picture.

For those of us interested in local and regional events, it is fun to watch well-known places and events reflected off Hulda's memory: the 1948 fire that roared down off Ben Lomond Mountain, the December 1955 flood that isolated the Waddell and the 1989 Loma Prieta earthquake punctuate the chronology. Her descriptions of the challenges of being the only woman on the Santa Cruz County Board of Supervisors from 1956 to 1963 are priceless.

Because we always think of Hulda and Chuck living in the Waddell, it is surprising to learn that between 1929 and 1943 they lived in Pasadena, California. During that time Hulda became involved with the Junior League and League of Women Voters. She was elected to the latter's statewide presidency in 1941, an experience that helped sharpen her political skills for her later forays into Santa Cruz County politics. Concern for her ailing father's abilities to operate the Waddell ranch property pulled the McLeans back to Santa Cruz County in 1943, and they never left.

With all of her family's international business interests and connections, one might have the impression that Hulda and Chuck were gentleman farmers, dabbling in agriculture while being nurtured by a flow of cash from elsewhere. Nothing could be farther from the truth, however, as Hulda and Chuck continually walked the narrow solvency tightrope suspended over disaster. Hulda's account of farming and ranching on Santa Cruz County's North Coast is a cautionary tale of the vagaries and difficulties of the agricultural life. Beyond the broken water lines, power outages and other discomforts of living in a remote place (she summarized it all up as "country living"), the annual crapshoot of getting the crop into the ground, harvested and out to market was always scary. And rarely profitable. However, through it all, Hulda kept her artist's eye peeled, and when one of their broccoli fields was left unharvested because the price of broccoli had collapsed, she sat down and painted the yellow bursts that heralded their failure.

And, if there's any doubt about Hulda's feelings about the Waddell Valley, one need only see how her writing fairly blooms when she begins describing the valley she loves so dearly. Beginning with those girlhood summers, Hulda began storing images of the beach, lagoon, stream, valley and redwood forests beyond. And, with her artist's eye and sense of mischief, she knocks off descriptions that forever linger: the bullheads that scurry along the bottom of the stream, leaving "clouds of sand"; the "short-tempered" yellow jackets, or the evening bats, "flying mice with worried faces." She includes a short list of recipes, including one for barbecuing rattlesnake. (Yes, she agrees that it tastes like chicken, albeit stringy chicken.)

Her father passed on his love of the Waddell to Hulda and her children, but the centrifugal forces of inheritance taxes and marginal agriculture forced the McLeans to the realization that the only way the valley could ever be preserved would be to move it into public hands. Eventually, over a number of years, most of the canyons, valley and finally the family home became part of what we now know as the Rancho Del Oso sector of Big Basin Redwoods State Park. And for those who think it is easy to move property into public ownership with any guarantee that the public agencies will manage the land with wisdom and care, be sure to read the section of the book describing the transfer.

If one had to make a list of Hulda's legacies, certainly the creation of the Rancho del Oso Nature and History Center, the Skyline to the Sea Trail, and the now public beach at the mouth of Waddell Creek would be at the top. Every year thousands of people play, hike, meditate and commune with a natural world that was conserved and preserved by her family. But I think that her greater legacy is her life story itself, her relentless pursuit of meaning that led her into art, politics, science and literature. Contrary to the old saw that one becomes a "jack of all trades and master of none," she mastered them all. But, consider for a moment what might have happened had she grown up at a time when being a woman and Governor/Senator/President was generally accepted by both politicians and the public.

Hulda concludes this work with a delightful over-the-shoulder look at her life and offers (though admitting her doubts about the usefulness of doing so) some pieces of advice. "Wash the dishes before you go to bed." "The time to hurry is before you leave the house." Or the haiku-like "Donate to worthy projects and to street musicians." But the one that could be the coda of Hulda's century on this earth is the simple suggestion "Leave things better than you found them." Hulda has done that. And how.

Preface

Every life is a tapestry woven of important events and trivialities, hopes and despair, joy and sadness. Every life is a story: it should be written down. Individual lives are the essence of history.

Writing my story has been fun and hard work. It has been a joy to return to the sunshine of a young family. It has been interesting to revisit, with the experience of years, so many events and undertakings, even though it has included some painful hours reliving difficult times. Facts and dates have been easy to check because I kept copies of journal letters written first to Mother-in-law Lillian McLean, beginning in 1931 when her first grandson was born, and then to my lifelong friend, Mally Proctor. Our albums of pictures, starting with my babyhood, have woven faces and places into the fabric of memory.

I am especially grateful to Rob and Jean McLean for harnessing computer magic to prepare narrative and illustrations, and to Diane West-Bourke, who insisted that this chronicle be written and who enriched its progress with her advice. My thanks also to Alverda Orlando, who was responsible for the initial stages of development, and to Kirk and Pat Smith, who shepherded the book to publication. The professional work of Judy Steen as editor and Stephen Pollard as designer was matched only by their personal interest in the project. Family and friends have helped me immeasurably with their memories, suggestions, and creative copy reading. To every one of these, I am sincerely grateful.

Contents

Hulda in her mother's arms, with Mindy looking on; 1906

1
Childhood
1906–1925

Mostly London, 1906–1917

I WAS BORN Hulda Brooke Hoover, several weeks late, in our home in Palo Alto, California, on August 19, 1906. Daddy didn't wait for me; he had returned to his mining engineer office in London, where he worked with his brother, Herbert Hoover. Mummie, five-year-old sister Mindy, and I followed when I was six weeks old. Sister Louise was born in London eighteen months later.

What are my earliest memories? They are of our flat in St. James Place, watching a nurse mix formula for baby sister, feeding goldfish by the window of the stair landing, hiding on a small shelf in the toy closet, eating dried prunes, riding in a pram with the baby, playing in a crib with the Noah's ark and balloons Daddy brought me to brighten whooping cough. It was fun to puncture the balloons with the noses of the animals. I remember watching what I have thought to be the coronation procession of King George, but which more likely was a Lord Mayor's procession. (I was sitting in the lap of Signor Antonio de Grassi, a musician friend of the family, and wiggling and wiggling because I did not like the way he smelled.) Daddy's office on old London Wall Street was filled with his friends. We watched from the windows, interminably, until horses and ornate carriages, plumes and swords appeared through the crowd.

When I was four, we moved from the St. James Place flat to a five-floor home near Kensington Gardens. Memories here begin with listening to artist Dorothy Ward tell me stories while she painted a miniature water-color-on-ivory portrait of me, a wide-eyed, serious little four-year-old with red-gold curls, wearing a daisy chain around her neck. For an exhibition Dorothy painted another portrait of me, wearing a brown velvet bonnet.

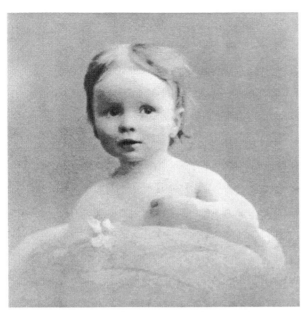

Hulda at nineteen months, 1908

I loved to sit and live her tales of enchanted castles and fairies. Louise was not charmed so easily. When it came her turn to pose, she was sometimes pulled from her hiding place under a bed.

We lived in modest elegance. It was during the last years of Edwardian society, when affluent families had a lifestyle of three worlds, separate but intertwined. There was the nursery world of children, nanny, and governess. There was the downstairs servants' world of cook, scullery maid, parlor maid, upstairs maid, nursery maid, and gardener. And there was the upstairs world of parents and their friends.

Mindy, bossy and beautiful, Louise, an angel-faced nuisance, and I lived with our nanny on the nursery floor. Mornings we were awakened by the nursery maid lighting the kindling for the coal fires. There were two fireplaces in our long bedroom, one at each end. There were many fireplaces in the house, one in nearly every room. They were the only source of heat, except for round smelly kerosene stoves used to warm bathrooms.

I don't know how we escaped watchful eyes, but sometimes, if there had been a grown-up party the evening before, Louise and I crept downstairs early in the morning and drank the sweet drops left in the bottom of tiny crystal glasses.

Afternoons we put on our coats and bonnets, leggings and mittens and went for a walk. Often our destination was nearby Kensington Gardens. We took a paper bag full of crumbs to feed the ducks. Cousins Allan and Herbert Hoover Jr. might join us there with their nanny. Allan, a few months younger than I, and Herbert, about Mindy's age, lived with Aunt Lou and Uncle Bert in the big "Red House" on Horton Street. It had a large garden where we played in the swing under a mulberry tree. Allan, Herbert, and Mindy sailed boats on the Round Pond. I made daisy chains

Hulda and Louise, 1910

in the grass and talked to the squirrels. We played tree-tag and ball or sat on the benches and paid a penny a seat to the ticket collector or watched the horsemen on Rotten Row. Rotten Row, the equestrian path, was a verbal degeneration of "Route du Roi."

Sometimes we went up High Street and bought celluloid birds, tiny teddy bears, and the horrible little pincushions and trays with which the English litter their bureaus. When we picked where we wanted to go, Louise would choose the penny bazaar, where we could buy six tiny naked white dolls for a penny. I usually chose a street at the edge of the slums (our governess, Miss Pickering, would not let us go further in). Slums fascinated me. I resolved that when I grew up I would get a big house full of bathtubs, gather all the dirty urchins in London, and give them baths.

Occasionally on our walks we would come across a stretch of street where straw was laid thickly over the cobblestones. This meant that there was someone seriously ill nearby, and the clatter of horses' hooves and wooden wheels were being muffled out of consideration.

There was dancing-class in the drawing room, with the polka and the Highland fling. It took baby Louise a while to understand that "one, two, three, hop" was a direction for the polka and that real counting was "one, two, three, four." There were hours in the garden surrounded by high ivy-covered walls, and there were dark afternoons by the fire in the nursery.

We spent the time, between our nursery tea and the grown-ups' dinner, downstairs in the library with Mummie and Daddy. Daddy sat at his desk smoking his pipe. Mummie sat by the fire, often reading to us—

Miniature of Hulda, watercolor on ivory, by Dorothy Ward; 1910

Hiawatha, Wind in the Willows, Idylls of the King. I had the privilege of filling Daddy's pipe with tobacco kept on the dining-room mantelpiece in a big blue stone jar from Cornwall, until, in an experimental mood, I carefully curled one of my hairs in the bottom of the bowl. The experiment was not appreciated.

Our house was in a parklike area across the road from Holland House, one of London's "great houses." Once or twice our canary flew out the bathroom window, and we appeared in Holland House gardens with a butterfly net and empty cage. Poor bird, he met an untimely end, squashed on a window ledge. I ran across him years later when putting fresh moth crystals in Daddy's collection of bird skins.

Our house was tall and square, built of brick, and covered in Virginia creeper. It was surrounded by an ivy-covered stone wall, had a small lawn in front and a larger garden in back. Counting the basement, which contained the kitchen, servants' dining room, and related rooms, it had five stories. Each floor had basically the same plan: a winding stairway, a wide hall, and four square rooms. The ground floor had living and dining rooms; the next floor had Mummie and Daddy's bedroom and guest rooms; on the next floor were the nursery rooms; and on the top floor were maids' rooms, a trunk room, and a large rainy-day playroom.

Another miniature of Hulda by Dorothy Ward; 1911

The plumbing was definitely period. I remember sitting on it, looking up at the pull-chain, and thinking, "When I'm seven, I'll be able to reach that high." The house was not planned with any idea of convenience. Carrying food from the kitchen to the dining room, the butler had to walk down a short hall, climb a flight of stairs, and go along a long hall to the dining room.

I was, most of the time, a good little girl and ate whatever was served to me. However, I couldn't swallow spinach. To a child's palate it can taste bitter. There was a small shelf-like place under the dining room tabletop and I would put my spinach there. It was gone by the next meal. That did not seem strange to me at the time. Later I realized that one of the maids

Hulda, Nanny, Louise and Mindy in the garden
of the house in Kensington; 1910

must have sympathized with my plight. Although we had Sunday noon
dinner downstairs, we children ate most of our meals in the nursery,
which was three flights of stairs from the kitchen. At teatime the governess blew down a tube in the wall, and the tube whistled in the kitchen.
You could talk down the tube and understand what other people were

Mindy, Hulda and Louise, with dolls; London, 1911

bellowing up through it, if you had an imaginative ear.

There was a glass conservatory off the library. In its moist warmness, Mummie grew ferns and precious geraniums, and Daddy raised goldfish. His engineer's eye was more tuned to pipes for aeration and circulating water systems than to aquarium beauty. On winter mornings Jack Frost's pictures on the glass were more exquisite than all the ferns. The conservatory opened out onto a small iron balcony with steps winding down to the garden. There was a moment on those iron filigree back steps when my mind first sensed infinity. I thought, "When I am grown up I shall remember this, and remember that I knew I would remember it, and remember that I knew I would know I would remember it . . ."; and no matter how many times I could bring the future and the present together, I would always be able to do it more times in the future.

The scullery opened into the garden. Sometimes the scullery maid brought her work out and sat in the sunshine shelling peas or stringing beans. She would let us help her until we ate too many of them.

Occasionally Louise and I would go up to the fourth floor maids' rooms. They were full of bric-a-brac and sentimental atrocities. They

7

Herbert Jr., Mindy, Hulda, Aunt Lou and Louise in Uncle Bert's motor car;
Miss Pickering is at the far right. Uncle Bert can just barely be seen
behind the steering wheel; England, 1910

smelled of powder and perfume and tea and closed windows. Once I asked a maid if I could pin her hat on when she was getting dressed for her afternoon off. As I had thought that grown-ups stuck hatpins through their heads like through a pincushion, the result was staccato!

Standing on tiptoes to look down, from the nursery landing we could see all the way to the first floor. Louise and I took our teddy bears, golliwogs (golliwogs were a bit like later years' Raggedy Andys, only they were black with wooly hair—we loved them), and other more or less indestructible soft people and dropped them down. Then we would tenderly gather them up and use them for patients in our nursery hospital. We put them to bed and bandaged heads and fed them caraway seeds and "hundreds and thousands" candies from pill bottles.

My babyhood ended consciously on my fifth birthday. In bed with measles, I was filled with the weight of my years. I have never felt older. I had stopped being a baby and was a little girl and I thought I should become more accomplished. Fired with the desire to be in all things admirable, I labored diligently and futilely to draw perfect circles.

These London years were studded with bright holidays. There was a heavenly and undisciplined interlude with cousins Allan and Herbert in Wales. Our governess must have been on vacation. The prominent mem-

Miss Pickering with Louise and Hulda; Kensington Gardens, London, 1912

ory is freedom, freedom to go barefoot and to run away from Louise and to climb down the steep cliff stairs from the lavender-scented cottage to the beach. I think we must have been in the lovingly permissive care of Aunt Lou.

On Eastbourne vacations we lived in a boarding house that smelled of brussels sprouts. The cook left salt out of the porridge. I sat on the beach and drew pictures of the lighthouse. At Chorley Woods there were damp country lanes through woods carpeted with primroses and bluebells. Fearsome cows tenanted the pastures. Signs on gates said, "Trespassers will be prosecuted," interpreted by me as "Trespassers will be executed," a drastic combination of the Lord's Prayer and Alice in Wonderland.

There were family excursions with Uncle Bert in his car, a rare and wonderful vehicle. With cousins Allan and Herbert, we picked beechnuts, fished for minnows, sailed boats, caught butterflies, and rode on a merry-go-round.

There were frequent Sunday trips with Daddy to the London Zoo. From a trip to Russia, he had brought us a small baby bear, but the cub's disposition had been soured by hardships en route, becoming unsuited as a pet for little girls (had he ever been?). The London Zoo got him, and we had tickets to visit him and to ride on elephants and camels. My memory of Daddy during this period is mostly of him returning from mining trips to Finland, Burma, Mexico, Belgium, and China. He brought queer, exciting toys home for us—a fragrant piece of sandalwood, a small carved elephant with ivory tusks, an aluminum box with a peacock on the lid, nested Russian dolls, flower-covered porcelain slippers too fragile for dolls to wear.

Often, Mummie went on journeys with him, and once we all did. In 1912, when I was five, we went to Australia. Because it was going to be hot, Mummie had matching seersucker dresses and bloomers made for us. They were scratchy. Louise's were blue and mine a henna color I detested. Because I had gold auburn hair, Mummie was convinced that I should wear shades of brown. We also wore "cholera belts," six-inch strips of flannel around our tummies to ward off the dreaded disease of foreign countries.

Mummie must have had an awful time. I had croup and the maid, Martha, had a serious appendix attack. The broadening influences of travel were largely lost on a child of five. The trip forms a jumbled pattern in my memory: the smell of the ship, the sting of spray, phosphorescent waves in our wake, sharks slim and ominous in blue or yellow water, glistening native divers, and armless little boys. I remember Mount Etna burning brightly against the black sky, bustling colorful odorous ports, rickshaw rides, pink coral in Naples, and Turkish delight sweets in Port Said, sold by men in red fezzes. In Gibraltar I was terrified while being carried down the side of the ship on a rope ladder by a sailor. And, always, there was the sound of music at night.

On the ship was a famous actor, Henry Irving, a kindly man who played with us. There were lesser, nameless friends—the man who sang "One More River to Cross" and the kind lady who brought me toilet paper when I was trying to make my need known by calling to Mummie, two decks above.

Australia was composed of flies, hot sand, ants, bright birds, pink pepper berries, and the fragrance of eucalyptus. There was a white cockatoo that thought that Louise's pink toes were fat worms. The hotel was full of mosquitoes and more flies. My first poem was composed in the hot dining room, looking at flies floating in the melted butter.

> My buttery fingers I wiped in my hair
> While I nearly fell off the chair

Mummie was stunned by her gifted daughter.
There was no fresh milk. There is no way to make a child eat or drink

something she does not want to. However, Mummie persuaded me to drink canned milk if it had peanut butter melted in it. Louise adopted a broad Australian accent that amused Daddy but distressed Mummie. She kept it for more than a year before it gradually disappeared.

I was six when Miss Pickering came into our lives and my heart. Not much more than a girl herself, Mabel Pickering was our governess for eight years and later came back to us to take care of Mindy's boys. In retrospect, it seems as though she was always with us. At bedtime it was Miss Pickering who heard our prayers, tucked us in, and left the door open a crack so it would not be too dark. Our childhood prayer was "Now I lay me down to sleep, I pray the Lord my soul to keep, If I should die before I wake, I pray the Lord my soul to take." A terrifying prayer. Miss Pickering alleviated my fear by assuring me that my guardian angel would watch out for me while I slept.

Any remembrance of my childhood lacks a sense of reality if she wasn't there. Her neat, prim prettiness, her calm voice, her gentle scolding, her steadfast affection, and her quick feet and busy hands are always part of the background as memory emerges from the haze of those early London years. Miss Pickering had numerous gentle rules you must live by if you wanted to grow up to be a lady. At that time Emmeline Pankhurst, the prominent pioneer suffragette, was determined to get people to pay attention to her battle for women's rights. She and her followers did a great deal of shouting and marching and very much annoyed the London constabulary. Mummie commented that such activity was unladylike. Emmeline and her friends were jailed. When they went on a hunger strike, they were force-fed, which the nursery maid described to us graphically. I decided that it would be prudent to pay more attention to the rules for being ladylike. It wasn't until I was well into adolescence that I began to appreciate Emmeline's foolhardy courage. From then on, I have been selective in deciding just what rules I will follow. Emmeline eventually prevailed. In 1918 English married women over the age of thirty were permitted to vote. Meantime, twenty thousand American women paraded in Washington for suffrage. "Don't they have anything better to do?" asked newspaper editorials. However, they, too, prevailed, and in 1920 American women over twenty-one won suffrage. Several states had it earlier, including the first one, Wyoming, in 1869, and, later, California, in 1911.

My education on life and public events came mostly on Miss Pickering's days off when the nursery maid took care of us. She was gifted with a

Daddy with daughters on beach;
Eastbourne, England, 1911

talent for the dramatic. She told us of the suffering of Peary's men on their trip to the North Pole and of the drowning people's screams as the Titanic sank. Sometimes she took us to the park and bought sweet biscuits, which tasted vaguely like soap, and she read us "penny dreadfuls" about maidens wrecked on desert islands or pursued by villainous men or in the clutches of a greedy uncle or, perhaps, all three at once. They were almost as fascinating as Dorothy Ward's stories of castles and fairies.

Early in 1913, after a trip to America, Daddy came home and spread the contents of a blue bandanna out on his desktop. There were curly shells, a tiny down-filled nest not much larger than a walnut shell, tree cones almost small enough to fit in a thimble, and a crisp transparent tube that Daddy explained was a snake's skin which it had outgrown and wiggled out of. He had brought them from California, near a town named Santa Cruz. He said that we would all go to visit the ranch soon. I asked, "What ranch? Where is California?"

Casa del Oso, 1914

In 1898 when Daddy was a student at Stanford University, he rode horseback over the hills from Stanford to the coast on a surveying trip and fell in love with the Waddell Valley. He decided that one day he would buy a place there for his family home. That same year, he telegraphed his childhood love, Mildred Crew Brooke, in Baltimore, to come West and marry him. They hadn't seen each other for seven years, but she came. He graduated from Stanford and they went to London, where Daddy worked as a mining engineer with brother Bert. They prospered. In 1913 Daddy bought the ranch in Waddell Valley that he had been dreaming about for those fifteen years.

Mummie and Daddy decided to take us all to spend the summer at this ranch in California. In the spring of 1914 Mummie set out with her three small daughters, a teenage maid, and Miss Pickering. Daddy had suddenly been called to Burma on mining business but would join us later.

First there was the long voyage across the angry Atlantic Ocean, then a wonder-filled trip across the continent. We children accepted adventure as it came, but the two English girls must have speculated occasionally about what they had gotten themselves into. Everything was different for them. There was mile upon mile of rolling prairie instead of neat English farms. There were towering mountains instead of English hills. The colored porters and conductors were strange and frightening, especially when they told us that the beef on the bill of fare was buffalo meat and that we must watch out for wild Indians along the tracks.

When we reached Santa Cruz, we stayed for two days at the old St. George Hotel while Mummie bought a houseful of furniture from Leask's store for the home she had built by cablegram from London. The furniture was all loaded on a big wagon drawn by four horses that set out, in advance of us, up the Coast Road to the ranch. The St. George was a Victorian high-ceilinged hotel furnished with antiques. The bathrooms, added recently, were spacious, raised little rooms. We explored the town, with its wealth of gingerbread houses, and we picnicked on the beach. We ate ice-cream cones, a delightful new discovery.

We took the train to Davenport, where Mummie bought pots and pans and other odds and ends from the general store. They were loaded, with us, into a wagon drawn by two gray horses, which took us another ten miles over a winding road through redwoods, over Gianone Hill to the quiet blue Pacific Ocean, and along it to the big gulch of the Waddell. I was certain that we had come to the outer edge of the earth.

We turned into the road up the valley and came to our home, the Brown House (nostalgically named for Daddy's childhood cottage). It was so new there was sawdust on the floor. It was filled with the fragrance of the redwood from which it was built. There were smooth cool walls and floors and the spicy taste of curled shavings on the floor. There was the warm beauty of the valley and grandeur of the hills. The air had a perfume I had never before experienced. The scent was ocean spray and redwood, blended with pine and fir, the incense of burning leaves, a suspicion of skunk, shale dust, damp leaf mold and stagnant marsh, the warm essence from haystacks and pasture and chaparral, the cool breath of creek and fern-lined springs. It is a perfume I am thirsty for when I am away and that greets and fills me whenever I return.

The day we arrived, Louise and I, infected by the general busy bustle of settling in, made a garden ready for lilies and strawberries in a spot that turned out to be the front path. Uncle Jimmy Hyde had made the long rough trip from Palo Alto in his automobile. He had brought a tremendous picnic lunch for us all, which we ate by the creek.

James Hyde, "Uncle Jimmy," and his wife, "Aunt Bessie," had been Mummie and Daddy's Stanford and, later, London friends. He was a huge and frighteningly jovial man; in London I hid when he came. Aunt Bessie was sweet and motherly. He later became a lecturer in Daddy's Mining Department at Stanford.

We collected experiences industriously. We were stung by nettles, frightened by cows, warned about rattlesnakes, and delighted by barn kittens. We went to bed in cots lined up in the spacious spicy attic, under new blankets and blue quilts. Before we went to sleep we listened for a few minutes to the murmur of the creek, the muted booming of the surf, and the whisper of trees.

The valley was full of strange animals, plants, and insects. We adopted them all. Miss Pickering stood up courageously to spiders, snakes, and wildcats, but the flea situation filled her with horror. In England, fleas are not respectable. The ranch was currently being farmed by two young Swiss cousins, the Rodonis, who were raising pigs. Fleas were rampant in farm buildings. A sortie into a barn after kittens rewarded us with a coating of fleas. They only used me as transportation, evidently not caring for the way I tasted, but they dined on Miss Pickering and Louise. In these modern days of insecticides, problems like this are easily solved, but in 1914 fleas had to be pursued and removed one by one. Farm activities were fascinating. Milking time, baby pigs, and all the other marvels of the barnyard were strange and wonderful. Louise, always less naïve than I, collected amazing information there. When she told me that babies came out of their mothers, that fact struck me as happily reasonable. I asked Mummie for confirmation, and she said, puzzlingly, "Yes, but don't tell Allan." I thought the news was worth spreading.

The creek was another center of curiosity. Barefoot, we splashed up and down it, feeling slippery pebbles, smooth sand, gooey ooze, and, occasionally, something squirmy between our toes. We caught tadpoles and salamanders. We put miscellaneous eggs in glass jars and watched them hatch into a variety of bugs and pollywogs. Often I lay on my stomach on the rough planks of a bridge, looking, between the cracks, through my reflection to life below. There were trout, still as shadows, until, startled, they darted into deep water. Tiny sticklebacks guarded their nests in the

The Brown House at Rancho del Oso, built of heart redwood
from plans Mummie cabled from London; 1914

shallow water's edge, chasing away foe and innocent bystander alike. Caddis worms moved leisurely over the bottom in their houses of twigs or pebbles. Bullheads raised a cloud of sand on the bottom as they scavenged. Water snakes glided across the water, leaving a V-shaped wake. Copper-brown salamanders with green eyes and tiny hands sauntered across the bottom or wiggled through the water. They left their egg clumps of green jelly attached to waterweeds where they hatched into green striped pollywogs. Water tigers, larva of big dragonflies, lurked among willow roots, a hazard to small minnows. Frogs swam by, using a matronly breaststroke. Turtles paddled upstream. Bright blue and green dragonflies skimmed on gossamer wings over the surface, touching it briefly to deposit eggs. Wraithlike water-skaters skittered on the surface, seen more distinctly in their shadows than in themselves. Crazy bugs, little round silver beetles, scooted around in circles, getting nowhere in a desperate hurry. Sometimes, long spawning salmon or steelhead, giants among the other inhabitants, moved majestically upstream. An occasional water ouzel dipped and hopped on the rocks, or a kingfisher screamed as he left his perch over the stream.

I often arrived home wet. I had leaned too far over the creek or waded into a deep unseen hole or I had slid off a slippery rock. Once I tripped with a skirtful of kittens. As I struggled out of the creek, they tried to climb onto my head.

We went swimming in the deep pools, puffing and splashing in icy coldness. We did not swim in the ocean; its undertow was too dangerous and anyway, it was even colder than the creek. The shallow lagoon, warmed by sunshine, was the best place for swimming. On the beach we collected shells along the tide line and delighted in more unusual salvage—green glass floats from faraway Asian fishing boats, whale bones, crates and barrels. (Once, in 1917, we found two hundred pounds of fresh butter sealed in a wooden box, undoubtedly lost from the deck of a ship. It was very useful in feeding the crew of men building the farmhouse and barns.)

We slid down steep smooth sand dunes, fished from the rocks jutting out into the sea, watched jewel-like life in tide pools, smelled the heliotrope-scented purple and yellow sand verbenas, saw sandpipers' tracks edging the wave-line with lace, listened to the cry of gulls, and felt the sting of wind-blown sand on our bare legs. My skin was not made for sunshine. Mindy and Louise went home from the beach with glowing tans: I went home sticky, magenta, and limp. I preferred misty days when the sea was pearl gray and the white gulls flew close to the foam.

Trails through the woods were inexhaustible sources of adventure. When we walked silently, we would see the birds and animals that lived there. Many, many birds. Daddy knew them by sight and by song. We grew up among birds: saucy chickadees with bandit masks, bushtits and warblers who traveled with the chickadees on their daily rounds, tiny wrens bobbing in the bushes, song sparrows on fence posts, finches in the trees, quail taking off with an explosive whir of wings, jays raucously warning of our intrusion, flocks of pygmy nuthatches fluttering high in the pines. It surprised me that most of my friends did not have bird acquaintances. They didn't even know sparrows from thrushes.

A crashing in the underbrush meant a startled deer. We saw them rarely in the woods but a herd at a time in our fields. They were a pest in crops and gardens. The Rodonis hunted them for meat and to protect their crops. Once they sat me on a dead deer and took a picture. I was scowling, and no wonder. The deer was covered with fleas and ticks.

Cuddlesome-looking bobcats would be seen watching at gopher holes or bounding along a trail. Coyotes, like thin dogs, were shadows in the distance. An occasional gray fox poked around looking for mice. Squirrels scolded from trees and chipmunks ran along fence rails. Badgers dug deep burrows in the fields chasing ground squirrels; brush rabbits flicked their cottontails as they disappeared into the bushes. Skunks sauntered arrogantly up the road.

Snakes were fascinating. Most of them were yellow-striped garter snakes who ate pill bugs and minnows. There were also larger garter snakes striped with red and blue. There were shiny earth-colored milk snakes, tiny red ring-necked coral snakes, small boas that could be worn like bracelets. There were long gopher snakes whose patterns were similar to a rattlesnake's and who bit with tiny needle-sharp teeth when I tried to shove them down gopher holes to do their job. There were rattlesnakes whose checkered skins in light and shadow made them hard to see on a sun-speckled trail. More than once we stepped over one before he startled us with his sharp warning. Fortunately, rattlesnakes at the ranch were sluggish and unsociable; they spent their energy, when disturbed, in getting away. I never saw one strike except when teased by some stupid person or foolhardy cat.

I spent hours watching insects. We found big ceanothus moths and their silver cocoons. There were innumerable crawly things to be found when I shook a branch or turned over a log. Spiders spun their dew-

Aunt Lou and five Hoover cousins: Mindy, Herbert, Hulda, Louise and Allan.
Rancho del Oso, 1915

spangled webs across trails or made small tunnels in clay banks. Trapdoor
spiders could be enticed out of their burrows with a straw. Pill bugs rolled
up into tiny shining balls. Six-inch yellow redwood slugs glided over leaf
mold. Butterflies were everywhere.

All year around there were wildflowers. Most flamboyant were blazing
California poppies, but my favorites were delicate pink fairy lanterns, so
much like Mummie's rose-quartz necklace. There was redwood sorrel
with its vinegar taste, white-flowered crisp Indian lettuce, dramatic wake-
robin, and pungent ginger. There were myriad toadstools and mushrooms. We ate yellow fluted chanterelles, white-fleshed puffballs, and
meadow mushrooms. We were unfamiliar with the many other edible

Butterfly expedition, with Hulda, Miss Pickering, Mindy and Louise;
Rancho del Oso, 1916

varieties. After a rain, the forest was full of these fungi and I loved the beauty or ugliness of them, delicate blue ones, dark red umbrellas, orange ruffles, sticky black balls, and the large red, white-speckled ones on which leprechauns surely sat.

When we played in the meadows, I usually found a shady spot while Mindy and Louise chased butterflies in the sun. I watched ants, listened to crickets, smelled warm grass, and chewed on wild leaves. There were many strange tastes to be found in the woods and fields. It is surprising I was not poisoned.

Bats, flying mice with worried faces, interested me. Sometimes we would find them behind a loose board. They liked to get under the shingles next to the warm chimney. If Louise and I climbed the steep slippery roof (where was Miss Pickering?) and poked gently under these shingles next to the chimney, a bat or two would sometimes find its way into the big attic, which was our communal bedroom in the Brown House. Soon there would be a great commotion with Miss Pickering, the maid, and Mindy running around the attic with brooms and butterfly nets. Louise and I, an appreciative audience, would watch from the beds. I wondered why they didn't just open a window and let the bats find their own way out.

Louise and I were often mistaken for twins. As a matter of fact, we felt much like twins, were very close, and knew each other's thoughts and dreams. The fact that her dreams were confused, drifted and re-formed like flotsam on the sea, and that her anomalous acts sometimes dismayed me did not reduce my love for her or my feeling of responsibility for her, then or throughout our lives.

A special joy (then and always) was when I would walk in the woods alone, watching, listening, and hoping I would see a mountain lion. I would play a game, finding how much I could know by discovering and trying to interpret clues around me. There were tracks in the dust. A doe and two fawns had walked the road; a possum and a bobcat and a coyote had been there. A raccoon had left scat on a rock and the coyote had left his in the road. The bobcat, like all cats, was neater and had hidden his. There were small rodent tracks and the shining curved track of a snake crossing the trail. There were quail and smaller bird tracks and intricate embroidery of beetle tracks. A rabbit track ended in a flurry with the bobcat tracks. Looking higher, I saw ceanothus, California lilac, pruned by hungry deer. In the bordering orchard were apple trees with orderly rings of three-eighths-inch holes neatly drilled by sapsuckers. Apple blossoms were probed by honeybees; I watched the direction of their flights home. Once, near the creek, were the remains of a deer, scratch-covered with leaves, sure sign of the recent presence of a mountain lion. Jays above me made their usual raucous announcement of my intrusive presence, ensuring that I would see no shy wildlife. If I sat quiet and motionless, the jays lost interest. A sociable flock of bushtits slowly made its way towards me, wary but curious. Rabbits came from bushes beside the road. A butterfly poised briefly on my knee. The increasingly vertical slant of sunlight through the branches would tell me that it was noon. As I made my way home to lunch, jays picked up my trail and resumed their warning.

I had longed for a tabby kitten ever since Miss Pickering read to me about one called Peter. One day, Jarvis Rodoni brought three kittens to us, and here was my Peter at last! No kitten was ever more loved, and no cat more well behaved and loving. He brought me his mice and gophers to admire. He climbed through the upstairs window to sleep with me. He followed me everywhere, until he was grown up and had an agenda of his own. Even then, when I called, he would come from the field for conversation and affection. After Peter, there were more kittens and cats, many of them descendants of Peter and some of them adopted barn cats. I remember Mummie once saying, "Hulda, fifteen cats are enough!" They were "outside cats." Mummie did not hold with cats in the house (she didn't know about Peter at night). They went about their jobs of catching mice and gophers and, evenings, gathered by the back door for milk and scraps. All of them except Junior. As a kitten, Junior had lost his leg in a gopher trap. Daddy adopted him as an "inside cat." He still ate gophers; Daddy caught them for him.

On summer nights Louise and I slept on the wide upstairs porch that used to wrap around two sides of the Brown House. We'd be snug under the patchwork quilts Mummie made, covered by a waterproof sheet against the morning dew. Our noses would be cold in the night air. We watched bats swoop and cry in their high voices and would listen to the other night noises. We'd name the trees on the hilltop horizon and choose a star for our own. We'd wish on falling stars; occasionally the sky was full of them. I might make a wish that we'd have rack of lamb and pan-roasted potatoes for Sunday dinner, or that Mindy would be less bossy, or that Louise's cut finger would stop hurting and, over and over again, that I would see a mountain lion as Louise and Miss Pickering had seen in the pasture above the Brown House. In late spring, very occasionally, we'd hear the marrow-chilling mating scream of a lion. It would make me want to lock the door and hide under the bed, which I knew was silly. Because Louise was so frightened, I would make up a story to comfort her, perhaps about her favorite raindrop sprites who lived behind the moon. Some nights, when mist obscured the stars, the sky would be faintly illumined every ten seconds by the light from Año Nuevo lighthouse, three miles away. Many years later, when I was on a cruise ship far out at sea, I saw this ray of ten-second light, and it gave me a warm, coming-home feeling.

The ranch, in 1914, was a world by itself. No neighbors for miles around; dusty roads that rain made impassable; no telephone; no cars except for a rare affluent visitor and the daily mail stage, when it could get through. We lived in an isolated paradise.

World War I, 1914–1918

We were at the ranch when World War I broke out on August 14, 1914. So much happened after that, that my mind is a bit confused about what happened when. Daddy, who was supposed to be with us by that time, was busy in London, collecting the fragments of his and Uncle Bert's fortune all over the world and winding up the business affairs of Uncle Bert, whose volunteer work of saving the starving people of besieged Belgium left no time for his private business.

Aunt Lou and cousins Herbert and Allan were still in London. When Allan and I were apart, we wrote many letters to each other, some in secret languages to keep our confidences away from Mindy and Herbert. Censors, on alert for German spies, were puzzled by cryptic mail in the Hoover family. They confronted Daddy with our letters for an explanation. We were told not to write in code in wartime.

We crossed the Atlantic several times during the war, with the ocean full of German submarines. At first, these U-boats did not bother American ships. (It was in 1917, after the Germans sank three American merchant ships, that America declared war.) Our first crossing was in 1915 to rejoin Daddy in London. Although now there was no nursery maid to regale us with tales of terror and disaster, at nine I was reading everything that came my way, including newspapers that carried headlined stories of torpedoed ships.

We had learned to swim at the Stanford YWCA. I had complete faith in my swimming ability (six breaststrokes without touching the edge of the pool), but I did not trust all those fish swimming around; I remembered the little diving boys in Ceylon with no arms. I was terrified. However, Mummie was calm, so I was somewhat reassured. As a matter of fact, she was not as unworried as I thought. On September 27, 1915, she wrote from our Addison Road home in London to her half-sister Eva, in Baltimore:

". . . Now we are here, safe and sound. I am thankful. I had special life-belts for each of us, and one to spare so that if our boat was torpedoed we would have a chance of life. The captain took every precaution and for the last two days of the voyage when we were in the danger zone, he had plenty of lifeboats swung out to hold everybody on the boat. A German submarine came up and looked at us but, as it was an American boat, they did not torpedo us. It was an anxious week for us on the boat, and for Theodore awaiting us here . . ."

London was made hazardous by German zeppelin night-bombings. I was unaware of them. Censored newspapers said nothing about them and there was no nursery maid to keep me aware of disasters. The grown-ups and Mindy sometimes watched them from the roof and once saw a zeppelin go down in flames. However, as an instrument of war, zeppelins were ineffective.

In England, the last of the elegant Edwardian era of my early child-hood had been swept away. There were no servants; the maids had better jobs in munitions factories, and the men had been drafted. Mother, Miss Pickering, and the maid (who soon left for a better paying job, too) did all the work. We ate in the servants' dining room in the basement, next to the kitchen. No point in climbing all those stairs, and fuel conservation left it cold upstairs.

We returned to Norland Place School nearby. There were friendly teachers and lessons as fascinating as stories. I was shy, almost afraid of the children. I loved working with my head and hands and the thrill of in-tellectual activity. I loved school all of my life, no matter how unpleasant some aspects of it could be. A memory that stands out is that of a little boy asking the teacher if he could sit next to me. I was warmly amazed that anyone would especially want to sit next to me.

Frances Friedel was Mindy's best friend at Norland Place School. When her father, a musician, died (he was a German, and when the war started, they said it broke his heart), Mummie invited Frances and her mother to join our family. Mrs. Friedel became our housekeeper. Her ca-pability and dignity made me forever unable to believe in any stigma on household labor.

In 1917 we all returned to California to live—our family, the Friedels, and Miss Pickering. The war had de-stroyed mining opportunities indefi-nitely, and anyway, Daddy said that he didn't want his children to grow up lit-tle English girls. We belonged in America. We returned to the ranch paradise, but because of school, we lived weekdays in Palo Alto. After liv-ing in borrowed and rented houses for a while, Mummie built our home

The Melville Avenue house;
Palo Alto, 1917

on Melville Avenue. It had seven bedrooms and five baths. It was a stucco house with a red tile roof and a huge garden. Our house was on a quiet street with nice but unostentatious homes on it. Our neighbors were apt to be professors, doctors, and bankers. Mummie was pleased that there were several within a couple of blocks who were listed in *Who's Who in America*. In addition to Daddy, there was Professor J. P. Smith, the biolo-gist, and Kathleen Norris, the author, and, later, Phimister Proctor, the sculptor.

Mummie loved flowers and had a natural knack for landscaping. When the garden was just raw land, she had wagonload after wagonload of street sweeping, mostly horse manure, spread on it, and then more wagonloads of good soil put on top of that. The garden flourished.

In 1917 Daddy took up a new profession as head of the Stanford Mining Department. He stayed in this work, later as dean of the Stanford School of Engineering and visionary planner of the School of Earth Sciences, until he became emeritus in 1936.

We had settled down to what Mummie certainly intended to be a quiet, genteel, and normal American family life. We four children, Mindy, Frances, Louise, and I, started our metamorphosis from secure and gentle English children to bewildered Americans.

Proud in the knowledge that California public schools were unexcelled, Mother entered us in the Palo Alto schools. I don't know what was most frightening about the public Lytton Avenue Elementary School. Perhaps it was the smell, a not quite clean smell of lunch boxes and grimy children, floor polish and chalk dust. Perhaps it was the children themselves. There were so many of them: little girls with frizzled hair and beribboned dresses; grimy vigorous little boys. They were distasteful to a child used to scrubbed and uniformed English schoolchildren and fastidious to a point where Daddy called me his "finicky princess." My red curls, freckles, and English accent were not social assets. Perhaps it was the strange new language of the lessons—dollars instead of pounds, George Washington instead of King Arthur, America instead of Europe. But, above all, it was the arbitrary rules that I was always breaking because I had never heard of them until it was too late. There were places that were off limits, confusing bells that meant I must be in one place today and some other place tomorrow, times to stand up, times to march, times to sit down. Breaking rules meant going to the principal's office, there to wait long minutes in dread. The lessons themselves were mysterious. The teachers were impersonal and did nothing to help my terror and confusion. They saw no connection between my consternation and my exasperating nausea.

My life was further complicated by severe earaches that would bubble all night and burst gooily in the morning. Other nights I lay on the bathroom floor, doubled up by stomachaches that Mummie called bilious attacks, but which I found out later was appendicitis. I have no idea why I didn't call Miss Pickering for help.

The bright spot in these dreadful days was lunch with Aunt Ann

Six Hoover cousins: Louise, Van Ness, Hulda, Allan, Mindy and Herbert; 1917

Minthorn Heald, who lived near the school. She was my Grandmother Hulda's sister. I never knew my grandmother, but I loved Aunt Ann. We had lunch and, afterwards, sat on the back steps looking out at her fragrant garden while she told me stories of her childhood.

In the course of a few months, Mummie took us out of public schools and enrolled us in Castilleja, a nearby private school. There the little girls wore uniforms and the little boys were clean and the teachers were kind. On Monday mornings a short passage from Shakespeare or the Bible or a poem was written on the blackboard. We recited it in unison every morning after prayer and the Pledge of Allegiance. By Friday we had memorized it. It was a cultural treat. But there was a serpent in Eden, a big girl who teased and bullied me. Each night when I said my prayers, I'd add, silently, "Please make Jane break her leg or something so she will have to stay home."

We lived a double life. Weekends, from Friday afternoon to Sunday evening, the family usually spent at the ranch, sixty miles over narrow winding mountain roads from Palo Alto to the coast. Daddy drove us in our big Studebaker, which, like all cars at that time, had running boards on each side. On a running board were three cans: the red one contained gas, the blue one oil, and the white one water. The only time in my life when I ever heard my father swear fluently was once when he stopped because the engine was too hot. When he took off the radiator cap, he got an eruption of steam up his arm.

These weekend trips were nightmares for me. The combination of the curvy La Honda Road, the mousy smell of poison hemlock that lined the road, and Daddy's pipe made me carsick. Our frequent stops were an aggravation for everyone. I knew I was an exasperating child. If Aunt Carrie happened to be on one of her frequent stays with us, I was mercifully left home in Palo Alto with her. I regretted that I could not travel by flying carpet, because I hated to miss days on the ranch, but Aunt Carrie was gentle and indecisive and I could entertain myself by getting into as much mischief as I felt would go undetected.

Carrie Goodhue, "Aunt Carrie," was a fragile spinster. She had been a friend of Aunt Lou and Uncle Bert and Mummie and Daddy at Stanford and, later, in London. She lived sometimes with them and sometimes with us—a friendly presence who loved flowers and gardening. I was fascinated when she told us that she couldn't take pills because there was a little shelf in her throat and the pills always got stuck there.

In 1917 Daddy's cousin, Roy Heald, an architectural designer and builder, directed the building of the farm headquarters—the Farmhouse, workshops, milk house, and barns. After it was finished, he and Cousin Kate, with small daughter Elsie Ann, moved in and managed the farm enterprise for several years, using Iowa farm-background skills. Then they moved back to Palo Alto, where he resumed his profession and built several of Palo Alto's public buildings.

In 1918 my dearest friend of childhood (cousin Allan was far away and we did not resume our friendship until we were grown up), Mary Ona Proctor (Mally), had moved into the big rambling house across Melville Avenue from us. Her father was the noted sculptor, Phimister Proctor, who had, all over the country, big statues of horses, Indians, buffalo, and tigers. Mally was a lovely girl, pretty and warm and sensible. I don't know why she gave me her friendship and loyalty. I was not sensible. I was adventurous and silly and wildly imaginative. Why couldn't I have had some of her sense? Why didn't she catch some of my foolhardiness? The Proctor house was my alternative home, and her family, Mody and the eight children, became as dear as my own. Het, the eldest, was a darling; overburdened by household and sibling responsibilities, she lost her chance to have teenage fun. Much of the work also fell on Mally. I enjoyed

Louise, Bill Shockley, Mindy and Hulda on the porch
of the Melville Avenue house; Palo Alto, 1917

helping her do chores that I avoided at home. Jean, a little younger than
Mally, was pretty in a pink and blue and gold way and was an expert at
avoiding work, as were the boys. Alden, the eldest boy, was nice to children
and we loved him. Phim paid little attention to us. He was busy getting en-
gaged. Brother Bill, several years younger than we, was a thoroughly obnoxious small boy. He delighted in sitting just out of our range and
serenading us with a truly remarkable repertoire of belches. "Wee Mac,"
Gifford, just out of babyhood, was sweet. Baby Anne was a plump cherub.

I spent a lot of time in their untidy kitchen helping Mally. I wonder
how I avoided learning to cook. My cooking talents were limited to cookies and candy. Meals at the Proctors were informal. Once Mody bought
a grocer's stock of canned goods at a fire sale. Since the labels were
burned off, it was interesting to open a can and find out what we were
having for lunch.

Louise (on roller skates) and Hulda
wearing masks during
the 1918 flu epidemic

In 1918 the great worldwide influenza epidemic hit. Schools closed and there were no parties or theatres open. We all wore gauze masks when we left the house. Twenty million people died. More of our soldiers died of flu than of wounds in the war.

Palo Alto, a town of less than five thousand people, was a delightful place in which to grow up. It was a prosperous, friendly college community next to Stanford University. The schools were good, the streets clean and tree-lined. Its houses were neat, surrounded by gardens of bright flowers. It had its Women's Civic Club, its Art Club, a weekly farmers' market, a public library where high school students did their homework in the evening, an excellent medical partnership, a Piggly-Wiggly grocery store and Sticky Wilson's ice cream parlor. Mally and I rode our bicycles exploring its hinterland, taking our paintboxes into fields of bluebonnets and poppies, studded with spreading oaks, or we rode narrow paths to the mudflats. We couldn't walk a block downtown without greeting people we knew. Our misdeeds were promptly reported to our parents. However, not all my misdeeds were discovered, like the time I found a dead skunk in the vacant lot next door and put it in a neighbor's icebox that she kept on her back porch. She was known for her unfriendliness to children. This prank did not make her any more friendly, especially to the neighborhood boys who were credited with the crime.

Mally and I took twenty-five cents each and attended the Congregational Church Youth Club every Thursday evening. Mally's uncle was minister of this church. One evening when Mally was home with a cold and not with me to be a good influence, I took my quarter and went a few blocks further on to the movie house. I happened upon Rudolph Valentino in *The Sheik*. Wow!

Louise and I had piano lessons from Cousin Bertha Heald, Aunt Ann's daughter. We went to dancing classes at the nearby military academy, where the boys wore white cotton gloves for dancing and smelled of cleaning fluid. We took ballet lessons. Elizabeth Norton had me as a pupil for watercolor lessons. I loved the afternoons with her in the hills doing plein air painting.

In 1918 Daddy was busy working out the curricula and lectures for his new Mining Department at Stanford. He went through his stacks of professional magazines (I don't think he ever threw away a magazine), marking pages or paragraphs with blue pencil. Then Mally and I for the lovely sum of forty cents an hour would carefully cut these marked passages out for him. Mally and I, again for the blissful sum of forty cents an hour, worked with Uncle Bert's staff sorting the trainloads of material and publications that relief workers had collected for him all over Europe. It later became the start of the Hoover Insitution on War, Revolution and Peace at Stanford. The work was fun and a financial bonanza at a time when an ice-cream cone was five cents and a tube of Winsor & Newton watercolor paint was thirty-five cents.

World War I continued for four long years of our childhood. We knitted scarves for our soldiers who were in the cold trenches of France. We had no sugar, and there were meatless, wheatless days. There were bazaars to raise money for Belgian relief. But in those pre-radio, pre-television days, there was little realization of the horrors of war. On November 11, 1918, the armistice was signed. There was wild rejoicing that the hostilities were over, no more killing. Miss Pickering's joy was mixed with sadness. I did not know that her fiancé had been killed in action. The Treaty of Versailles, ending the war, was signed the next year. I knew little about it except that Daddy and Uncle Bert did not like the treaty. Daddy said that its conditions to Germany held the seeds of the next war.

In 1919, the Eighteenth Amendment, Prohibition, was added to our Constitution. Uncle Bert characterized it as "an experiment noble in purpose but impossible to enforce." (By 1933 it had become obvious that it was not working, and it was rescinded by popular demand. Wine appeared on our table again, and Daddy went into the woods above the Green Cottage to dig up a case of whiskey he had hidden in 1919. It had disappeared.)

During vacations we happily reverted to ranch life. Often Mally was with me, and Elizabeth Hyde (Uncle Jimmy's daughter) with Louise. Occasionally we had house parties for our special friends from school. Sometimes Miss Pickering was away on her own vacation, as were Mrs. Friedel and Frances. There would be a vacation cook at the Brown

House, helped by a young woman sent by the Stanford Student Employment Service. There might be Stanford students building fences and trails and helping Daddy with his projects. We were usually a large household, increased by frequent guests. Other friends with families often camped in Maple Grove Camp, across the creek from the Green Cottage. There were children for us to play with and fathers whose main interest was fishing for trout in the Waddell or for perch in the breakers. Later, when the creek was closed for fishing, some of them didn't visit us any more. "I guess they were just friends of the fish," said Daddy sadly.

Woods, stream, hills, redwood forest, chaparral, sunny shale cliffs, marsh, fields, beach, and farmyard never lost their fascination. Days were spent exploring, studying, and making pictures of them. Evenings and rainy days were spent reading. Daddy's library was esoteric and inexhaustible. Evenings were not long enough; I read into the night with a flashlight under the bedcovers. There was no restriction on my wandering, except I must come home when the big bell reverberated up and down the valley. And I must not go on the beach alone. It was no longer deserted. The occasional casual picnicker was regarded with suspicion by Daddy.

One morning in 1920, an army hydroplane made an emergency landing on the beach and could not take off again. After the army had taken the engine and all the odds and ends it wanted, Daddy scavenged the rest. There was a small, wooden, brass-bound water cask. There were the wings, made of shellacked linen on balsa-wood struts. Daddy put the wings on top of the chicken run to make an area sheltered from sun and rain.

Transition, 1920–1924

I was fourteen when Mummie decided that we did not need a governess any longer. Our deeply loved Miss Pickering, the idol and guiding beacon of my young life for eight years, went back to England, leaving an aching hole in my heart. I felt orphaned. Without her goodnight hug, I felt cold; without her welcome when I got home from school, I wandered the house forlornly. There was no one to share my joy and troubles with, no one to give me advice or to comfort me when I was hurting. Why didn't I turn to Mummie? It never occurred to me. She was the cool and competent head of the household, a friend of mine, but not a confidante.

Mindy and Frances graduated from the private school, Castilleja. Mindy went on to Stanford and Frances to the School of Nursing at Stanford Lane Hospital. Mrs. Friedel, too, left us and became housemother at the student nurses' home.

In 1921 Mummie with some friends organized the Palo Alto Art Club. At fifteen, Mally and I were enthusiastic members and painted diligently for its exhibits. There were excellent artist members: James Swinnerton, who did southwest landscapes and the "Little Jimmy" cartoons; Phimister Proctor, Mally's father, sculptor; Elizabeth Norton, painter, sculptor, and printmaker, who gave me art lessons; A. B. Clark, who taught art at Stanford; John Lemos, art teacher at Palo Alto High School; our friend May Shockley; Dr. Bailey Willis, who was a skillful watercolorist and the father of Neal, my future brother-in-law. (Now known as the Pacific Art League, the eighty-year-old organization continues to flourish.)

Some of the Art Club events were held in Mummie's gorgeous garden at our home. Every autumn the Art Club held a Harvest Festival as a money-raiser. Daddy brought a truckload of produce from the ranch— varied gourds, colorful corn, apples, pumpkins. Dressed as an Indian, I manned one of the booths; Louise was too shy and Mindy was too busy with her Stanford social life. Mindy was very, very popular.

The early Palo Alto Art Club was a happy era of my childhood and encouraged me in serious painting. However, the main artistic creations of Mally and myself during this period were plaster piggy banks which we painted pink, with daisies and pansies on them, for fifty cents an hour at a Palo Alto gift shop.

One morning, sitting in the swing on the Brown House porch, I decided not to be a little girl any longer. I cut off my curls, bought a lipstick, discovered boys, and turned into a 1920s "flapper." My parents were flabbergasted. Aunt Lou later told me that I had suddenly become an entirely different person. She said it was like watching a small caterpillar turn into a strange butterfly. Mindy said it was like a mouse turning into a bobcat. Castilleja was a fine school, but it had what I considered silly rules and I decided to ignore them. Castilleja decided it could get along without me.

I was sent to boarding school in Los Angeles. The night I got there I was doubled up with a severe attack of appendicitis, which the housemother diagnosed as homesickness and treated with a hot water bottle. I was not in the least homesick; Miss Pickering was gone and there was nothing to be homesick for. Girls Collegiate School had a nice campus, excellent teachers, and interesting students. Courses were fun and I got good grades in spite of not studying. Once there was a surprise test on the

Punic Wars. Not having read the assignment, I knew nothing about them, so instead I wrote about a little Roman boy sitting on a hill overlooking the Mediterranean and thinking about war. I was a facile writer and Miss Gartzman, the teacher, gave me an A, with a note that she wished I had gotten to the Punic part. Years later, Miss Gartzman was in charge of the board of education parent-child play group that I and my toddler first-born son attended. She told me then that she had always remembered that essay.

Girls Collegiate, too, had rules. One that especially riled me was that the front door was locked, and we were not allowed to go outside without a chaperon. However, the lock was simple and I got a skeleton key to fit it and let myself out for unobserved early morning walks in sunlit freedom. One time there was a party that I'd been denied permission to attend. I let myself out of school and registered at a downtown hotel, which I went back to after the party, not wanting to break into the school after midnight. The party was fine; I slept well in the hotel room and let myself into school undetected in the morning. Everything would have gone well if my brother-in-law, Neal, had not phoned me the evening before and my absence was discovered. Again I was expelled. I stayed the rest of the term with patient newly weds Mindy and Neal and was tutored to keep up with my classes.

Our home in Palo Alto had been sold, and Mummie had rented Dr. and Mrs. Willis's home on the campus while they were in Europe. It was a charming Victorian house, furnished in Mrs. Willis's good taste—antiques and things of beauty. Mummie was not fond of Mrs. Willis, who had remarked, concerning Mindy and Neal's betrothal, "It will be a good thing to bring peasant blood into the Willis family." Mummie was proud of her noble ancestry and aristocratic forebears.

Returning home, I found an understanding friend in the principal of Palo Alto High School. He suggested that I pour my energy into double classes so that I could finish my last year of high school at half term. This I enjoyed doing. But, at the same time, I fell crashingly into first love—unrequited. I think I stayed half in love with Alexis Klotz most of my life—sometimes a way with first love.

Throughout my teen years I was haunted by waves of depression. First there would be shallow darkness, then deeper until I was immersed in it. I would sink into social lethargy, avoiding friends, and drowning in despair. When the black tide finally receded, I was dizzy with relief. I was told I was having a spell of the "blues." It was not blue, it was black.

I had experienced a bad case of adolescence. It is not something I would ever want to go through again.

Steve

It was during these adolescent years that Howard "Steve" Stevens and his widowed mother came into our lives, two of the many good people whom Mummie and Daddy took under their wing when there was a need. Steve, two years older than I, was a slim, serious, nearsighted boy. He was fiercely protective of his mother and a helpful near-brother to me.

When he was in his teens, he cleared a campsite at the ranch along May Creek, Stevens Camp. May Creek is a main-flowing spring. Then, it ran by the campground as a shallow stream over pebbles; later it cut a deep channel for its path. Steve and his friends and all of us have made great use of this fine campsite.

Mummie and Howard's mother had hoped that Steve and I would fall in love. We chose friendship. He tried to interest me in some of his fraternity brothers. I introduced girls to him. He was a very good friend and helped me out of scrapes, although he could not figure out why I'd been stupid enough to get into them, such as the time he extricated me from the hedge. One weekend I was home alone in our borrowed campus Willis house. It was 1923. I decided that I would see if I could drive Mummie's little Austin car. I'd watched carefully and thought that I could probably do it. So I got in and put the clutch into neutral gear, started the engine, and shifted to low gear. The car leapt forward, crash! I had put a bulge in the corrugated iron garage. I put the clutch into reverse and the car shot backward across the alley and into a deep cypress hedge. Then it refused to do anything. I phoned Steve at his fraternity house and he got the car back into the garage, showing no sign of its misadventure. Next weekend he came to the ranch and taught me how to drive on a long lonely stretch of highway on the way to Pescadero.

Steve graduated in economics from Stanford, having also taken all the finance and business courses that Stanford offered in those pre–School of Business years. Daddy and friends were busy establishing the Palo Alto Building and Loan and were looking for a manager. I persuaded Steve to apply for the job and gave Daddy my unasked-for advice about how hard-working, intelligent, honest, and well-qualified Steve was for the job.

As manager, Steve developed Palo Alto Building and Loan into a profitable and flourishing institution.

Steve married Margery, a nature enthusiast and rock hound. As time went on they had a son. They bought an attractive home in Los Gatos, then a small development in an apricot orchard. We were happy recipients of boxes of apricots from time to time. When Steve retired, they indulged their appetite for travel and for rock hunting. Eventually Margery fell into Alzheimer's disease and gradually became helpless, needing Steve's constant care. When he was diagnosed with inoperable cancer, he shot and killed Margery, and then himself.

Stanford University, 1924–1925

Stanford in 1924 was an exciting new world. There was a beautiful campus, glowing with sandstone pillars and bright flowers, cool lawns and winding paths. Life was vibrant with new friends, new knowledge, a newspaper to work on, parties to go to. I loved it. However, my first grades were dismal. Mother was upset. Daddy was furious. So I settled down to

Hulda, 1924

study, working very hard indeed. A new friend, upperclassman Allene Thorp (who later married Dave Lamson and was tragically murdered) was concerned about my intensity and lack of rest. She showed me how to better organize time and strength. Academic grades were never a problem after that.

I lived in Roble Hall, where the non-sorority women and the freshmen lived. I welcomed and helped the new freshmen. I persuaded the resident senior sponsor, a Theta, Peg Watson (who later married cousin Herbert), to be my roommate. I organized residents' get-togethers. I was general friend and troubleshooter.

At Stanford I found really good lifelong friends, including Allene, Marietta (whom I had known at Castilleja); Hope Williams (I became godmother to her Randolph children); Mary Decker (who married John Steinbeck); Marion Nicholas (who married Cranston Holman, tennis star and, later, New York surgeon); Loraine Cleaveland (sister of Norman Cleaveland, Olympic star), who married George Keffer; Nip McHose (member of the Stanford basketball team and tennis champion); Allen

Campbell; Bunny Miller (later, Aunt Lou's secretary); Lefty May (baseball star and later our financial advisor and good friend); and many others, along with dozens of casual friends and "dates" no longer remembered.

At that time there were five hundred women at Stanford and about ten thousand men. Mrs. Stanford had specified the female limit. For us it made an active social life, never a dateless weekend. I'd usually double-date with another couple, or we would go in a group of several couples. We went for hikes and picnics in the hills behind the campus. We rowed on Lake Lagunita. We attended campus plays and parties. We went to the movies in Palo Alto and, afterwards, ate banana splits at Sticky Wilson's. We'd go dancing in San Francisco at the St. Francis Hotel or the Mark Hopkins Hotel or a night club. We'd stop for a drink at an illegal, Prohibition-years speakeasy. Or, best of all, we'd have a house party at the ranch.

Sunday evenings I'd do class assignments or study desperately to keep up with my work. I didn't have the sense to realize that Stanford would have been a richer experience if I had less social life and looked more deeply into its intellectual treasure.

Louise, 1924

One afternoon I was walking down Palm Drive from the campus to Palo Alto when a friend stopped to give me a ride. With him was a Chi Psi fraternity brother, a nice looking young man with a comb and a toothbrush sticking out of his shirt pocket. I was introduced to him, Chuck McLean.

"Happy to meet you," said Chuck. "This is the third time we have been introduced; it would be nice if you'd try to remember me."

I loved working on the "Dippy," the campus newspaper, writing news and features, but I didn't like counting out headlines. I loved late night talk sessions, parties, and lonely vigils by Lake Lagunita. But most of all I loved the challenge and joy of learning. It was impossible to choose a favorite subject—each took me to new levels of mental exploration—psychology, art, economics, biology, music, political science, history, literature. Each was a different angle of human experience and horizon. It was hard to work out a semester program because I was greedy to embrace them all.

Louise and her new husband, Ernest "Snick" Dunbar, gave a Halloween house party in Wilson Gulch, the northern boundary of the ranch. My date was with a Chi Psi. When he and I had an argument and broke the date, I was happy to go as a "single" to help Louise with the work, picking up and washing up after the guests, an untidy bunch. Then Chuck McLean arrived; he said he'd been enlisted by my former date for the weekend. I was surprised. I remembered him from our Palm Drive encounter, and I knew that he had been the freshman golf champion and was also said to have received the highest grade ever on the Stanford entrance exam. At the house party, he spent most of the day helping excavate a car which one of the guests had managed to run off the road while avoiding a mud puddle.

I was busy turning a sundry supply of groceries into dinner for twelve, as helpful companions disappeared by twos along the hillside trails. The job was a bit difficult because the cottage was without electricity or hot water. The dark came early, and with it the late October chill. Dinner was lit by jack-o-lanterns and firelight. The beverage of choice was a mixture of apple cider and gin. When more gin was needed, Chuck drove me back along the beach and to the Casa. Chuck talked to Mummie and Daddy while I went upstairs to my room to get the bottle hidden in my closet.

"Such a handsome and well-spoken lad," said Mummie.

Back at the cottage, the guests, now fortified, decided to go swimming. Chuck and I, not enchanted by the cider-and-gin mixture, chose not to dive into the cold North Pacific Ocean. We stayed on the beach and built a huge driftwood bonfire, around which the shivering, blue, dripping, and now sober house party gratefully gathered.

When they trooped back to the cottage, Chuck and I stayed by the glowing coals. We talked. The fire died down and we built it up again. We talked some more. The coals lost their heat.

"Time to go in, I think," I said.

"You know," said Chuck slowly, "I always thought it would take longer to find you. I would like to marry you."

"Fine idea," I said, and we laughed.

Back at Stanford I thought a lot about that magical weekend; but I didn't see Chuck again until a couple of weeks later, when we met around the Big Game bonfire.

"Hey," said Chuck, "when are you going to marry me?"

"Next Friday?" I suggested.

"Sorry, I already have a date."

After that we spent a lot of time together. The joke (he said it had never been a joke) about marriage became a semi-joke, and then an idea, and then a plan.

On December 5, 1925, without telling anyone, we drove to Yuba City and were married by a kindly minister. His wife served us sherry and fruit-cake. I wrote:

> Happiness found me when you came,
> Filling my life with love and laughter
> Brighter than moonlight, gentler than flame
> We shall live happily ever after

We decided not to announce our marriage until after finals were over in order not to risk losing our credits. At that time, Stanford did not look favorably on student marriages. When we got around to telling our parents, they were exceedingly angry and upset. This surprised me. Here we were intelligent adults (both nineteen!). I didn't see why our plans and activities were the business of anyone else. However, with customary poise and grace, Aunt Lou rose to the occasion. She gave a wedding reception for us in her lovely Stanford house on the hill.

Our first need was to find jobs. When satisfactory employment did not offer itself, we took what we could get. We needed immediate money for food and rent. Chuck became night watchman and mechanic at a garage. I took care of a family of unruly children. I got paid weekly, Chuck biweekly. One Friday my employer announced that my pay would have to wait until Monday, because, otherwise, her household account would get too low. Chuck would not be paid for another week. No money for Saturday grocery shopping. Our Saturday and Sunday menu was sliced tomatoes, oatmeal porridge, and leftover Christmas fruitcake. Altogether it was not a satisfactory lifestyle but the best we could do at the time. Education would have to wait.

Billie, a Stanford friend, suggested that we help her drive her family back home to the St. Lawrence River's Thousand Islands, for no salary, but with all expenses paid. It sounded like fun, so along we went. Our party was Grandma and her elderly companion, Billie and her boyfriend, Billie's younger sister and her boyfriend, and their demon younger sister. The trip was interesting. Grandma had bought three new Marmon cars for the journey. (Her husband had left her with a lot of money when he took off with his daughter-in-law. He had made his money by inventing laundry machinery.)

In 1926 the national highway system was, to put it gently, spotty. On the desert in Arizona and New Mexico, roads were often wooden planks laid on the sand. Going through cities, we usually lost our way. Asking directions was not a considered option, so we saw a lot of interesting neighborhoods. When we got to Chicago, we rested a few days in the Brown Hotel and explored shops, beaches, and zoo before we took off again cross-country. Our trip was marred toward the end when I got ill. Roadside food and little rest or exercise had completely upset my interior.

The island on the St. Lawrence was beautiful. Their home was a huge summer "cottage." I slept and walked and painted and started to feel better. We needed to make plans and get jobs. Chuck went over to the mainland to investigate possibilities. But soon I was ill again.

My illness got worse and worse. Chuck was frantic. It was a kidney infection, dangerous in those pre-"wonder drug" days. He finally phoned Aunt Lou in Washington, D.C., since she was my nearest relative and had been kind to us in the past. She told us to come to them.

2
Pasadena
1925–1943

Washington, D.C., 1927

STAYING WITH Aunt Lou and Uncle Bert, under doctor's care, I recovered slowly. My twenty-first birthday came while we were there in the welcoming S Street home. Because of the diet I was on, which did not include birthday cake, Aunt Lou had her chef make a decorated arrangement of white rice, not as delicious as cake, but a loving gesture. Uncle Bert gave me a wristwatch. It was a nice birthday.

Uncle Bert was secretary of commerce under President Coolidge. He was working to make our emerging industries more efficient. Two things he did that I remember were to get the eight-hour workday generally accepted and to standardize the sizes of products, making them more interchangeable. He did a great many more important things that were beyond my interest at the time.

When I was well again, Aunt Lou asked us what we planned to do. We told her we intended to find jobs and get money to go back to school. She said that she thought it best if she would lend us the necessary money so we could concentrate and finish our studies quickly. Splendid! We became two of the many, many young people whom she helped through college.

McGill University, Montreal, 1927

Chuck's uncle, John Nicholson, was registrar of McGill University. We went to Montreal to investigate registering. We could not go back to Stanford yet because Chuck had flunked out the semester we got married and needed a semester of good grades somewhere else before he could re-register at Stanford. Uncle John helped us get into McGill. Dean McKay

Hulda, 1926

said, "McGill is forty years ahead of any American university so you'd better just take elementary courses here." We took the advanced courses we needed to fit into our Stanford majors and ended the year with A– averages.

We both worked, so that our debt to Aunt Lou would be as low as possible. I typed thesis papers. As important to me as this income were the papers I typed that gave me knowledge in fields beyond my class sched-

Chuck, 1926

ule. Chuck worked in an exclusive menswear shop. This job provided an extra dividend; he accumulated a good supply of excellent, long lasting clothing at special prices. Good taste in clothing, along with courtly manners learned from his father, and innate kindness stamped Chuck as a gentleman. His cheer and gentleness made him beloved of children, dogs, and elderly ladies. His charm and humor and friendliness filled our life with friendships.

It was a good year. We lived in a dark, minuscule apartment near the university. Chuck's Nicholson relatives welcomed us into their homes and lives. We made delightful friends at school. Winnie Kydd, a graduate student, became a special and lifelong friend. We hadn't realized that she was a member of the Montreal social elite. As her friend, we were welcome in McGill society. "Barbarians from the States" (Californians to boot!), we surprised them by not being noticeably uncouth. The condescension with which these Canadians regarded citizens of the United States astonished us.

Our courses were excellent. Our economics professor was Stephen Leacock, an erudite, warm, and funny man. He became our mentor. I competed with an earnest boy for the highest grades in his classes. Our social science professor, Dr. Dawson, was a macho and pompous person but a good teacher. He disapproved of my year-end thesis, "Women—The Dominant Sex," but said that he, reluctantly, had to give me an "A". My anthropological research for the paper had been extensive.

By the time school ended in May, we were thoroughly tired of snow-slush, still on the ground, and were yearning for California. We boarded the train for home. After settling me on board with our luggage, Chuck went back into the station to buy cigarettes. The train pulled out without him. The conductor was distraught. I was cross, but there was nothing I could do about the situation. Chuck had our money; I had the tickets. I settled back to read the funnies. Chuck turned up at the next station. He had raced the train in a taxi.

Home Again in California, 1928

California. It was pleasant to be home in the warmth and to know that snow and slush would stay up in the mountains where they belonged. Somewhere on our trip home we must have passed by spring. May was still slushy winter in Montreal. At Stanford it was summer. We reveled in the blue skies, sunshine, green trees and grass, and all the flowers.

It was good to see Louise. I had missed her. Her marriage to Snick Dunbar had produced an adorable baby, Dellalou, lovely beyond description. I loved her with yearning envy. Chuck and I knew that our babies had to be far in the future.

We had a happy summer, spending as much time as we could at the ranch. Mindy was there with her two little boys, lusty, red-cheeked, and rambunctious. They were beautiful natural-born *enfants terribles* with talents for destruction. Mindy coped with them serenely.

As an adult I appreciated my parents for qualities I finally saw in them. They soon became very fond of Chuck, recognizing his gentleness, thoughtfulness, and intellectual abilities. He enjoyed working with Daddy on ranch projects and fly-fishing in the creek with him—things that his other sons-in-law did not care about.

As soon as school started, we registered at Stanford to graduate. Again, we both worked to keep our debt at a minimum. My job was as secretary to Dr. Clelia Mosher, medical advisor to Stanford women, at $170 a month. She had been one of the first women in the country to earn a medical degree, and it had not been easy. She was a militant feminist before there were many such heroines, and she had my complete devotion for it. Chuck worked in a garage; the pay was better than for more genteel pursuits, and the knowledge he gained was useful all his life.

I graduated in mid-year and used the $300 Daddy gave me for a graduation gift to buy a car. Chuck, with grades to make up for flunking out the previous year, did not graduate until the end of the school year. He got an airplane pilot's license with the $300 graduation gift from his parents.

As soon as we graduated we found jobs. Chuck became an inspector for the California Department of Agriculture and I the assistant manager of the San Francisco Emporium Style and Comparison Office. Neither job was a step in the direction of our life ambitions, but both were good for now. My job was assigning routes and evaluating results of a corps of "shoppers" who monitored the other San Francisco department stores to make sure that our prices and stock were competitive. It was a completely new world for me. The work was interesting, but its unfamiliarity and my lack of experience made it much more difficult and time-consuming than it should have been.

We rented an apartment in San Francisco on Telegraph Hill on the corner of Hyde and Greenwich Streets. We furnished it sparsely (our bed was a mattress on the floor) with furniture Mummie could spare. When Chuck's parents came to visit us, they bought us a table. We had inadequate heat but a gorgeous view of the Golden Gate and spectacular sunsets.

Chuck was busy all over the state during the week, so we were together only on weekends. My Stanford friend, Marion Holman, shared the apartment during the week. Weekends she spent with her new husband, Cranston, who was an intern at Stanford hospital and busy day and night during the week. Marion was a good apartment sharer. She was quiet, intellectual, and interesting. She worked at a bookstore. She had a strange sense of humor but so do I, so that was okay. We had some goldfish that Marion said kept her awake at night saying, "Gup, gup, gup." One day they were gone. She said they'd been happy the last she'd seen of them being flushed down the toilet. Once when there was a rash of break-ins and rapes in the neighborhood, she hung a sign on her door: "There is a younger and more attractive prey in the next room." She was not much of a cook or housekeeper, although she tried to be helpful. She told me, much later, after she had her own home, that she had not realized how little of her share of the work she had done.

It was often hard. There were times when, worn out from work and with sinuses throbbing, I stood in a crowded streetcar with my arms full of groceries and dripping vegetables. I had an evening of cooking and housework ahead of me, and Chuck was far away. I sometimes felt sorry for myself and would let a tear or two trickle down my cheeks. The friendly streetcar conductor would call out, "Green witch Street," and pat my shoulder as I fought my way to the door. Wind howled up from the bay and met itself in icy whirlwinds as I made my way to our front door. After a struggle with my hat (one never left the house without gloves and a hat), purse, groceries, and key, I would be in the cold hall of our silent apartment.

I had another appendix attack. My usual remedy of reading a thriller to take my mind off the pain didn't work. Marion phoned Cranston to send a doctor. He proved more helpful than pulp literature. When a month or so went by without a bill, we told Cranston that we were afraid it had gone astray in the mail. Cranston mentioned it to the doctor, and we were touched by his reply, "Oh, I couldn't send them a bill. Why, they had hardly any furniture in the house." We paid the bill.

Weekends were a joy. Then, with Chuck, I could appreciate San Francisco. We explored the city, doing all the things that could be done without using money. We window-shopped the elegant downtown and hiked up Nob Hill to admire the mansions. We went to the zoo, art shows, museums, and the aquarium. Once, when people were standing around watching fish flopping around the bottom of an empty tank, Chuck called the management—something no one else had seen the need for. We poked into the stores and alleys of Chinatown, walked the Embarcadero and waterfront piers, North Beach and Golden Gate Park. We gave Sunday morning waffle breakfasts for our many Stanford friends in "The City." We walked up to Coit Tower to look at the Daughters of the American Revolution historic plaque I had designed. We went to parties given by our friends. Sometimes Mindy and Neal came up from Los Angeles and we went dancing at the Mark.

In November 1928, Uncle Bert was elected president of the United States. We spent the evening with them and friends at their home on San Juan Hill on the campus, listening to the election returns as they came in over the radio. John Philip Sousa marched his band up the hill playing "Hail to the Chief," and most of Stanford paraded past the house, cheering.

I was transferred to Capwell's in Oakland as manager of their style office. I worked ten hours a day on a job that should have been done in eight if I had been more experienced. But I enjoyed it. The store manager was a fine person to work for, and his staff reflected his courtesy and enthusiasms. No more battles with the menswear buyer over whether to mark his shorts thirty-five cents or fifty cents. Here he cooperated. The window dresser did not share the Emporium's fondness for taxidermy masterpieces, stuffed dogs, in sports goods displays. Even the tearoom manager was responsive when I suggested that pickles and potato chips should not be served with afternoon tea.

After Marion left, Loraine Cleaveland, another Stanford friend, became our apartment mate. She was tired of teaching in Marysville, and I got her a job selling men's underwear in the Emporium basement. "Well," she said, "at least it's a change." She left when her application for a better teaching job was accepted. After her, a girl who had been recommended moved in with me. She only stayed a short while, then disappeared with some of my clothes, owing her rent, and leaving a note, "I don't like you and find your friends uninteresting."

A neglected sinus infection hung on; finally, lost behind a terrible headache, I went to a doctor. He put me in Children's Hospital with septicemia. With no money put aside for hospitals, I was in a charity ward with five others with similar conditions. The only financial obligation was forty dollars upon release. Chuck brought me the forty dollars and I put it under my pillow. Next to me was a fragile Mexican girl. During visiting hours, her young husband sat beside her, holding her hand and telling her about their baby at home. When the time came for her release, they did not have the forty dollars. I overheard their conversation (hard not to—he was sitting not three feet from my bed) and offered them my money until his payday. Their gratitude was tearful, but I wondered if I would ever see the forty dollars again—and what would I tell Chuck if I didn't? But that weekend the young man came back with it. He reinforced my belief in the innate goodness of people.

After the hospital, I was too feeble to go back to work. "A rest and a warm, dry climate," said the doctor. Mindy wrote, "Why don't you both come down and visit us for a while?" We went to Los Angeles. I have never forgotten Mindy's kindness to us then and in the following years with our three small children in the Southland.

Hollywood, 1929–1931

We stayed several weeks with Mindy and Neal, enjoying their social life, their boat, and their two little boys. Then it was time to get back to work. Chuck decided to give up his travel job with the Department of Agriculture and to work with Neal in his Norden Corporation, a company for discovery and development of oil. Neal was a genius at discovering oil and in the promotion of his discoveries.

I got a job with the Los Angeles County School District as assistant director of a salary survey. It was pleasant and profitable. The salary was ten dollars a day! The director taught me how to put my Stanford courses in statistics and research methods to practical use, from gathering the raw data to processing and publishing it. Our team worked well together, except that the rest of us complained that the director's White Owl cigars smelled as if the feathers had been left in.

We made a trip to share a vacation with Dad and Mother McLean on Wing Point, Bainbridge Island, Washington, where Chuck had spent his boyhood summers. We visited Mally (Proctor) and Campbell Church in their beautiful home on Seattle's LakeWashington. Mally and Cam had a charter boat adventure business in the Inside Passage along the Alaska coast—a series of wilderness camps. We wished that we could afford to share an adventure with them.

After my experience with the salary survey, most of the jobs I did were in statistical research. This was ideal work for me because it could be done between babies and other responsibilities. I liked work and we needed the money, but family was our first responsibility. We took our promise "to love, honor, and cherish through sickness and health, for richer or poorer" seriously all our lives. Whenever I could during the depression years, I did my part in keeping us financially afloat. Chuck's job was demanding, and he was often away from home; but when home, he did his full share of helping me with family chores.

Some of the surveys were dull and some very interesting. Work for the Gallup Poll was fascinating, but Chuck was so distressed when I had to take my work sheets into slum areas that I didn't stay in that job long.

For the California State Employment Department, I completed a domestic services survey on work conditions and satisfactions. The survey went unnoticed for several years, and then the Pasadena schools adopted its recommendations for training sessions and educational publications.

The Pasadena Playhouse had me make tables and charts of audience reactions, but I have no idea what use they made of them. The best thing about the job was all the plays I enjoyed.

Some other jobs included ghostwriting a book, doing society page features for the *Pasadena Star-News,* and working as secretary to a man bent on proving that Shakespeare's work was written by Bacon and that Bacon was a member of the royal family. But that job was short-lived because my shorthand skills were not equal to his arcane vocabulary.

The Depression, 1929–1939

We moved to Pasadena and had not been there very long when, in October of 1929, the stock market collapsed. It suddenly made many of our affluent friends as poor as we were—some poorer. Chuck still had his job. The subsequent Depression caused widespread, desperate hardship when banks closed, businesses failed, and people lost their jobs and savings. There were many sad suicides. It is hard to imagine, nowadays, such a worldwide calamity. Experience has caused governments to put into effect a network of political, economic, and social bulwarks designed to temper a repetition.

In the years immediately following the collapse, while Uncle Bert was still president, one measure after another was tried to remedy the hardships. Some failed and some succeeded. The principal hurdle was cruel-hearted politics. Franklin Roosevelt, the Democrat running for president, encouraged the Democratic Congress not to pass legislation proposed by the president for recovery. Nevertheless, most economic signs pointed upward by 1932. They collapsed again when Roosevelt was elected. Gradually, in part because Congress passed the previously refused recovery measures, things got better. However, the Depression was not entirely over until World War II galvanized industry in war supply production.

In the absence of effective remedies during the Depression, there was an upswelling of people helping people. Private charities and individuals, although terribly overburdened, kept the fabric of society from unraveling.

I only really knew what was happening around me in our little world. The members of the Junior League, many of them newly impoverished, used their experience as trained volunteers to keep clinics and food distribution functioning. Doctors donated their time. Employment agencies, when there were no jobs, created them—paid work projects for the jobless, and they canvassed businesses and individuals for help in creating new job opportunities.

Families took in other individuals. Chuck and I did our small part by giving a home and minuscule wage to one desperate woman after another until each found a better job. People went through their belongings and gave clothing and bedding through "clothes closets." Carpools proliferated. Parents prepared lunches for schools; grocery stores gave vegetables and dented cans to hungry people; bakeries handed out their surplus; churches had soup kitchens.

The ranch was a welcoming shelter for friends whose incomes had evaporated. Stream and forest and Daddy's vegetable garden fed them. Daddy's university job continued at a reduced level. Mummie said their only real disaster was that trusts they had set up to make their daughters independent were wiped out.

People hung on and helped each other when they could.

While Uncle Bert was President, 1929–1933, Daddy and Mummie went to the White House to visit and so did Mindy and Neal. We were much too poor to think about such a trip. But I continued to write to Aunt Lou to keep her up with family news. Sometimes I'd get a note back from her, usually asking me to do something connected with one of her projects or to look up a friend or relative and see how they were. If I reported that they were not okay, I knew that something would be done about it—but not traceable to Aunt Lou. As First Lady, she avoided public notice but was very busy. She was active in the Girl Scout organization and other projects for girls and women. She fostered schools in the backwoods of Appalachia. She was saddened by newspaper protest when she invited wives of black legislators to her teas for congressional wives. She spent a great deal of time and money tracing and recovering historic White House furniture.

When the storm of the Depression and the politically orchestrated attacks on Uncle Bert's character defeated his plans, he was serene in the knowledge that he had done his best and had designed many of the programs that his successor was following. Aunt Lou, however, was desolated by the vicious lies about the man she loved. My father and, to a lesser extent, the rest of the family were also targets of politically planned attacks. As cousin Allan said, "the worst thing that ever happened to our family was Dad winning the election."

First Baby, 1931

In 1931 we had been married for six years. Chuck had a job and I had saved some of my earnings. We had moved to Pasadena and lived in a cottage on Cornell Avenue. I had finished a survey job. We decided it was time to start our family.

We had delightful neighbors, specially the Wilsons. When my pregnancy became obvious, Mr. Wilson (who was retired and spent most of his time in his blooming garden, when he wasn't working in mine turning it from a weed patch to beds of flowers) became very solicitous. He was convinced that I didn't eat enough. He brought me big, nourishing, gooey sandwiches for lunch. I appreciated his concern but saved the sandwiches for Chuck. He had a better appetite than I.

Everyone helped us get ready for the baby. Many of our friends had young children, and they showered us with outgrown clothes and equipment. Babies grow too fast to wear things out. We received a baby basket, crib, baby bath, stroller, and playpen. Cousin Allan's baby, Allan, provided welcome contributions. Louise sent Judy's things, which had been saved for the purpose. Yellow had been the baby color selected for the new Princess Elizabeth of England, a happy solution to the "pink or blue?" question. I washed and ironed and replaced ribbons. Our baby had a beautiful layette.

Doctors had decided that cesarean surgery would be necessary. I wanted Dr. Almon Roth, family surgeon in the Palo Alto Clinic, to deliver the baby. When the time approached, we drove to Stanford, and I stayed with Mummie and Daddy at their Salvatierra home, a tiny house on the campus which served them during the week when they had to be away from the ranch and busy with their responsibilities at Stanford. Mother was occupied researching and writing *Historic Spots in California*.

Waiting on the campus for my baby to be born was a happy time. It was a beautiful autumn. Trees in the arboretum were turning red and yellow. Golden-crowned sparrows woke me at dawn with their haunting calls.

Thanksgiving 1935: the whole family on Mindy's front steps, Pasadena
Back row: Theodore Hoover, Snick Dunbar, Mildred Hoover, Chuck McLean,
Louise, Mindy, and Neal Willis
Middle row: Hulda holding baby Allan; Judy and Dellalou Dunbar;
behind them, David and Ted Willis
Front row: Tookie and Anne

There was leisure to renew Palo Alto and Stanford friendships: Margery and Howard Stevens—Steve, who had always been a big-brotherly friend-in-need; Dave and Allene (Thorp) Lamson, who now lived next door on Salvatierra Row; Hope Williams, who had not yet found the happiness her family would bring her; Elizabeth Hyde, and Louise and Snick with their adorable little ones. I spent pleasant hours with cousins Roy and Kate Heald, Daddy's cousins who had managed the ranch for him in the early days. Cousin Kate had been a sympathetic grown-up confidante.

Charles Alexander McLean III was born September 19, at the Palo Alto Hospital, certainly the most charming and beautiful baby in the nursery. I lay looking out at the mist curling around the eucalyptus trees in the arboretum, and Chuck bought me a paint box so I could make a picture of their tranquil beauty. Indications of a bad appendix had caused Dr. Roth to remove it during surgery. That was the end of my appendix attacks.

Back in Pasadena our friends came to welcome and admire our baby. He was quiet and cheerful. Among our friends, Nip and Mary McHose stopped in on their way to Hawaii. Mary called our baby "buttercup" in his pale yellow sunsuit. Nip named him Tookie.

When the Cornell Avenue house owners sold it, we moved to Dale Street and found another group of friendly neighbors, specially Miss Kerr, across the street, who was happy with the job of caring for Tookie when I had to be somewhere else. Dale Street was a quiet cul-de-sac ending in the locked back gate of a large estate. Our pretty cottage with its big screened porch and fenced garden was the most modest home on the block.

Not being experienced with babies, I didn't realize that when people, including the pediatrician, said that Tookie was an extraordinary child, they really meant it. He was quiet, curious, thoughtful, full of questions, and quick to learn. I did not know that a two-year-old would not usually say such things as "Does tonight go all around the world?" "Does the moon lay eggs?" "This wiggly turtle has no legs [a snake]." "Look at the teeny baby moon, soon it will squash up big." More two-ishly, he told me that he hunted pretend tigers and pink bears with curly tails.

Very helpful to a new mother was the Pasadena preschool "Play Group" program. Once a week a group of mothers and small children gathered in Tournament Park. The children played, the mothers watched, and two teachers guided, interpreted, and advised. I noticed that Tookie was apt to sit a little apart to observe what was going on, and then he would join the project and often ended up in charge of it. Among the parents in the group was Mrs. Linus Pauling with her tiny daughter, Linda. "Linda is so passionate," remarked Mrs. Pauling when Linda hit a trespassing boy a resounding whack with her plastic baseball bat.

Pasadena Social Life, 1930–1943

In Pasadena we had a host of friends and led a cheerful social life. We gave and attended dinner parties and we played a great deal of bridge. Chuck was an excellent card player and I bid by math and was fairly good. We went to picnics and on excursions. There were elegant Junior League parties and informal gatherings of friends and relatives. Our calendar was full.

Our closest friends were Marietta and Russ Harriman. She was beautiful. We had been friends through Castilleja boarding school and Stanford. Chuck had been in love with her. Russ was also from Stanford, handsome, somewhat surly, and very ambitious, both socially and as a young lawyer. He judged worth by wealth and power. When we introduced them to Mindy and Neal, Russ realized that their friendship would be more useful than ours would be and set out, not entirely unsuccessfully, to discourage Marietta's time and friendship with me.

There were cousin Herb (Herbert Hoover Jr.), his wife, Peg, and their children. Peg (Margaret Watson) had been a senior sponsor and my roommate in Roble Hall at Stanford. She was a beautiful, serious young woman who kept an invisible wall around herself. She had no intimate friends, although she was fun to be with and gave lovely parties. Herbert was quiet and dear. He had been deaf since childhood. Years and years later, a new invention gave him back his hearing and he became outgoing and full of humor. One day when Peg dropped in with her four-year-old Peggy Ann, for a visit, the little girl greeted me with "Aunt Hulda, does your little boy always run around with no clothes on?" Eighteen-month-old Tookie had discovered how to take his clothes off and had met them, naked, at the front gate.

Virginia Watson, a friend from Girls Collegiate boarding school, and her husband, Punch, were special friends. Once when I was very much annoyed by four-year-old Allan's depredations, I offered him to the Watsons along with a set of dishes. (Punch, several times later, said he regretted that the deal did not go through.) Virginia was not a nature lover. While we were visiting them one evening, a toad that had been happily settled in my coat pocket in the front closet got adventurous and joined us in the living room. From Virginia's reaction, one would have thought we'd been invaded by aliens.

There were Harriet (Huntington) and Al Doerr. They were poor and cheerful like we were. Once we were given, by Mally and Cam Church, a box at the Santa Anita races. The Doerrs were included in our party—Harrimans, Willises, Doerrs, and us. Some years later Harriet inherited a great deal of Huntington money. When she was widowed, she became author of best-sellers, including the haunting *Stones for Ibarra*.

Mary Barstow, another Stanford friend, had married Norman Rockwell, the artist. They came frequently to Pasadena to visit Mary's mother. During these visits we had fun together. One evening, driving to a party, we were stopped by highway police—for what reason we never knew. We were asked for identification. Norman had none, but volunteered helpfully that he had a birthmark on his shoulder. The police laughed and decided we were not the people they were looking for.

The Shockley family lived near us in Pasadena. I had known May Shockley ever since I was a baby in London. No family ever had a truer and more beloved friend than May. As May Bradford, she had known my parents in Stanford. She married a mining engineer twenty years her senior. Daddy always said that Dr. Shockley had the best mind he had ever known and an encyclopedic knowledge. A kindly, white-bearded gentleman, he was a lecturer at Stanford and knew seven Chinese languages and once tried to teach me one. Mrs. Shockley had a compulsion to serve others and was always involved in some useful and strenuous activity. During World War I she did a magnificent job organizing food conservation programs. She was a fine artist. She had a brief, rich, period of doing glorious oil paintings of flowers and the precious Chinese porcelain Dr. Shockley had collected in China. Her paintings sold for high prices in Gumps gallery in San Francisco. She gave me a painting of cinerarias that was lost when the Casa burned. In between, and along with, her projects, she was a tower of strength when her friends needed her.

Their son, Billy, who was a spoiled baby and an obnoxious teenager, became a fascinating, arrogant young man with imagination and a wicked sense of humor. Sometimes, when Chuck could not be there, he was my escort to social events. Later, in 1947, Dr. William Shockley, while working at Bell Labs, invented the transistor, which made computers possible and changed our world, and was awarded the Nobel Prize in 1956. He went into genetic research and demonstrated that racial differences are more than skin deep. This discovery was not appreciated by the public but was the basis for medical advances.

With Loraine (Cleaveland) and George Keffer we made adventurous camping trips together, including one into the desert near what was, at that time, the small wild town of Las Vegas in Nevada. We toured Hoover Dam while it was being built, that colossal engineering triumph which, when completed, paid for itself by selling power to light cities and run industries. It prevented flooding, created a lake, irrigated almost two million acres, and had cost the lives of dozens of its builders. We roamed around Las Vegas; it was a small dusty and somewhat bleak village—its glory as a gambling mecca was years in the future. Loraine had been a very popular Kappa at Stanford and had shared our San Francisco apartment. She was outspoken and smart. Her brother, Norman Cleaveland, captain of the

Stanford football team and Olympic hero gold medal winner, had become a mining engineer. Eventually, he became Tookie's brother-in-law. George was manager of a branch bank.

Two other Stanford friends in Pasadena were Allen and Mildred Campbell. Allen was the son of Tom Campbell, former governor of Arizona. Tom disapproved of the extensive lawn around the Casa, viewing it as "expensive and unproductive." When Chuck mowed it he agreed with him. But the lawn was Daddy's pride. Allen had been a Beta at Stanford and a close friend of cousin Allan. Mildred had been Aunt Lou's social secretary in Washington. In Los Angeles, Allen was a high school principal. We enjoyed their company. He was a clever, light-hearted, and slightly bawdy entertainer at the piano. Mildred was quiet, serious, and firm-minded.

All these and a host of other friends were lovely to us and embraced our children, who, fortunately, had excellent company manners. Sundays, we took our older, carless friends on frequent drives into the country around Los Angeles—to beaches, hills, and wooded canyons. They were pleasant excursions to unpopulated areas where villages later grew.

Daddy's sister, Aunt May, lived in Santa Monica with Uncle Van Leavitt and cousin Van Ness. Uncle Van had been a favorite of the children when he visited the ranch. He seemed happier playing with us than in the company of adults.

During this time, Chuck was working with the State Petroleum Inspection Service. The office was so politics-ridden that it was not conducive to social friendships. However, Bill Stuart, an older man, was indifferent to this maneuvering and Chuck enjoyed his company. Bill was well-educated, well-traveled and humorous. He was generous in sharing his professional experience with Chuck. When Bill wanted a loan, Chuck was glad to help him, to repay him for kindness. Bill left for his vacation. The time for promised repayment became long past, and we needed the money. Chuck wrote him a note. We got a letter back from Bill's wife. Bill had emptied their joint bank account, borrowed from all his friends, and disappeared. We were shocked, sad for everyone, and more than a little financially dismayed.

Again, our rented home was sold. Mummie suggested it would be a good idea for us to buy a house, and she lent us the down payment for a two- bedroom, newly built tract house on Linda Vista Avenue in Altadena, a Pasadena suburb. We bought the adjoining vacant lot for a play yard for the children. It made a pleasant and adequate home, but we looked for one that would suit us better.

And, again, we had delightful neighbors, the Gwinns. He had retired as Fresno superintendent of schools. They got up at 5:30 in the morning. I was horrified when I discovered that four-year-old Tookie had dressed himself while we were asleep and joined them for breakfast! But they assured us they enjoyed having him and had adopted him as an additional grandchild. Tookie ate another hearty breakfast with us a couple of hours later.

I had been somewhat surprised when I was invited into membership in the Pasadena Junior League. Junior League was a nationwide organization of socially elite young women, which I certainly was not. But I accepted membership for several reasons: Mindy and Marietta wanted me to; many of my friends belonged and seemed to have fun in it; and I liked its organizational purpose, which was to put money and volunteer service effectively into local health, education, and welfare agencies. I couldn't donate money, but I was more than happy to accept assignment to volunteer jobs, and I profited enormously from the professionally directed training courses. Knowledge and techniques learned in them were useful all my life.

One of my most worthwhile volunteer work assignments as a new Junior League member had been in a hospital birth-control clinic. We worked with teenage mothers and with young women drained of strength by too many pregnancies and with young couples who wished to postpone pregnancy until they could afford to care adequately for a family. It was a somewhat hazardous job because there was a risk of fines or imprisonment. At that time, giving contraceptive advice was illegal. I considered that law to be illogical. Abortion and abortion information were also illegal; it seemed to me that widespread knowledge of contraceptives would tend to somewhat lessen the need for the tragic choice of abortion and that both reduced the number of unwanted, abused children.

However, laws affecting women's and children's welfare have not, historically, been consistent with logic, justice, or compassion. But we can take heart, in spite of glaring exceptions, that civilization, little by little, appears to progress toward justice. Worldwide, the situation gradually, very gradually, improves. There is no longer the torture of foot binding in China; there is no longer official sanction of suttee in India. The world condemns female circumcision in Africa and the murder of unwanted wives, concubinage, purdah, and the denial of female medical care and education. In our country, contraception is no longer a crime. Women with the sad necessity for abortion no longer must seek dangerous help in back alleys. Women now have a say in what happens by our right to vote. Equality in education, medical care, and economic opportunity are still lacking, but the gaps are slowly closing. We, along with all men and children, would benefit if the abilities and energy of women are allowed to contribute fully to general welfare.

Murder, 1933

On our frequent vacation visits to the ranch we'd often go to the campus to see our friends there, especially Dave and Allene Thorp Lamson, who with their adorable baby girl lived across the street from the Salvatierra Row campus house. Chuck and I knew them well at Stanford; both were prominent in campus life. They were both intelligent, handsome, gentle-mannered, and very much in love with each other.

Memorial Day, 1933, beautiful Allene was found bludgeoned to death. Dave was arrested for murder. His friends could not believe that he was capable of such a crime but could offer no factual defense. The prosecutor believed he had done it, but he could offer no argument beyond the fact that there was no evidence of the presence of anyone else in the home.

While Dave was in prison, Louise and Snick and Chuck and I and countless other friends supported him with our confidence and affection. After a three-week trial, he was found guilty and sentenced to hang. He was sent to death row in San Quentin State Prison. While there he wrote his thoughts about life and death, about his fellow prisoners, the guards, and criminal justice. In 1935 he compiled them into the best-selling book *We Who Are About to Die.*

In 1934 the California Supreme Court ordered him a new trial, stating that the evidence presented against him had been "no stronger than suspicion." After eleven months on death row, he was transferred back to the Santa Clara County jail and was more accessible to his friends. The second trial lasted three months and resulted in a hung jury. Dave was put on trial the third time in November 1935, but this trial was stopped because of jury irregularities. The fourth trial, in 1936, also resulted in a hung jury. (The prosecution against David Lamson was dropped on the same day that the murderer of the Lindbergh baby was executed.)

The mystery of Allene's death was never solved. Prosecutors believed David was a murderer. His friends believed he was a tragic victim of unsupported suspicion. Dave took his five-year-old daughter, Jenny, and moved to Southern California, where he eventually remarried and rebuilt his life.

State Emergency Relief Agency (SERA), 1932–1933

In the depth of the Depression, projects were invented to make jobs for women on welfare. The manager of the Pasadena Employment Agency asked me if I would, as a volunteer, manage a statistical research project to employ about a dozen office workers. It was an opportunity to be of significant usefulness and I agreed to do it.

Women assigned to the project came in, shocked and embittered by job loss and bewildered and humiliated by welfare procedures. Working together, we gradually became a family, teaching and encouraging each other, rejoicing when a real job opened for one of them, taking in new arrivals, and, with understanding and affection, knitting them into the warmth of the project. I taught them to be skilled statistical clerks. Leadership gradually emerged. They were interested in the project and loyal to me, and they formed an efficient team. One of the women, Christine Martin, was specially competent; she ran the office when I wasn't there.

Our statistical methods were ludicrous compared to modern computers, which hadn't yet been invented. We wrote items of information on cards and then sorted them into piles. The results were tabulated and correlated, using a big calculating machine. In the evenings I taught those women who were interested how to turn tabulated results into usable information. Among the women in the class was a pretty, not very bright stenographer. Christine Martin asked her why she was interested in this material. "Oh," she said, "I just like Mrs. McLean and I like to watch her nose wiggle when she talks." Although the mechanics of statistical research have changed radically, the real skill remains unchanged. Interpreting the meaning of the figures must still be done by a human brain. Without interpretation, the figures are meaningless.

In the flood of welfare problems, ours was such a minor project that officialdom left us pretty much alone as we worked. The growing octopus of SERA usually ignored us. Occasionally a timekeeper would come from headquarters to check our records and be upset by our informality. They wanted eight to five work, with an hour off for lunch, five days a week. Most of our project women had family responsibilities that sometimes made this difficult. We kept time sheets and, as long as the work was done and each woman was putting in the required forty hours each week, I let the hours be flexible. Mine were, too. As the trained women took over more responsibility, I was able to spend more and more time at home.

Our report was published and well received by the powers that be. The women went on to other work projects. I was wanted by the head office in Los Angeles to develop a project about fraud in welfare applications. As there was no paradigm at headquarters for volunteer work, I was paid fifty dollars a week, which I used for transportation and to pay Miss Kerr for taking care of Tookie.

The next three months turned out to be an amazing experience. I learned about inefficiency to the nth degree, vicious office politics, the helplessness of clerical staff, the despair of welfare recipients, and the general idiocy of bureaucrats. As my secretary said, "Sometimes it's almost funny and sometimes it ain't."

One of my superiors was Mrs. Shencup, volatile, vituperative, dedicated. I liked her. She was friendly, fair, and helpful. Another supervisor was Mr. Cooley, cold, power-greedy, and vindictive. Mrs. Shencup constantly struggled against Mr. Cooley's machinations in empire building.

I had my first direct experience with this feud when I arrived one morning to find my office occupied by someone else and our project shut down; I was transferred to another office as a file clerk! It took Mrs. Shencup several days to find all of us, locate our files, and get the project set up again. Another time Mr. Cooley sent us all out into the field to survey food prices in grocery stores. Mrs. Shencup gathered us up again and the welfare fraud project was resumed. One of the staff said she was glad I was back because I had a calming effect on Mrs. Shencup. By that time I had just about decided that the pitiful lies the needy were telling to get onto welfare were insignificant compared to the waste of funds, inefficiency, and political warfare of the department. Everything fell into chaos again. A state election was in the offing, and the social workers were told to relax rules and get five hundred additional people onto welfare rolls immediately! We were all assigned to do the paperwork.

On my noon break, I often sketched—dejected clients waiting in line, furniture being moved out of offices, a social worker interviewing a client surrounded by dogs (listed as her dependents), fat Mr. Cooley and his cigar, Mrs. Shencup in a fury. Mr. Cooley was not amused.

Mr. Cooley won. Mrs. Shencup was assigned to a small windowless office with practically no staff. I was "terminated," which fortunately meant fired, not executed. Perhaps the sketches had something to do with it.

I really liked fiery, valiant Mrs. Shencup and I dropped in to see her from time to time. She gradually worked her way back out of exile. She planned interesting well-paid projects for me to direct, but she was never able to implement one.

It was a relief to escape from the turgid whirlpool of SERA. Marion Holman, in New York, where Cranston had his medical practice, had a friend who asked me to market her line of elaborate and expensive Christmas cards. No harm in trying. Feeling somewhat like a Fuller Brush salesman, I took my book of samples and Tookie and rode busses and streetcars and walked miles and miles. I placed orders in the most prestigious stores in Los Angeles, Pasadena, Santa Monica, Westwood, and even in San Francisco and Palo Alto. The enterprise was profitable and would have been more so if I had more adequate transportation and more time and strength.

"Our Baby," 1935

Tookie was pleased by the prospect of a baby brother (a sister was not considered) and happy to spread news of "our baby" among his friends.

At the time, I was doing a survey of opportunities and need for volunteers by Pasadena social agencies. When it was done, I organized and managed the Pasadena Volunteer Employment Bureau, for Junior League in cooperation with the Pasadena Chamber of Commerce. When Allan's birth became imminent, Marietta Harriman replaced me as manager.

I took the train to Palo Alto, spending an uncomfortable night watched over nervously by an apprehensive Pullman porter. Again, I stayed with Mummie and Daddy in their Salvatierra Row campus home. Chuck brought Tookie up to be with me and stayed a few days himself before going back to his job in Pasadena. Tookie had a new audience of neighbors to tell about "our baby, about to hatch."

This second cesarean, October 10, was a nightmare for me (and for Doctors Almon Roth and Blake Wilbur). There was some kind of poisoning. I had a very hard time and a slow, slow, incomplete recovery. Chuck was with me as much as he could be. I arrived from the hospital in an ambulance, which thrilled Tookie. He and Chuck went home to Pasadena.

When I was stronger, the baby, Allan Hoover McLean, and I took the train home. It was an awful trip. Trouble on the line delayed us for hours. We arrived in Pasadena in a rainstorm. Our car was at the end of the train, far from the sheltered station. There was no Chuck to meet me; he had been told the wrong time. I didn't have the strength to carry the baby

Louise's daughters, Dellalou and
Judy Dunbar; 1937

to the station. The porter put him in his basket on top of his cart. The basket slipped and the baby rolled down between the suitcases. We fished him out, wet and slippery. Chuck eventually arrived. Home and love and warmth and bed had never been so appreciated.

It was frustrating to be so weak and for moving to be so painful. But the children were a joy. Tookie adored "our baby." When he cried, Tookie would talk to him and lay his head beside his, and baby Allan would sigh and go to sleep. Sometimes Tookie would sing to him, too softly for me to hear the words, but I caught snatches of "down at the bottom of the sea with the shells . . . Big bear good bear, little bear bad bear."

One morning when I did not wake up to Allan's first complaining noises, Tookie came to me with pins and a diaper and said, "Mummie, I can't put this on, it's too compilated." He was often awake at dawn when I nursed Allan. He told me that "when the sun comes up the dark melts into the floor."

At seven months, Allan was not a kewpie type. Chuck was annoyed when I said, "Chuck, have you ever seen such a funny-looking baby?" He was more annoyed when, forgetting my previous remark, I said that Allan resembled him. Fortunately, by the time he was a year old, Allan was a satisfactorily beautiful toddler. By then Tookie had reverted to normal mischief. Once when I corrected his behavior he said, "I'm just getting that way, Mummie, boys do."

Mrs. Williams's School, 1936–1938

Not long after Allan was born, our dear Dr. Benjamin told me that he knew someone who needed me. Mrs. Williams had a school for about a dozen handicapped children and needed someone to run the office for her. He said she paid well but might be difficult to work for. Was she ever!

Getting ready to drive our trailer from the ranch to Pasadena.
Casa driveway with grape arbor in background; 1938

The hours when I was working, Tookie and Allan were cared for by Mrs. Hanson, a capable, loving grandmother neighbor.

Mrs. Williams's accounts were in chaos. Her accountant practically wept with relief when I said I'd do what I could to straighten them out. The unemployment tax had newly been instituted and detailed personnel records were essential for the first time.

I got an early sample of her mind processes one day when I was surrounded by piles of receipts and bank records and bills and she said, "Don't bother with all that, just send them the totals." And, again, when I heard her side of a phone conversation: "Operator, give me Terrace 5065 or 6056 . . . I said . . . Of course I know the number, it is Terrace 5065 or 6056 . . . well, if you can't get me the number give me someone who can" . . . Bang. "I don't know what the world is coming to."

She announced one day that she was no longer going to pay tax on the wages of Agnes the cook and several times tried to deduct from agreed-on wages because she disapproved of something. I had found another screaming boss. But, where Mrs. Shencup had been a frustrated, profane longshoreman, Mrs. Williams had the tantrums of a demented child. Fortunately, neither of them screamed at me. But the personnel turnover of nurses and teachers was dreadful. I became a buffer between her and infuriated staff members. And yet, she could be a sweet, cultured lady. She dressed beautifully and had, except when screaming, a lovely voice. She took Chuck and me to ballets and operas and symphony concerts. When we gave a party, she made us table-centerpieces. She treated the children under her care with expert attention, but she was rude to their parents. They put up with it because of the loving care given the children by the staff in this handsome home. She had dreams of buying a large estate and expanding her program. Several times she was on the verge of getting individual or foundation help for this, but her erratic behavior always, eventually, frightened off prospective support.

My work was not with the children, but I lost my heart to them—Down-syndrome children who were affectionate and obedient, spastic paralysis victims who struggled so desperately to talk and act, autistic little ones, silent in their nightmare worlds. The children responded to me. "I love you because you smile," said one.

I decided to establish a Girl Scout troop (it included a boy or two) because they needed something interesting to do, and they needed some way to learn an ethical code of behavior that made sense to them. They loved it and it helped them. There was one thrilling day when a previously silent autistic child stood up with the others and recited the Girl Scout pledge. I taught them, in months of work in my kitchen, to cook and serve a simple lunch: creamed tuna on toast, sliced tomatoes, frozen peas, snow pudding for dessert. Finally we were ready to invite parents to lunch. Some of the parents wept.

The Girl Scout Commission, of which I had previously been a member, was interested in the experiment. Up to that time there had been no handicapped children in scouting. Most of the commissioners were delighted, but two said that "other Girl Scouts should not be exposed to 'that kind of child.'" We were not allowed to wear Girl Scout uniforms or insignia, but I made the children alternatives.

Working for Mrs. Williams was extremely nerve-wracking. After almost three years, I'd had all I could stand. I told her that my mission there was completed; there was nothing more I could do. I wanted to go on to other things, and she must look for a new office manager. I worked with another Girl Scout leader until the children accepted her happily. I trained my assistant to take over the books and cope with Mrs. Williams's peculiarities. Then I told Mrs. Williams that it was time for me to leave her in order to cope with my own family. I gave her two weeks' notice. She was stunned and didn't believe it.

She was shocked into a few days of more rational behavior. She stopped accusing all of us of stealing and she apologized for past accusations. She stopped telling us to spy on each other. She stopped screaming and having tantrums in the office. After a week, she decided that I was not changing my mind, and she fired me because I had "no loyalty, was too young to understand child psychology, and had no idea of personnel management." Being fired instead of resigning, I was entitled to two weeks' salary and to unemployment insurance, which she protested vigorously, but which were extremely helpful until I could find another job.

Dear Dr. Benjamin said that he was amazed at how long I had stuck it out. Those were welcome words. Mrs. Williams soon forgot that she was angry with me. She resumed doing nice things for our family.

Another Baby, 1939

Winter, spring, and summer 1939 were spent in a nightmare pregnancy. In addition to nine months of nausea and fainting spells, there was increasing pain from adhesions resulting from difficulties of the pregnancy four years before.

Early in July we drove to Palo Alto. Since the house on Salvatierra Row had been sold, this time I stayed with Cousin Kate and Cousin Roy Heald until it was time to go to the hospital. They were dear to me. Daddy's cousin, Roy, had always been a favorite relative, and Cousin Kate was a large, comfortable, capable, and loving woman who knew everything about everybody. She entertained me with illuminating gossip. She also told me how devastated Mummie and Daddy had been at our marriage, and how, after we returned from Montreal and visited them at the ranch, Mummie had said, "Oh, Kate, just to know that boy is to love him! Hulda will be happy." Cousin Kate added, "How ever did you find such a nice man?"

Allan and Tookie with Chuck's mother, Lillian McLean; 1939

In Pasadena, Chuck's darling, fluttery mother had come from Boise to take care of the family. To help her was Ellice, a competent, pregnant young woman who was lovely with the children and did the cooking and cleaning. They got along without me beautifully.

Robertson Brooke McLean was born July 22, 1939, in the new Palo Alto hospital on the Stanford campus. My recovery, although slow, was without the pain of last time. Dr. Roth told me he used completely different materials than with Allan's cesarean, believing that part of the trouble may have been an allergic reaction. He was also able to release the binding adhesions that had caused so much trouble afterwards.

From the hospital I went to stay with Aunt Lou and Uncle Bert in their gorgeous campus home-on-the-hill. Chuck and the little boys drove up to get us, stayed a few days, and then we all drove home. Robbie's birth brought me the gift of recovered health.

South Pasadena Avenue, 1938–1943

In 1939, our friend Varick Martin told us that the two-story gingerbread Victorian house next door to him was going to be for sale. A Cal Tech

Our home in Pasadena, 1938–1943

professor who had been living in it for years with his mother, who had recently died, wanted to move into a small apartment near the college. We talked to the professor and he told us he would be glad for us to live in his house and that he would sell it to us for $3,500, including any furniture he didn't take with him. The house needed repairs, but the price was fantastic, less than half what it was worth, even in the deep depression market. The problem was, we didn't have $3,500. However, George Keffer said his bank would lend it to us, and we could repay part of it when our Linda Vista home sold and the rest in installments. We had no collateral. He said it was "a character" loan. Our friend Varick now became our neighbor. He was a widower with an elderly deaf housekeeper, who turned her radio on so loudly that it sometimes shook our windows. Varick had three sons. The youngest, teenage Howard, was an admirer of mine. When I turned thirty, he told me that I was well-preserved.

On Pasadena Avenue, which was in the older part of Pasadena, were large, comfortable homes surrounded by gardens. One block away were the elegant mansions on Orange Grove Avenue. A few blocks in the other direction was a poor Mexican settlement. A neighbor, fascinating to the little boys, was a firehouse with two large, shiny, red fire engines. It was staffed by firemen, patient and friendly to the awed children.

We bought the house full of antique furniture. It was soundly built of heart redwood. It had been the farmhouse for the 1860s farm formerly there. The roof, electric system, and plumbing had recently been

Hulda with Allan and Rob
at the Pasadena Schools Play Group, 1940

redone. We hired our Linda Vista unemployed carpenter neighbor, at the going depression rate of fifty cents an hour, to work on the house and to supervise workmen doing things he could not do. The multicolor peeling paint outside was scraped and the house painted white. A fireplace was added. A sleeping porch was screened in. The banister of the curving stairway was repaired. The hardwood floor was sanded of its green paint and stained to enhance the oak it was made of. Interior ivory paint was refreshed. We cleared the half-acre garden of seventy-five spindly trees, leaving a huge magnolia and a mimosa in front, an orchard and a large pepper tree in back, and several camellia trees against the house. It had an extensive basement.

It was beautiful. We settled into it and loved it. It would be a blissful place for the children to grow up. For help with housework and children

Tookie, Rob and Allan with pup Blacky in the garden
of our Pasadena home, 1940

while I was working, we had a series of maids, some excellent, who sooner or later left for better-paying jobs. Others were woefully inadequate. The problem eventually was solved by Christine Martin. After being my right hand in the SERA work-relief project, she had become a school librarian. But surgery had left her weak and jobless. She came to live with us. She could not do heavy work, but that was okay, Chuck and I could do it on weekends. She was fine with the children and was constantly tidying and polishing and cooking and cleaning up and was a cheerful companion for everyone. In the intervals when Louise was with us, they worked together. Louise was always welcome, a delightful companion. I loved her as a sister, enjoyed her off-beat ideas, and was alternately horrified and amused by her escapades. As Christine got her strength back, she resumed her own business and social life, but she continued to stay with us, doing more than her share. Between all of us, our home was well cared for and the children flourished.

With my strength almost miraculously back after Robbie's birth, our social life picked up, and I resumed jobs, both volunteer and paid, with new enthusiasm. The all-important responsibilities of wife and mother took on an additional glow. The children were a constant joy and an occasional exasperation. They were healthy and happy in a world of love and wonders.

Robbie progressed from "Wobbie want cookie" at one, to two's "Whee, here I come," as he threw himself at me, to three when he had an air of self-approval and took everything in stride, whether or not he had any idea of what was going on. At four he was full of questions: "When is sometime?" "Who watered the watermelons?" He was an excellent mud pie maker; his neat row of "punkit" pies would dry on the back steps. One afternoon he announced, "Tell Daddy get a new bed now." Investigation revealed a room full of smoke and a heater lifted onto the bed and covered with a blanket.

Aunt Lou registered Robbie and Alice Campbell (Allen Campbell's toddler) in Broadoaks, a fine Quaker nursery school. Robbie's first report said that he was a happy, cuddly child but resented adult interference in his projects and that "he and Alice often team up to defy authority." Mildred Campbell picked them both up from school and fed them lunch and put them down for naps. I picked Robbie up from Mildred's when I got home from the office.

Allan, as a toddler, had been a destructive cyclone. The pediatrician called him "a sparkler." He had an exploring mind and wanted to find out everything about everything. His explorations frequently resulted in mayhem. At three, he had complete self-confidence. On our first visit to Mindy's new home in Sierra Madre, he watched the divers in the swimming pool, trotted out onto the diving board, and dove off. Three clothed adults jumped in to save him as he bobbed up, spluttering and laughing. That was the pattern of his life.

When he got to school, his energy found constructive outlets and most of the destruction stopped. His school report said that he was doing well and was socially successful, "perhaps too much so," and was a leader in the children's projects. He was smaller than most of the children and he got his longtime nickname "Mouse." Watching children in the school playground, I noticed that wherever Allan went, others followed.

At seven, he told me that he had a little bit of God in his head who told him what to do. I don't think it was the "little bit" that told him to put a handful of chicken feed in my gas tank. For months I carried a bicycle pump in my car to pump out the gas line when the engine stalled. He had said that his conscience "pinched" him. Sometimes it evidently didn't pinch hard enough.

One afternoon, dressed for tea—hat, gloves, high heels—I paused to kiss Allan goodbye. "Oh, Mummie," he said, "you look like a lady." It reminded me of times in London when my mother on her way out to a dinner would come upstairs to kiss us goodnight. She was beautiful and smelled of violets. She had diamonds around her neck and a circlet of them in her hair. "You look like a princess," I told her.

With Chuck's help, Tookie made himself an office, four by eight feet, under the stairs. It housed a desk, chair, lamp, and rug. It was his getaway from little brothers. He could lock up his microscope and other treasures there. He wrote (under his school name "Alex") a poem for his brothers, a parody of a currently popular song, "You're the Cream in My Coffee":

To My Little Brothers—Alex
You're the sand in my spinach
You're the cracker crumbs in bed
You're the sulfur in the water
You're the cold in the head.
You're the slug in the salad
You're the mouse in the stew
You're the bane of my existence
I don't appreciate you.

His teacher reported, when he was ten, that Alex was at the head of his class but socially timid. I had noticed that, unlike Allan, who jumped into the middle of things, Tookie liked to watch for a little while to figure things out before participating. As head of his Cub Pack and vice president of his class, I didn't think he was timid. At ten he was the lead in his school play. A parent sitting in the audience near me said, "Who is that little boy? Isn't he marvelous?" His mother glowed.

Tookie was observant and thoughtful. One afternoon when he was eleven, I was ill with a sinus headache. He insisted I go to bed while he took care of Allan and Robbie, got dinner for them (soup, toast, and canned cherries), put Robbie to bed, and then got himself and an unusually cooperative Allan to bed.

Sometimes the children would go to church with me, not to Quaker meeting, because I couldn't find one. Since Mummie and Daddy were Quakers, that would have been my choice. I went to church as often as I could; although I did not believe in the Christian mythology, I did admire the Christian ethic. I took joy in the literature of the Bible and delight in the company of good people and church music. One of the ministers said, "We come to church to try to find God." I pondered the metaphysical.

Allan's first church experience had not been a success. Four years old, he asked to come with me, getting appropriately scrubbed and dressed. We settled ourselves into a pew and he asked, "Where is God?" I said, "In your heart, darling." He grasped his stomach and looked puzzled. People smiled. The choir started a complicated chant. Allan said, "If they don't stop that racket, they'll scare him away." After the choir chant, the minister came slowly, solemn, benign, white-bearded, down the aisle. Allan jumped up on the pew and pointed, "There he is!" I gathered us up and went quietly out.

The children clamored to go with me on trips and to the office. Sometimes, of necessity, I took them. Robbie was still nursing when I had to go to Sacramento to a legislative hearing. I left him in a hotel room with a baby-sitter and came back to furnish nourishment periodically. The state medical director found out what I was doing and assigned me a state car and chauffeur. It thus made things simpler. I had known him before, as the Pasadena medical officer. We had worked on several projects together.

Tookie and Allan were astoundingly good when they went with me. They listened quietly or played chess or, if there was a nearby park, played there. I wondered what they found so interesting on these excursions. "I learn a lot of things," said ten-year-old Tookie. Once, in the office, four-year-old Allan was not so good. He locked all the doors in the ladies' room, crawling out under them. My secretary, Barbara Henry, was smitten with Allan and found things for him to do to "help" her. If it was necessary to bring Robbie to the office, he sat placidly on my lap, perhaps chewing on my keys. "Pacifiers" were not the universal baby-quieter they are now, when every baby seems to have one stuck in his face. We didn't even own one—our babies didn't appear to need pacifying.

Daddy gave us his small three-wheel house trailer. He had become disenchanted with it because the single rear wheel kept getting hot and blowing out. Chuck redesigned it for four wheels, and we used it on weekends for family camping on a beach or in the hills behind Pasadena. Perhaps our favorite spot was Palm Springs, which had not yet been "discovered." We camped under palm trees by a small stream whose bed sparkled with flakes of fool's gold and was full of pollywogs to delight the little boys. These were idyllic times.

Every vacation was spent at the ranch. There was no other place we enjoyed so much or where the little boys could have so much fun. The twelve-hour drive was tiring, but we took along toys to amuse them and they could sleep when they got weary. For us, the trip was enlivened by the series of Burma Shave advertisements along the way—signboards spaced a few thousand feet apart along the roadside. I remember two of them: "Within this vale / of toil and sin / your head grows bald / but not your chin / Burma Shave." And "Does your husband / misbehave / shout and rumble / rant and rave? / Shoot the brute / some Burma Shave."

The grandparents were patient with the small boys. Mummie said that she did not clean grubby fingerprints off windows and walls for a while after we left, so that she could still feel their presence in the Casa!

World War II, 1939–1945

One day in Pasadena, in 1939, I was ironing the carpet in Louise's room with a hot iron, trying to get rid of the fleas that her kitten had bequeathed to us (insecticides were being developed, but were not yet on the market), when news of Hitler's invasion of Poland came over the radio. England and France declared war on Germany. France fell. Other nations joined in. The United States became "the arsenal of democracy" in a frenzy of production of arms and supplies for England. Our ambassador to Japan informed President Roosevelt that there would be a possible Japanese attack on our West Coast.

Aunt Lou, who came to Pasadena often to visit her sons, Herbert and Allan, usually dropped in to see me, too. We were good friends. I could depend on her for advice, and she would give me family news and tell me of her concerns. She knew I was an interested listener and would be discreet. She told me that Uncle Bert was worried that the president and Secretary Cordell Hull did not understand Japanese character and perhaps did not realize that recent messages had been badly worded and would be considered insults by the Japanese.

I was in our Pasadena kitchen, cleaning up after breakfast. Chuck and the children had gone in our car on an errand, when the radio news flash came—8 AM, December 7, 1941, the Japanese air force attacked Pearl Harbor in Hawaii, sinking a large part of our navy and killing more than a thousand men. America declared war. Japan overran Hong Kong, Singapore, the Philippines, and many Pacific Islands. It seemed to me that in times of dire emergency sober common sense and action are required. There probably was sensible planning and action taking place somewhere, but more obvious was hysteria: for instance, all Japanese, and

American citizens with Japanese ancestry, were imprisoned, with no adequate provision made to protect their possessions and property. I made myself unpopular by protesting this outrage.

The children were frightened by what they heard. "Have the Japs reached Grandaddy yet?" asked Allan with apprehension. The Japanese increased this hysteria by flying a few of their airplanes over the Pacific Coast, by lobbing a few shells onto a beach, and by sending some submarines to the West Coast. One submarine surfaced near Waddell Creek at Greyhound Rock. We were told it had been destroyed near Año Nuevo Island, but as no wreckage ever washed ashore, I doubted that assurance.

Our friends' husbands who had skills that were needed enlisted. Other friends went to work in war industries. Neal and Chuck were busy in official conferences about wartime use of oil and gasoline. Chuck was an air-raid warden. Daddy became a colonel in the Army Ordnance Corps.

In order to mitigate the children's fears, we held a family conference about what we could do to help. We decided on several things. We would raise a vegetable garden. We already had one, but we would make it much bigger. Food was being rationed, and fresh vegetables were hard to find. We would obey the "Make do, or do without" war slogan. We would buy war savings stamps. Aunt Lou sent us all bicycles in case the gas shortage made other transportation unavailable. I thought that it would be a long bicycle trip to the ranch if we needed to seek refuge there.

The existing vegetable garden, surrounded by Allan's sunflowers, was made bigger. Allan planted radishes with enthusiasm. When they sprouted, Robbie pulled them up to make sure they were growing. As with all successful vegetable gardens, our crop exceeded our needs. We shared with our friends. The boys loaded their red wagon and peddled vegetables to neighbors, buying war stamps with the proceeds.

Mummie Dies, 1940

We were in the Brown House for a long summer vacation in 1940—three children and Mrs. Hanson. Chuck came for long weekends. Mummie was making a good recovery from the stroke she had suffered months before. She spent most of her time on a couch where she could look out over the fields to the ocean and where she could watch the little boys when they played on the lawn.

Then she had another stroke. Daddy was devastated—prostrated. He wanted Mindy to come up, but she couldn't leave Pasadena. We couldn't find a nurse willing to come out to the ranch. The servant couple flatly refused to help in the sickroom. I did my best alone. I stayed with Mummie day and night and tried to keep her comfortable, hid my tears and surrounded her with love, although she showed no signs of being aware of much of anything. A nurse finally came. The servant couple left. I did the cooking and cleaned up a filthy kitchen.

Mummie got pneumonia. The nurse insisted, over Daddy's heartbroken protests, on calling an ambulance to take her to the Stanford Hospital. I rode in the ambulance with her, a long ride because the ambulance driver got lost and went to Watsonville by mistake.

It was difficult. Mummie got steadily worse. Daddy and I stayed in the Salvatierra campus house, and I tried to comfort him. He wouldn't talk to anyone. Mindy finally came. I turned the cooking over to her, while I undertook to return phone messages and do much-needed housework. Mindy hired a cook. Chuck had taken an unpaid vacation and was at the ranch, caring for our family. They were all in the big Casa in order for him to cope with the telephone and a constant stream of concerned friends.

Doctors had been conferring with me because Daddy would not face reality and would not talk to them. They told me that the pneumonia was better and that Mummie could be kept alive indefinitely, but that she would never regain consciousness. I made the choice to let nature make the decisions. When she died on September 3, 1940, I knew I had done what my proud, elegant, and practical mother would want—what I would have wanted.

The funeral was held in the Casa and her casket carried up Emeritus Trail. She was buried on Grateful Mountain as she had wanted, on the ridge overlooking the valley and the ocean.

I returned to my family at the ranch and found the bewildered children covered with itchy pink patches—ringworm from the adopted barn kitten. Chuck took us back to Pasadena. Tookie could not go to school: the children were in quarantine. Dr. Benjamin had never seen such an overwhelming case of ringworm. It took two months of drastic treatment to get rid of it. The treatments were painful; the baby screamed, Allan whimpered, Tookie shed silent tears. My heart cried with them.

Mildred and Theodore Hoover

Mummie and Daddy are intertwined with this narrative, but I want to write about them specially. The one real regret of my life is that I showed them so little love and appreciation—I didn't appreciate them until too late. They were remarkable and good people.

Mummie, Mildred Crew Brooke, whose mother died when she was born, was raised as a foster child on a farm in Iowa. She taught school and then went to live with a wealthy half-sister in Baltimore, where she enjoyed high society. In 1899 she came to California to marry her childhood sweetheart and raised three daughters. When the daughters married, she took up her interests in social life, art, and history. She founded the Palo Alto Art League and joined the Daughters of the American Revolution and became its state regent. She was primary author of *Historic Spots in California.* She liked friends, community work, beautiful things, gardening, order, and hooking rugs that were objects of art. She disliked mediocre results, "common" people, bad taste. She was gracious, beautiful, and efficient.

Daddy, "Tad," Theodore Jesse Hoover, an orphaned boy, worked on his uncle's Iowa farm. In his teens he went to Oregon to gather his young brother, Bert, and small sister, May (who had been displaced to live with relatives), back into a family again. They all worked hard, under the harsh guidance of their Uncle John Minthorn. They moved to California, where Tad, working as a linotype operator, helped his brother Bert through the newly established Stanford University. Then it was Tad's turn for Stanford. They both became gold-mining engineers. They had interests all over the world and made international names for themselves. When World War I broke out, Bert went into public life and eventually became president of the United States. Tad became a college professor and, eventually, dean of the Stanford School of Engineering. He wrote numerous books and articles about engineering. Daddy's interests were his beloved Rancho del Oso, knowledge, and the natural world. His dislikes were my boyfriends, small talk, poachers, game warden McDermott, "New Deal" politics. Things were either right or wrong—no middle ground, no excuses.

As a child, I was sure Daddy knew everything and could do anything. I wasn't far from correct. He could either answer every question or explain how to look it up. Where Mummie was elegant, friendly, and social, Daddy was simple, shy, and gruff.

They had both been raised as Quakers and passed that ethic on to me. A Quaker is guided directly by God, which is the "still small voice within": there is no greater tyranny. They were raised in situations where there was little expressed affection. As a result they were unable to show their love to us children. But I remember that they suffered my teen

Theodore Hoover, 1935

years, endured my friends, helped us buy our first house, helped pay for our babies, adored our children, and always welcomed us into their home. I have wondered, too, if, perhaps, they paid Aunt Lou the money we owed her—and that that was the reason she would not accept it from us when we finally reached a point where we could begin payments.

They enjoyed having our children around them. Daddy would show them things to make and do. Mummie just liked to watch them. She once said to me that she wondered at my patience with them. I replied, "It is hard to know where patience ends and resignation sets in."

Mildred Hoover, 1935

I should not have taken my parents so much for granted—they were uncommonly fine people. I suppose it is in the nature of things that one must live most of life before one appreciates parents. By then, they are gone and there is no way to tell them of your love and appreciation. Perhaps, if there is a Heaven . . .

Pasadena League of Women Voters, 1940

I directed a couple of research projects for the Pasadena League of Women Voters. I was delighted by the effectiveness of the league in acting on our facts to bring about needed action by government agencies. At that time, the early 1940s, every league action, local, state, and national, was based on a completely nonpartisan and thorough study of each problem. In later years, decisions were increasingly made at the national level, rigid nonpartisan principles were relaxed, and individual members were relieved of much responsibility.

Our Pasadena Police Department study was an example of local power. One evening in 1940, Chuck and I were visited by a young police officer. He suggested that, as part of the league's study of city government,

we pay special attention to the police department. He said that he could help us by suggesting questions to ask and places to observe. He said that danger might be involved if we discovered wrongdoing. However, by exposing facts, we could bring great benefit to the people of the city. That sounded very challenging. Chuck, understandably, was not enthusiastic about my getting involved, but he realized the potential importance of the project. I talked it over with a fellow league member who, I knew, had intelligence and courage. We two volunteered to be the committee to study the police department as part of the "Know Your City Government" project.

With best wishes Lou Henry Hoover
Herbert Hoover

Christmas 1940

We steeped ourselves in knowledge of the laws under which the department functioned and the statistics of its operation. The cooperating police officer frequently phoned me with suggestions. We never worked alone. If we could not both go on an assignment, we drafted another league member or friend or even a reluctant husband to go with us in case a witness was later needed. We made a journal of events: time, place, description (names and badge numbers, if possible, which it usually was not). I wish I could remember all the interesting things we found. We noted policemen conferring with officials, drinking on duty, having out-of-city assignations, accepting money, showing up in strange places with strange people, and being rough in arrests. Sometimes we could take verbatim conversations, such as the time we sat in an adjoining booth and saw and heard blackmail money paid to a police officer by a homosexual man.

We made our end-study report of the police department to the league, including the duties and responsibilities of the department, the budget, statistics of operation, and the details of dereliction we had witnessed. The league sent a committee to share our information with the city manager. He was courteous and noncommittal. Shortly afterward, in slow stages, the police chief was fired, a new one was appointed, and the force reorganized.

Our cooperating police officer told us that he had originally come to us at the suggestion of the city manager, who had told him that, on account of the political strength of the police chief, he could not make changes without public support and that the best plan would be to encourage the League of Women Voters to look into it. If we discovered the problems, our information and support would enable him to make the needed changes. Our report, added to other information, gave him the necessary strength to take action.

California League President, 1941–1943

In 1941, I was elected president of the California League of Women Voters. My election as state league president was a surprise. I hadn't been a candidate. Two factions battled for their candidates and then drafted me as a compromise—not an auspicious start. The first challenge was to bring the warring factions together. I told them that the split was irrelevant to our league's job—that there were enough issues on which we were in complete accord to absorb all our energies and resources and that we must put aside the controversial issues for further study. As a result, we all worked together successfully.

There was the challenge of fitting my league work into our family plans. Weekdays were full of school for the children and work for Chuck.

I firmly kept weekends free for them, and I urged the other league officers not to work more than a five-day week. The work was hard and took careful planning to fit it into our other obligations.

It was my responsibility to turn concern into action. I appointed capable women and committees who did their jobs competently. I presided at board meetings, conferences, and conventions; I guided local leagues in action with county and city governments. I represented our program to public officials, newspapers, and the public. I appeared at innumerable state legislative committee hearings.

To accomplish these duties, there was the help of a strong board of directors and, specially, my Stanford friend, Loraine Cleaveland Keffer, whom I appointed as our chief lobbyist in Sacramento. Her husband, George Keffer, was busy as commander, or something, on a warship in the Pacific Theatre. The focus of the California league is in the state legislature. Loraine did the bulk of the work there, and it was because of her knowledge, skill, and charm that our program there was so successful.

We aided the legislators with information on issues with which the league had knowledge, including finance, transportation, public health, industrial relations, child labor, and labor laws. It was helpful that the league was given a desk and space in the assistant district attorney's office. With our successes, our public recognition grew and we gained new members.

Work hours were horrific. I sometimes gave three speeches a day in different towns. There were speeches to local leagues to tell them what was going on and to encourage their work, conferences with government or private agencies, and talks to other organizations and groups to enlist support for our projects.

One group I specially enjoyed was the Non-Partisan Roundtable, a monthly meeting of presidents of statewide women's organizations who gathered to talk over their programs and how best to work together. The members of the roundtable were the Business and Professional Women (BPW), American Association of University Women (AAUW), Parent-Teacher Association (PTA), Daughters of the American Revolution (DAR), Nurses Association, Federated Women's Clubs, and several smaller groups. It was beneficial to me when a league project was compatible with their programs and we could get their active support. It was gratifying that every one of these presidents joined the league.

Another important project was serving on Governor Earl Warren's Citizen Tax Committee. The fact that I had previously directed a league study of "Financing Government" was valuable here. The committee brought about a reduction in state taxes—not a common phenomena for government committees!

Travelling in wartime was an adventure and a frustration. I had to do a lot of it. The trains were crowded, slow, and rarely on schedule. Troop cars attached to trains overloaded the engines. The passenger cars were full of soldiers and women with their children. I didn't take Tookie or Allan on many of my trips during this time. When I did, they loved the train; it was a continuous party. I, however, was overburdened by suitcases full of literature to distribute, and I would have rather slept than been entertained.

Personally, the rewards of my work were great. There was the sense of accomplishment and the heady stimulation of new friendships. Among my new friends were: Llewellyn "Soozie" McMahon, California State Chamber of Commerce legal research director; Judge Harold Landreth; Governor Earl Warren; Pasadena Assemblyman Fenton Knight; and many other special people. Some of them remained our lifelong friends.

My two years as league president came to an end. At the final convention, the term reports and accomplishments came together. They were impressive, and the delegates were articulate in their appreciation. I felt blessed; not many people in volunteer public service get thanks for their work. New officers were elected and I was free! What unutterable relief! With friends, I celebrated freedom in the cocktail lounge. Cousin Allan was also there with some friends. He said, "This should be toasted with French seventy-fives." I don't like the taste of alcohol, no matter how disguised, and French seventy-fives, champagne and brandy, were especially awful. But I appreciated the gesture.

I was now back as a full-time mother. What bliss. The work I resumed for the local league and a course I taught at the Pasadena Junior College, called "It's Your Government," were easy to fit in. Louise was with us again. Her current war job was as a riveter at Lockheed Industries. Her husband, Ken, was coming home on furlough, and she wanted to look especially pretty. She gave herself a permanent wave. When it was finished, the curls came off in her fingers. Disaster! Woe! Desolation! I took her to my hairdresser, and he was able to coax her remaining hair into tiny soft curls to cover her head. She looked lovely.

Now we called a family conference. Mindy and Neal, Louise, Chuck and I. What to do about Daddy? What to do about the ranch? The dairyman renter was grossly inefficient. Daddy was sad, lonely, and unwell in the huge Casa. What could we do? What must we do?

3
The Casa
1943–1955

Decision, 1943

SOMEONE HAD TO BE FOUND to be with Daddy and to run the ranch for him. (Finances were no problem; he had these under control.) Finding capable help would be difficult in normal times and totally impossible during the war. I suggested that we three daughters take turns—an ongoing schedule of a week for each with Daddy and then a week by himself. It was a good idea but insufficient and impossible to carry out. Louise doubted that her job could accommodate such a schedule, and we knew she would not be a happy choice for Daddy. Neal said flatly that he would not let Mindy, who would have been Daddy's choice, assume such a obligation. So, it was up to Chuck and me.

We had to assume responsibility for Daddy's welfare and ranch operation. It was a difficult pledge to make. And, oh, the wrench of pulling up fourteen years of Pasadena roots. We were happy there. We had a beautiful home. The children were doing well in good schools. We were constructively involved in the community and had a host of friends. The greatest sacrifice would be Chuck's. He would be trading a bright future in a career in Pasadena for a new start as farmer on the ranch. But, if we didn't do it, how could we be happy, knowing Daddy's sad situation?

Louise said she'd come with us to help us get started. Mindy and Neal said that if we ever needed help, we should ask them for it. We sold our home for $8,850, and also sold most of the furniture; there would be no room for it in the already over-furnished Casa. In August 1943 we put the chickens and three turkeys on top of our loaded luggage trailer and set out for our new life.

Settling In, 1943

The pain of leaving our Pasadena home, friends, and dreams was buried deep under the joy of embracing the ranch, paradise of my childhood. With the fragrance of the air, warmth of the sun and cool kiss of wind, familiar song of birds, glimpse of our fellow residents the deer, bobcats and bush rabbits, brilliant stars at night and phosphorescent light in the waves, and pink dawns and daybreak chorus of song—the sheer beauty of everything—we went to work.

Johnny, the Portuguese dairyman, welcomed Chuck's partnership, another strong back for work and a purchaser of essential working tools. To make farming pay, we knew that a priority was to upgrade the dairy, get a good bull, and cull non-productive cows. We must clean up the place to reduce the milk bacteria count. We borrowed Marietta's horse-trailer and brought up an Adohr bull, Adohr Lubis Roscoe. It was our first experience with the local ration board. In response to our need

The Casa, built in 1925; destroyed by fire in 1959

for extra gas coupons to pick up the bull, we were given only enough for a one-way trip! So we used up our rations and borrowed from our friends. There were no coupons left for the weekly shopping trip to Santa Cruz. We wouldn't starve: we could rely on Daddy's garden, our chickens, our freezer, and the canned food supply. Adohr Roscoe was a fine bull. Johnny made a sub-rosa income when neighbors brought their cows to him.

Chuck set farmworkers to the unfamiliar task of cleaning up the farmyard. He worked with them. The little boys and the farm children all pitched in. When cleaned up, it was a handsome farm. Daddy and Cousin Roy had planned it well when they built sturdy barns and workshops in 1917. For help in plans to upgrade, Chuck relied heavily on the state dairy inspector's advice. For the best utilization of fields and orchards, the guidance of Ed Koch, county farm advisor, was invaluable. All it took was very hard work and the savings we had accumulated over the years.

Chuck rose every morning at 4:30 to get to the dawn milking before breakfast. The boys were up soon afterwards. Then I made breakfast for everybody. Chuck went back to work. The children and I cleaned up after breakfast and tidied our rooms before they went off for adventures, and I faced the housework.

The Casa had been built in 1925. It had four stories, twenty rooms (Chuck's count) or thirty (my count—every furnished space a room). It had been hard to know where to start. Daddy had organized it for his

comfort with an engineer's practicality. He used, and kept immaculate, his bedroom, the kitchen, and the library. Unused furnishings like bedding and clothes he wrapped neatly in newspapers tied with string, which kept out the moths and silverfish, or sometimes kept them in. The overfurnished rooms and halls were tidy but musty, thick with dust and cobwebs and dead flies, in-

Another view of the Casa

habited by spiders, moths, mice, and an occasional bat. Louise took a good look at it and went back to Pasadena.

I decided to start with the top, the little roof-room that was now Tooke's, and work downward three floors to the library and the garden room. I moved furniture around. Daddy said that it looked as though I cleaned house by moving everything into the next room. I cleaned and dusted and polished from the top floor down. At the end, I transferred piles of stuff to the Brown House and the Green Cottage, which would be cleaned and made attractive later on.

Anticipating a possible Japanese invasion, the coast was in complete blackout. Not a chink of light could show from a window. No car lights after dark. If a grim set of circumstances kept one from home after dark, the unlighted drive home was completely terrifying. Since white lines on roads had not yet been invented, there was not even that guidance. Daddy had covered the windows of the rooms he used with blackout cardboard that made them gloomy all day. To replace these I made opaque curtains that could be pulled back to let in the morning sunshine.

Occasionally I had the help of a farmworker's wife. I learned to take full advantage of these very brief domestic help interludes. Almost all farmworkers who had escaped the draft were wanderers. Their families never stayed long in one place. The man worked to accumulate a few months' wages—then they moved on. Their children picked up inadequate snatches of schooling wherever they could.

However, at last, the Casa was shining clean again.

We Start Our Ranch Lives, 1943

Tooke and Allan went to the little one-room Seaside School in Swanton Valley. There were eight students. Allan was the only third-grader. Tooke had the Wilson twins with him in the seventh grade. The teacher was elderly and strict. There are no frills in such a school, but no child is neglected; all had to do the grade work assigned. They received a sound basic elementary education. But not until Helme Smith became the teacher did they also get music and art and a love of nature. I drove them and the other ranch children to school every morning, and for these first months, they came home on the mail stage and walked the mile to the Casa. I remembered taking that walk in my childhood, only it was to the Brown House, along the old road running up the center of the valley. (Daddy plowed it up to increase field acreage and made a new road through the farmyard and at the base of the hills.) There were bluebirds feasting on thistle seeds; bright-striped garter snakes, green and yellow or, occasionally, red and blue and green and yellow; a bobcat trotting along the road ahead of us; the infrequent staccato buzz of a rattlesnake.

Ranch work kept all of us busy. Chuck's back soon protested the unaccustomed heavy labor. Dr. Roth prescribed a brace that solved that problem. My day was full—care of the children and the huge Casa, cooking special gallstone diet for Daddy and hearty food for the increased appetites of our family. I made new curtains and slipcovers to freshen our home's appearance. I helped at the farm when I could. I snatched odd moments to design study-kits needed by my successor president of the League of Women Voters.

On a farm, children work. Our boys took to the idea enthusiastically; it was mostly another form of play. Eight-year-old Allan organized the younger farm children (pay—a piece of candy and a nickel), took his red wagon for gravel, and filled potholes in the road. Twelve-year-old Tooke assisted wherever he saw a need. Four-year-old Robbie "helped" me by carrying things around and leaving them in undisclosed corners. On weekends I wrote a list on the kitchen blackboard of chores that needed doing before they went to play. It was apt to get them up early, because the first one down got the fun jobs. When there were children guests, there was quite a competition, while their mothers watched in amazement. But this was later, when we were ready for guests.

Allan and Tooke could be a real help to Chuck on the farm. They enjoyed the work—and play with the farm children, Johnnie and Zelma, active, adventurous, mischievous children. A soon obvious problem was Portuguese-English speech patterns, liberally sprinkled with anatomical terms and what we consider to be blasphemy. The children learned a colorful vocabulary. Chuck told them that this was "barn language" and not for general use. Except once or twice when the boys were unaware that I was in hearing distance, I never heard them use this vocabulary. However, I heard it once from Chuck, spoken vehemently. Chasing a pig, he

The Farmhouse, built in 1917, razed in 1994

slipped, fell down, and skidded in the mud. Chuck also occasionally spoke strongly when running after a horse trying to catch it. It is hard to outrun a horse. I had found that if one sits quietly in the corral, the horse will eventually come to you to find out what you are doing.

Animal anatomy was not completely learned right away, which was demonstrated when Allan told me he knew how to tell a cow from a bull. "That's interesting, how?" I asked. "You can tell by the expression on their faces," Allan informed me.

84

Soon after we moved up to the ranch, Daddy planted a new orchard across from the Brown House and named it Hulda's Orchard. There were a few trees still there from the old orchard, a quince and a couple of plum trees. Because gophers nibble at their roots, fruit trees do not live to be ancient on the ranch. Daddy waged a constant gopher war in Hulda's Orchard and in his garden. He was an expert trapper. When he checked the traps and took out the gophers, he would stand up and yowl loudly. This told any cat within hearing distance that there was gopher on the menu, and one or two—probably Peanut and Goober—would soon turn up for their treat. Passersby must have been puzzled to see an elderly man standing in a garden meowing. He built a chicken pen and enlarged his garden. He did not complain about the children; in fact, he seemed to enjoy

Another view of the Farmhouse, showing its natural location

them, in spite of toys left around to trip over and a high noise level when they played. We explained about courtesy and consideration for someone not accustomed to chaos, and they became tidier and quieter, most of the time.

In a totally masculine environment, I longed for the conversation and company of other women. Wartime gasoline shortage ruled out social trips to Santa Cruz, where I could have found friends in church, the

The Green Cottage, used on the ranch as a cheese house in 1913,
restored as a guest house in 1915, and still lived in

American Association of University Women, and other activities, so I was
delighted to learn about the Swanton Fortnightly Sewing Circle. All the
women on farms for miles around met at each other's homes for sewing,
gossip, refreshments, and information. It was fun. I took my piles of
mending and had a lovely time with other farmwives and daughters,
mostly families who had been there for generations: the Gianones and
Scaronis of Swiss descent, the backwoods Purdys, the Big Creek Timber
McCrary family, and newcomers like Mary Vickrey and the Wests and me.
There were ten of us.

Our other local social life was the Davenport Farm Center. It was one
of innumerable local groups which fed their ideas to the Santa Cruz
County Farm Bureau, the California Farm Bureau Federation, and the
American Farm Bureau, which is the national farm lobby watching out
for the promotion of food production and the welfare of farm families.
Daddy had been a member since 1918, when it was started. Our farm center met monthly, sometimes at the Davenport School and sometimes at
Charlie Bella's Oceanview Hotel with its handy bar. At the first meeting
we attended, Chuck was drafted as secretary. Center meetings concentrated on local problems, with the men and women discussing such
things as rationing problems, how to control poachers, and where to buy
scarce feed. The women also had their Santa Cruz County Farm Bureau

Home Department, which met monthly and taught skills such as uphol-stering, chair caning, and lampshade making—useful crafts for my Casa rehabilitation projects.

Christmas at Seaside School was a high point in community life. The teacher arranged an elaborate program. Costumes were concocted from the costume trunk in the Casa basement storeroom. When it was opened, there were mouse nests and several dead mice. I washed and ironed the large amount of salvageable material—costumes and lengths of silk and sequins. There was a pale yellow silk, pearl-encrusted cape I recognized as one worn by Mummie in England's social life. I scrubbed crowns and wands, masks and glittery stuff.

At the Christmas program, the trunk clothed an array of angels, shep-herds, kings, dancing peasants, and carolers, all roles taken, with rapid costume changes, by the eight pupils. It was a fine program, well appreci-ated by the Swanton area population. There were at least fifty people in the audience. Allan, as an unlikely, gumchewing, chunky angel was an un-intended comic hit. The school was inadequately heated by a round woodstove, but the room was crowded and the chill soon wore off. I wore a green wool coat lined with fleece. Mindy had sent it to me with a supply of other lovely discarded clothes.

The preparations for Christmas at the ranch took me back to child-hood. We made wreaths, decorated the tree with homemade ornaments, sacrificed our largest turkey gobbler, who had terrified Robbie with its fierce gobbles, made pies and English Christmas

Rancho del Oso: looking toward the ocean from Grateful Mountain

pudding. Then we got flu, all but Daddy and Chuck, who kept as far away from us as they could. I moved the boys into our big bedroom and the four of us suffered in this ward together. Chuck phoned our invited friends not to come for Christmas. May Shockley came anyway, not for Christmas but to help. She made us chicken soup and custard, cleaned up after Chuck's housekeeping, and just generally cheered us up. God bless her.

Christmas Day we still felt awful. I didn't try to cope with making Christmas dinner and being a hostess. The little boys were well satisfied with a toy or two from those under the Christmas tree. By New Year's Day we were almost recovered, so we took the turkey and pies and Christmas pudding out of the freezer and finally enjoyed our Christmas tree and its pile of gifts, a treasure trove of toys.

Twelve-year-old Tooke had researched and written a slim book about the history of the ranch and had sent it to people for Christmas. Ranch

Rancho del Oso: looking up Waddell Valley from Highway 1

history had not been gathered together previously. Producing it had not been an easy job. The reason behind the project had been to develop his writing and organizational skills, which were not up to grade. It had taken a great deal of encouragement and insistence on my part for him to complete the task. His hard work paid off, and he permanently overcame whatever had been handicapping him. Enthusiastic thank-you letters from the people who had received the books for Christmas delighted him. The project was a great success in every way.

Robbie liked my perfumes. I tried to keep them out of reach—I did not need a perfumed little boy. When little boys are clean they have their own warm fragrance. When they are dirty, Chanel does not help. But one day Robbie got into my Chanel No. 5—Chuck's gift, a wartime extravagance—and poured it all over his head. I cut off his hair and made sachets out of it. Rob found a lot of mischief to get into, but not as much as Allan had found in his preschool years. Rob was a favorite of his Grandaddy's, who said, "He's the only one of your children I can hear." We stopped trying to change his piercing voice, which modified itself in time into clear, pleasant tones. Daddy wrote some verses about him:

Robbie, the Robin,
A board and a nail
Make wonderful things
Like a boat with a tail.   1/1943

Robbie, the Robin,
The dog and the cat
There's something a-doing
Wherever they're at.   6/1944

Robbie, the Robin,
The least of the bunch
Is full of chatter
Instead of lunch.   12/1944

Robbie, O'Robin,
As fleet as a fawn,
He sprinkles his knickknacks
All over the lawn.   1/1945

Robbie, the Robin,
Your heart to entwine
Like the tendrils and turns
Of the pumpkin vine,
I send you this card
As your valentine.   2/1945

Brucellosis, 1943

Farmer Johnny had never had the cows tested for either tuberculosis or Bang's disease, brucellosis. Humans can contract undulant fever or TB from drinking raw milk from infected cows. (It had been a woman scientist, Alice Edwards, who, in 1917, had shown that undulant was caused by milk from cows with Bang's disease.) We had our herd tested and found them free of TB, but several of them reacted positively for brucellosis: that meant that they either had the disease or had been inoculated against it. It worried us, so I asked the creamery that bought our milk whether any of it was sold raw. All of it! The creamery owner assured us that was okay; all Santa Cruz milk was safe raw. Chuck talked to the county health officer. He told us that Santa Cruz milk was awful; there was no pasteurization ordinance to make the milk safe, and undulant fever was pandemic in the county. Chuck bought a small pasteurizer for the family.

It is part of Quaker upbringing that if you are concerned about something you should do something about it. So, that is what first plunged me into Santa Cruz politics. I appeared at a Santa Cruz County Board of Supervisors meeting and told them about the raw milk situation. They were uninterested. I told the county farm bureau board about it and received their support in pressing for a pasteurization ordinance. The health officer organized support from health agencies. We went to board of supervisors' meetings again and again—and again. A vocal opposition to us developed; it seems that milk pasteurization was a Communist plot to deny proper nutrition to our children. Headlines in the Santa Cruz Sentinel announced "Hulda McLean named Communist," a charge which would have surprised the Pasadena Young Republicans' Club on whose board I had served. Finally, the board of supervisors passed, reluctantly, an ordinance requiring milk pasteurization.

Aunt Lou Dies, January 10, 1944

Daddy came upstairs from the library, shaken. He gave us news that he had just heard over the radio. Aunt Lou had died in New York. I phoned Coby, cousin Allan's wife, who had just heard the radio, too, and was trying to find Allan. Chuck knew where he was—on his way to his ranch in Fresno County. We found him and he took the next plane for New York.

Aunt Lou had come in from a concert at Carnegie Hall. She stopped to talk to Uncle Bert and then left to dress for dinner. When she had taken a long time, Uncle Bert went in to get her and found her dead. As far as anyone knew, there had been no warning. But I thought perhaps she had known; for the past few months she had been very busy getting things out of storage and sorting them.

I loved her very much and am very glad that she knew it. Too often one forgets to tell a person while they are alive. And she was fond of me; perhaps I was the nearest thing to a daughter that she had. She gave me a wonderful double compliment once when we were sitting in the bright breakfast nook in her campus home: "I like watching the sun on your lovely hair and listening to your discerning mind." She was a good friend to Chuck and me, always ready with sound advice or a boost over a rough place. When we started to pay back money she had lent us to finish college, she didn't accept it, but told us to use it to have the babies we wanted and eventually to pay it back by helping somebody else.

She was, as Daddy said in his telegram to his brother, "a great and gallant woman." When Uncle Bert flew to Stanford, Daddy made one of his infrequent trips there to be with him. The brothers were two great men who had, as ambitious and talented farm boys, loved and married elegant women and had been cherished and civilized by them. They mourned together. Then Daddy came home. Chuck and I went to the memorial service, held in the Stanford Memorial Chapel. We left Tooke and Allan with their grandfather and deposited Robbie with cousin Allan and Coby's children in Palo Alto.

Work and Friends, 1944

One afternoon Robbie sat on the back steps looking forlorn. He said, "I miss Barbara." I doubted that he really missed Barbara, my Pasadena secretary, but realized that he was probably trying to put a name on his feeling of loss for the Pasadena life we had left behind. We all felt it, even when this yearning was buried under our busy ranch life.

In the Casa there were three guest rooms and a guest suite, the rehabilitated servants' quarters. There was the refurbished Brown House. We decided to re-establish the social contacts we all missed, schoolmates, Pasadena and Stanford friends, league companions. We started inviting them to visit us, warning them that it would be a different kind of visit, that we were busy farmers and our guests would be entertained either by working with us or watching us work, but that we would take time off to have fun on weekends. Our friends were anxious to see the ranch and what we were doing and so they came.

Rancho del Oso: Waddell Creek

Some only came once, and that was enough for them, for instance, Barbara. She had a Dresden china approach to farming—long fingernails she didn't want to break, fear of spiders and snakes. She said that her main prayer was that she would not meet a rattlesnake, personally. She was dubious of cows and couldn't climb ladders. But she was fun and decorative and a great moral support while we climbed ladders picking pears or painting the Green Cottage. But our house parties were not her cup of tea.

Others returned again and again during these ranch years. Among them were some of Chuck's Stanford fraternity friends, George and Walter Hays; my Stanford friend, Hope (Williams) Randolph and her family, who usually stayed at the Brown House; Punch and Virginia Watson, my friend from boarding school days; Allen and Mildred Campbell; Marion Holman and her babies; Marietta and Russ Harriman; Varick Martin and sons, Pasadena neighbors; the Shockleys, lifelong family friends; and especially Bill and Soozie McMahon.

Bill and Soozie were San Francisco lawyers, and she had been my League of Women Voters' right hand. They had decided that as a war contribution they would spend their vacation with us helping with farm chores. They worked hard and were a delight. We loved Soozie and her brilliant mind and Bill with his happy humor. They came again and again until the Casa was their second home and I couldn't imagine undertaking a project without them. The children and Daddy adored them. They shared our problems and labors. Once, when returning home from a ranch work vacation, they sent us this poem:

> We're home at last and lonesome for
> Our little cabbage patch.
> We thought of all the fun we had
> And then sat down to hatch
> A plan that would express to you
> Our deep appreciation
> For such a super-duper time,
> And for our graduation
> As pullers of the cabbage green
> And pickers of the berry.
> We're sending you this package to
> Advise you of our very
> Kind feeling toward the tribe that lives
> On the Rancho of the Bear.
> There's a special thanks for each of you
> Except we did forbear
> To add a bone for Rusty or

A snake for Chiki, but
We send regards to both of them,
And the son of puss Peanut.
We liked the work, the eats and drinks,
The restful picnics on
The sand, the trips to town,
The paint (it's almost gone),
The rides for milk, Siberia,
The jigsaw puzzles too,
The muscles and the merriment.
We're sorry that it's through.
We hope we helped a little bit.
(How are the dishes now?)
Please let us know what happens when
The hounds flee from a cow.
We know that Emily Post does not
Advise this sort of thing,
But hope you realize it has
A heartfelt sort of ring.

Another friend sent us a description of her visit:

"Come for a nice restful weekend on the farm, the bus comes right by the gate," she had written.

I got off the bus at the gate and swung eagerly down the two-mile path to the farmhouse with my three suitcases and two dozen chocolate eclairs. It was a beautiful summer day with buzzards flying overhead and rattlesnakes and scorpions dozing beside the road in the sun. As I topped the hill to the farmhouse the dogs ran out to meet me, playfully nipping at my ankles and scalloping my skirt.

"Hello, hello," jovially cried my host, "you're just in time to work up an appetite for dinner. We are off to plow the north forty. Slip into your overalls and come along."

A trampling horde of children burst down the back door and brushed past me. I got up, wiped the mud out of my hair and followed my hostess up three flights of stairs to my room, tastefully furnished with a stepladder and two gallons of paint. "I'll get up early and help you with the ceiling," she said.

Before dinner we gathered in the big ranch kitchen while my hostess, tastefully dressed in a sequin gown and tiara, was cooking dinner on three stoves while stepping carefully over fourteen rare Afghanistan cats, the trampling horde, four blue lura caterpillars and her twelve guests, including myself, three sailors, a visitation from the lowlands and a Very Important Person who paced the floor waiting for a phone call from Tibet.

"Naughty, naughty," said my hostess to the kittens who had pulled the roast off the table, "you'll get the floor all slippery."

Dishes were done well before midnight, and we were all ready to retire except the Very Important Person who did not like his bed and commandeered a posse to bring a special one up from the basement.

I slept peacefully, lulled by the music of a country night; coyotes, screech owls, and a rare Afghanistan cat having kittens under my bed.

The following noon, after an invigorating and back-strengthening morning picking peas, we climbed a mountain to the picnic spot where we were joined by a troop of Boy Scouts and six elderly ladies who were practicing for the local yodeling festival.

All too soon the weekend was over. The visitation departed for the lowlands, leaving behind them mounds of seaweed and wet tennis shoes; the thundering horde mounted their bicycles and rode over the horizon; one by one the others melted away, leaving me with my hostess to carry the Very Important Person's bed back down to the basement and to nail the back door up on its hinges.

Reluctantly I boarded the bus with my three suitcases, a bushel of cabbages, and a rare Afghanistan kitten.

As we had warned, we were busy. Each dinnertime everyone, family and visitors alike, drew a slip of paper saying what his or her domestic job would be the next day. There was much conversation about them and some job swaps. Chores might be sweeping halls and steps, washing silver and glassware in the pantry or dishes and pots in the kitchen, dust mopping, picking and arranging flowers, picking and cleaning vegetables—all things that would leave me more time for cooking, keeping the place tidy, and directing the children (whose jobs were posted on the kitchen blackboard). Daddy was somewhat amazed at this form of entertaining, so different from Mummie's elegant parties with the help of cook and butler.

Guests worked along with us on farm and garden chores or watched, giving us cheer and cold drinks. Each season had it own jobs. We weeded cabbage seedlings, picked apples, made cider, gathered blackberries, fed pigs and chickens, harvested beans, pumpkins, gourds, peas, and brussels sprouts, drained ditches, filled potholes, hoed emerging thistles, cleaned the water tank, cut and hauled wood, mended and built fences, sorted scrap, posted signs, evicted poachers, loaded trucks, painted sheds, broke up log-jams, repaired bridges and other storm damage. A few specially privileged guests were allowed to drive the tractor, plowing, disking, or mowing weeds. Soozie and Bill were experts in all these skills. Strange as it seems, they, and the others who returned often, must have enjoyed this taste of farm life.

On the dunes just beyond Steele's fields, there were wild strawberries. We'd pick them, quarts and quarts of them. Home again, we'd dump them into a big pan of water and wash them over and over again. It was hard to get all the sand out. It was best to eat strawberry shortcake without chewing it.

Varick and his sons and their girl friends came. They were not very helpful with any hard work, but they were entertaining and full of gossip about Pasadena.

Louis and Barbara Lundburg and son Brad came. Barbara had been a Kappa at Stanford and voted to keep me out of this sorority. Louis, who was president of the state chamber of commerce, was Soozie's boss. At the ranch they relaxed and we enjoyed them as friends. When they arrived for their first visit and asked for me, Robbie had told them, "Mom's up the creek with a sailor and Dad's under the house." Brad crawled under with him and helped fix the plumbing leak.

Frances Friedel, our foster sister for so many years, came sometimes. She had finished nurses' training years before and was now assistant to a San Francisco physician. She was always loved and welcomed. Eventually she married and went home to England.

Dellalou and Judy, Louise's daughters, visited from Australia, where they had been for eight years. They were in California briefly. I welcomed them back to the family; I had missed them terribly.

Louise's visits were welcome. She was an entertaining and industrious companion. When she got bored with her riveter job, I suggested that she enlist in the Women's Army Corps, the WACs. She enlisted and wrote us fascinating letters about her adventures. She was sent to the South Pacific war area, where she drove heavy equipment into battle zones. Louise's husband, Ken, was stationed in Alaska. Whenever he could, he'd hitch a flight down to see us. Ken worked effectively at whatever farm job needed doing. He was a good young man.

Mindy and her family came frequently. If it were a long vacation, they might stay in the Brown House and sometimes brought servants with them. They left it immaculate, which I appreciated. For short visits they stayed with us at the Casa, and that was different. They left chaos in their wake. But in spite of that, I loved having Mindy with us. And the boys were fine playmates for their young cousins. Mindy spent most of her time with

Daddy, which delighted him—and me. It was heart nourishing to see him so happy. Teddy, David, and Anne (Mindy and Neal's children) roamed the ranch with the rest of the youngsters. Our children enjoyed every minute of a Willis visit. Chuck escaped to the farm. I coped with chaos.

Daddy's friends were always welcome; they brought him much pleasure and cheer and were thoughtful guests. Among them were his longtime Stanford friend, Professor Fred Tickell; the Reverend Elton Trueblood, Quaker minister and family friend; Uncle Jimmy Hyde and his wife and daughter Elizabeth; May Shockley, our dear outspoken friend; Elwyn Rodgers, who had made the original survey of the ranch, had been its manager for a time, a nurseryman, and was now associated with Daddy in the Polar Star mine; and Dr. Bailey Willis.

Rancho del Oso: Canyon Road

Dr. Willis, Stanford geologist and earthquake specialist, was Neal's father. At that time in his nineties and an erratic driver (as he had always been), he was indignant that his driving license had not been renewed, although the rest of us were somewhat relieved. One time when he had been driven to the ranch to visit Daddy for a few days, he needed a driver to take him home. I was elected. Dr. Willis did not trust freeway traffic and directed me on circuitous routes avoiding freeways and towns. It was time-consuming and nerve-wracking, but it was scenic, and Dr. Willis's conversation was, as always, entertaining. One interesting thing he told me is that nearby Mt. Umunhum is moving seaward at a rate of about two inches a year.

Winnie Kydd, our McGill friend, came to visit us several times. She had just been knighted in England for her work with refugees. She was now Dame Winifred Kydd. She brought a world point of view that broadened our understanding. She was cross with me for "not doing anything" and complained that "there's nothing but scenery here!" But we loved her anyway.

Very late one night, driving home from Santa Cruz, I passed a crying Mexican girl walking down the highway in high heels. I turned around and went back. As I approached, she flagged me down and got in. She wanted to know if I was a Catholic and went to church. I told her that no, I wasn't a Catholic, but I went to church when I could. She said, "I am very frightened, will you take me home with you?" Her feet were blistered, she was worn out, covered with dust. The Casa was full of guests,

Mrs. Shockley and her sister, Bill Shockley's wife Jean and their two boys, and Soozie. I made a bed for the bedraggled girl in the sewing room. She didn't want anything to eat, nor a bath. All she wanted was bed.

In the morning she came into the kitchen, where I was getting breakfast. She was shiny clean and very pretty. She told me, "Last night I went to a dance with nice people, but they weren't nice people so I opened the car door and

Rancho del Oso: Redwood thinning project. Young trees grown up around the stump of a tree cut by Willliam Waddell in the 1860s

got out. I was very frightened." She asked if she could stay and work for me. I really needed help, but then there was no way I could pay her wages. I drove her home to Pescadero, where she lived with her sister and brother.

Christmas and Easter holidays we had special guests, foreign students from Stanford or the University of California. Hosts had been requested for these young people so far from their homes. We could easily accommodate several of them. We enjoyed them, and the experience was a fine one for our own boys. Among the foreign students I particularly remember were two young Mexican men who were studying forestry and were interested in our unique Monterey–knobcone pine cross-species. They persuaded a plump Egyptian student to go with them as they scrambled up a mountain collecting specimens: he did not enjoy the excursion, although he was usually a cheery fellow. We found out later that he was an army officer. There was Yah-Yah Babahani, an Iranian boy, who came to us often and wrote us when he returned to Iran and married his sweetheart, not a common occurrence there, he told us. But America had strengthened his sense of independence. We lost track of him during an Iranian-American crisis. His last letter to us had asked us to look up and protect his son, a Stanford student. We looked him up and left messages for him to phone us, but he never got in touch with us; he was probably not enthusiastic about adult friends of his father. There was Takeo Matsumoto, a journalism student. Tooke visited him when he was on R and R from his marine stint in the Korean War, and when Chuck and I later went to Japan, we were delighted to visit Takeo and his charming family.

As houseguests, these young people were a delight. They accepted their dinnertime job slips good-naturedly, although some had to be shown how to do the simplest of chores. They had come from wealthy families and had no experience in housework.

Evening entertainment was no problem at all. After a brief time in the library with Daddy in front of the fire, everyone, tired out, went to bed. "Fresh-air poisoning," Soozie called it.

Sundays we rested, somewhat. We went on excursions. I packed a big picnic, and we went up the canyon to a favorite spot—tiny sandy beaches along the creek or to Owl Feather Falls under cool redwoods, Slippery Falls and its super swimming hole, along Last Chance Road to catch butterflies, or to the fishing rocks on the beach where we could fish for perch.

It was at one of these picnics up the canyon on the beach below Eagle Tree, July 18, 1945, that we listened to the radio telling us about the first test of splitting the atom. The event had been announced for days. Remembering science fiction stories (Tooke and I were science fiction fans), I wondered, apprehensively, if perhaps splitting an atom might be something like dropping a knitting stitch and the whole fabric of the world would unravel.

During winter, things slowed down a bit. Rain irrigated crops, relieving us of a major chore. Trespassers were not such a problem. Danger of forest fire was slight and our watch could relax. There was more time to work on maintenance and repairs, although it seemed that we never could quite catch up on everything that needed doing.

We spent our evenings in the library downstairs with Daddy. He had appropriated the special comfortable chair that Chuck had brought from our Pasadena home and sat in it doing crossword puzzles or listening to the radio. On Sunday evenings there were special radio programs for us to listen to: Red Skelton, Jack Benny, Duffy's Tavern, Fred Allen, Charlie McCarthy. Chuck read or did farm accounts by the fire. The boys did homework. I was usually mending or darning socks, a never-ending task. Socks were made of cotton or wool. Synthetic hole-proof fabrics had not been discovered. We conversed in a leisurely fashion of the day's events. If Daddy was in a sociable mood, we listened with fascination to what he had to say. His worldwide experience and voracious reading had made him an inexhaustible font of tales and information. Questions would lead to memories, and we would be enthralled by his adventures.

Free Summer Camp, 1944

During summers we invited friends of the children to the ranch. Our boys needed their companionship. The farm children were fun, but not everything we needed. Mindy's Anne came every summer; she was my beloved "summer daughter." She amused and delighted us with her struggle to adjust to a lifestyle so different from the elegance at home.

The children drifted up and down the valley like a flock of birds. They built their elaborate projects, had picnics, and went beachcombing and swimming. They caught delicious crawdads in the creek, pressed wildflowers, and found snakes for the snake cage (released periodically for a new batch). They rode bicycles on the bumpy roads, hiked the trails, explored uncharted territory. They all did their chores, sometimes reluctantly, and ate prodigiously. I felt that we were running a free summer camp.

Occasionally, the children's choice of amusement was to join us in farmwork. For this, I thought I should call the Labor Board and find out if there was red tape to cope with. The Labor Board asked the ages of the youngest and I thought of Marion Holman's toddlers dragging weeds. "Three," I said. They laughed and said that the work seemed to be voluntary and sporadic (very) and that I was breaking no law.

As a child, I had enjoyed raising caterpillars to see what they turned into (mostly brown moths). Some of the children enjoyed this, too. We went on butterfly hunts. We identified and carefully mounted under glass the ones we caught. They were prized possessions to take home. I wrote a story about the children's butterfly enthusiasms and adventures, "Butterfly Summer," and it was published in *Nature Magazine*, June 1946 issue.

Among the children who came more than once was Anne's special friend, Linda Pauling (daughter of physicist Linus Pauling), who had shared our Pasadena Playgroup experience long ago. A pretty, blond, very intelligent girl, she entered enthusiastically into ranch projects, especially the butterfly collections we made. There was John Brooke, Tooke's friend from Pasadena, quiet, musical, full of humor. There was little Myra Randolph, Hope's daughter, who could never quite keep up with the older children and who made her frustrations known by screaming.

And there was young Walt Hays. His mother gave me a long list of directions about his care: he must wear his sweater and overshoes, must not swim in cold water, was a selective eater and had a delicate digestion, must not get over-tired and should take a nap every afternoon, and should not have contact with rough children. I told his father that these directions would be hard to follow, and Walter said just to turn him loose with the other children. This we did, and Walt turned out to be an adventurous little boy with a huge appetite, outlandish ideas, and an inexhaustible supply of knock-knock jokes.

It was just as well that his mother was not there one day when he returned from a swim in the icy creek, barefoot and carrying a butterfly net with a young rattlesnake in it. The children had all been told sternly to keep away from rattlesnakes. The snake was put in the snake cage to be admired for a couple of weeks and then I took it far up the canyon and let it loose. Chuck and I had different points of view about rattlesnakes. He killed them on sight—I felt that this was their home, too, so I just took them away from our paths and released them.

I have only been frightened once by a rattlesnake. One time, when toddler Tooke was playing in a sandbox, I leaned down to pick him up and saw one stretched out hidden by a side board. It was frightening to think what might have happened had the baby reached out for it.

Home again, young Walt, suffering from a childhood illness, told his mother, "I just pretend I am at the ranch under a tree listening to things. Then I feel better." When he was on the ranch, we had often sat "listening to things."

Because it has always seemed to me that males are prone not to notice small things, I hoped that our sons would grow up more observant. When I was taking walks with them or with the other children at the ranch, I would say when we sat down to rest, "Listen to the silence. What do you hear?" We heard the far away surf, a nearby insect, a lizard rustling in the grass, wind in treetops, the call of a quail, a high airplane, a distant tractor, the song of a wren-tit. Silence was often a quiet symphony. I had written verses about it.

Listen to the Wilderness

Listen to the wilderness
Filled with muted music's song;
Stay—and hear the quietness
Softly sing the hours along.

Listen to the wilderness;
Breakers curling on the shore.
Far above the leaping spray
Keening seagulls wheel and soar.

Listen to the wilderness;
Gentle whisper of the stream,
Rippling, flowing rondelay,
Shadowed depths and surface gleam.

Listen to the wilderness;
Gold-crowned sparrow's haunting prayer.
Mountain far, the hawk's harsh cry
Tumbles through the buoyant air.

Listen to the wilderness;
Raccoon chirrs to venturing kit,
Bats call high in twilight sky,
As, star by star, the night is lit.

Listen to the wilderness:
Hear, at night, coyotes sing,
Frogs, symphonic in their song,
Chorus praise to rain and spring.

Listen to the wilderness
Throb on drowsy summer days;
Crickets strumming shrill—beyond,
Dancing, humming, living haze.

Listen to the wilderness;
Music rung by nature's art—
Wave-song, bird-song—such as these
To rejoice a listening heart.

During these busy ranch years, I did a great deal of cooking for Chuck and the boys, for visiting children and other guests, and for Daddy's diet.

Family and friends at a picnic under the Casa grape arbor;
the four on the left are Mrs. Shockley, Louise, Ken and Daddy; 1943

In the big Casa kitchen there was a woodstove that also had gas burners. And there was an electric stove. The three ovens were useful on Saturday baking days.

There was extensive work canning products of orchard and garden, including sixty quarts of plums for Daddy: he ate them every day. Plums were easy to do, after fishing out the seeds. Peeling and coring apples was more of a chore. Canning peaches was not fun—Louise helped me once and called them "pitches." There were more dozens of quarts of pears, blackberries, apricots, raspberries, strawberries, and tomatoes, all neatly stored on the big pantry shelves. Daddy's garden yielded bushels of vegetables. We raised chickens, turkeys, lambs, pigs, calves. In season there was venison and salmon. There was milk and cream and butter from the dairy. No wonder that, in subsequent years, at the rare times I was alone, I was content to live on carrot sticks and Hershey bars! There were no such things as Bisquick or other ready-mixes. I made our own mixes for biscuits, pancakes, chocolate pudding, and basic cake. They were kept in the pantry in big glass jars.

We gave no thought to reduced fat diets or calories (except when Robbie got too chubby) or vitamins (except C—we had tomato juice to start each dinner). I made mountains of breakfast pancakes or biscuits. Lunch was apt to be sandwiches and homemade soup (potato soup every Saturday) and salad. Each Saturday morning I baked mountains of cookies and when the Casa was full of guests, a dozen pies and pans of cinnamon rolls.

We didn't "dress-for-dinner," although we made sure that the children cleaned up and wore fresh clothes, as we did. If it were a family dinner we ate in the sewing-room at what, in London, had been our nursery table. There was ample room for the six of us. But if there were more guests, we ate in the really handsome dining room at its huge mahogany table, which could be stretched even further with leaves. Frequently there would be ten or fifteen of us. If there were too many, the children would eat at the nursery table. Daddy, practical, pragmatic engineer that he was, was also superstitious. If there would be thirteen seated at the table, he would not eat with us. Chuck solved that problem by setting an extra place and bringing Robbie's biggest teddy bear to join us.

Later, when some of the summer ranch children had grown up, they would tell me of their ranch food memories—plain food made ambrosial by appetites sharpened by ocean air, hard work, and vigorous play. There were some favorite recipes:

Gingerbread. Lovely when eaten warm, with applesauce. Put 1 C sugar, ½ C butter (or scant ½ C cooking oil), 2 eggs, 1 C milk, 1 C molasses in a bowl and beat well. Sift together and add the following: 1 t each of ginger and cinnamon, ½ t cloves, 2 t baking powder, 2 C flour. Bake in a shallow pan at 300° for 45 minutes.

Steamed Chocolate Pudding (John Brooke's favorite). Cream together 3 T butter, ⅔ C sugar, 1 egg. Dump into this mixture, 1 C milk, 2½ C flour, 4½ t baking powder, 2½ squares unsweetened chocolate or ½ C ground chocolate, ½ t salt. Beat all this well. Steam for two hours. Serve with vanilla sauce or vanilla ice cream.

Vanilla Sauce. Mix ½ C sugar and 1 T cornstarch; add a cup of boiling water gradually, stirring constantly. Remove from fire and add 2 T butter, 1¼ t vanilla, pinch of salt. (To make lemon sauce, leave out vanilla and substitute lemon juice for part of water.)

Mother Lillian's Cheese Soufflé. Beat together 2 C milk, 3 eggs, 1 t dry mustard, 1 t salt, ½ t pepper. Pour them over 3 large thick slices of buttered bread, which have 2 C grated nippy cheese spread over them. Set for 5 hours, or over night. Bake in a bowl set in water 1 hour at 350°.

Popovers. Sift 1 C flour and ½ t salt in a bowl, dump in 2 eggs and 1 C milk and mix together gently. Pour into hot greased muffin pans and bake 20–25 minutes in 450° oven. This is also the recipe for Yorkshire pudding.

Sour Cream Pie (a tangy mince-like pie). To 1 C sugar, ½ t cloves, ½ t cinnamon, salt, add 1 C ground raisins, 1 C sour cream, and yolks of 2 eggs. Mix thoroughly and pour into pie crust. Bake at 350° until crust is done. Spread meringue (whites of 2 eggs beaten stiff and 2 T sugar added) over warm pie and set in oven to brown slightly. If you use grocery store sour cream, add juice of a lemon.

Rattlesnake (which tastes something like stringy chicken). Skin and clean the snake and cut into two-inch chunks.

Barbecue. Wrap each chunk in a strip of bacon and cook over barbecue or on a stick over the bonfire as you would a hot dog.

Canapés. Cover with water and boil for 5 minutes. Shred meat and mix with chopped hard-boiled egg and a little mayonnaise. Pile on Melba toast and stick a tiny piece of parsley or a thin slice of stuffed green olive on top.

Cookies. When there were visiting children I made extra supplies of cookies, quantities of oatmeal cookies, sugar cookies, chocolate chip cookies, ginger snaps, olio cookies, and quick cookies.

Olio Cookies. Make into crumbs any stale or unpopular cake, cookies, dessert, perhaps add a little oatmeal. In a saucepan heat and mix brown sugar and a little butter, enough so that when the crumbs are stirred in, it makes a *very* thick dough. Drop this in walnut-sized lumps on cookie sheets. Bake 10–15 minutes at 350°.

Quick Cookies. After cake mixes became available, the very quickest cookies could be made by pouring a box of cake mix ("as is"; forget the eggs) into a bowl and stir in a little water or juice to make a thick dough. Drop in walnut-sized lumps onto cooking sheets. If available, put half a maraschino cherry or walnut or some colored sugar sprinkles on each. Bake 10–15 minutes at 350°.

Some Side Effects of War, 1943–1946

In March 1944 a Navy bomber crashed on Waddell Beach. The pilot was uninjured and most of the plane intact. However, pieces were scattered up and down the beach. The wreckage provided entertainment for the children but was a nuisance for us. Government workers enlisted our help and the use of our equipment, tore up our roads until they were impassable, and poured gallons of precious gasoline out into the sand because they could not give away government property. We could happily have skipped this week of contribution to the war effort.

Things were going smoothly at the dairy. The herd was being improved by Roscoe's calves. Dairy methods had been made more efficient to raise the quality of milk. Ranch income from the dairy had increased. Chuck had done all he could for as long as farmer Johnny, with his folklore based methods, held the lease. The state dairy inspector promised to see that standards were maintained. We dissolved the dairy partnership and turned to other farm projects.

During the war there were strict controls over what farmers could raise. Beans were a crop assigned to our area. Beans, however, usually mold in the coastal mist. Another permitted crop was cabbage. The armed forces used a lot of dehydrated cabbage. We once asked a sailor whom we had picked up on the highway whether he liked dehydrated cabbage. "I dunno, haven't tried it—allus throw it overboard," he said.

We decided to sharecrop cabbage on our neighbor Will Steele's land. Our ranch fields were all still under lease to Johnny. Like all agricultural endeavors, it was hard work. We planted seed, weeded, pulled and transplanted, fertilized and irrigated. With wartime labor restrictions, we did most of the work ourselves, with the help of our friends, the boys, and occasional farmworkers. Some of it was fun. I enjoyed driving the tractor pulling the planter, with Tooke and Allan riding it, plopping a plant in a hole everytime the bell rang. Our cabbages flourished. Neighbors came to admire them. Contract braceros helped in the harvest. Then early rains came; it rained and rained and rained until fields were swamps, and it was impossible to get into them to finish harvesting. We made enough money to pay for the crop; no more.

Spring came. We plowed up rotting cabbages and planted broccoli. When harvest time arrived, there was no money to pay bracero wages. Remembering Mindy and Neal's offer to help, we asked them for a loan of two thousand dollars to pay wages, but they refused. The unharvest-

By the bell tower at the Brown House:
Hulda, Tooke, Rob, Allan, Peggy Crowell
and Chuck; 1944

ed broccoli crop sat happily in the field and burst into bloom, a beautiful sight, a soft yellow glow against misty blue hills. I painted a watercolor of it.

I remembered what cousin Allan had said: "Farming is a cinch if you have unlimited capital so you can sit out the bad years and make money in the good ones." Our capital was gone, and we had no collateral for credit.

War rationing and shortages of gasoline, food, equipment, labor, all of which were inconveniences in our farming, were devastating to the agricultural economy of the country as a whole at a time when food was critically needed all over the world. There appeared to be no intelligent government thought being given to this situation. I wished that Uncle Bert were president again.

When we received heavily censored letters from our friends in war zones, we realized how insignificant were our inconveniences. Some excerpts:

George Keffer: "I can't write anything dramatic or even interesting—it would just be censored out. That is why we write on one side of the paper, so holes will only effect one side message. Navy food isn't bad."

Louise's Ken, stationed in Alaska: "Nothing has happened since I last wrote. In fact, nothing ever does. One would think there would be some way to provide better food for us."

Louise, from training camp: "We moved to our new barracks, built for WACs instead of horses, as the old one was . . . Lt. told me to take off nail polish and spit out gum. Yes, Ma'am . . . Cleaned latrines again. So far avoided toilets by grabbing Bab-O and doing 25 washbowls . . . I got tired of making my bed for inspection, so sleep on top of it with a blanket . . . The cream of our country is the officers. They deserve the respect the army insists they receive. Their job is all work and no play and be clean and tidy at all times . . . The food is indescribably awful."

Louise, from overseas, Philippine area: "The first night our tent blew down. We'll be in barracks soon . . . Went for a walk this morning, and took this paper off a dead Jap." Louise came home with a necklace made of finger-bones.

John Matthias, New Guinea: "I feel much safer here than I did at the last beachhead. I came ashore and found my place in the jungle and dug myself a hole . . . None of my old squadron are here, they are all new men. The only thing we have in common is our complete lack of faith in our ever getting home . . . The food is God awful . . . I am terribly impressed by the scale we are able to do things—I am in awe of our greatness. If we ever convert our energy into the field of better living for all, we could change the face of the earth. . . . Bitterness is such a constant companion one can't help being depressed. We are terribly far away, buried in a deluge of indifference in this land of unhappy men. . . . "

We received worrisome letters from Miss Pickering in England:

"We moved to the country from London to [censored]. I haven't been very well lately. Some food is unavailable and some is hard to eat, but in most of the letters I write I try to be a good Pollyanna . . . Clothing is so difficult—one can't buy much . . . We had a few incidents a week ago . . . We are alarmed."

I wrote asking is there anything we could do to help. She replied that most imports were forbidden to civilians, but that what they most needed was fat! And there was no taboo on that. So when we butchered, we sent her tubs of rendered lard or suet. She was grateful for them. How little we could do!

End of World War II, 1945

In April 1945, President Franklin Delano Roosevelt died. While the public mourned their demi-god, my feeling was relief at an evil spell broken. However, we would long suffer from his lies and disastrous decisions, including: killing our last chance to avoid World War II when he scuttled the London Economic Conference; promising "a job for everyone" in the

Tooke and Capri, Allan on Teddy, and Rob with beagle Boo
in the Casa driveway; 1945

winter of 1933 when there were no jobs; stating, in a "fireside chat," "I give you mothers my word that your sons will not die on foreign soil"; perverting the public mind to believe that thrift and competence were selfish vices and that poverty and incompetence were virtues; condemning thousands of children to starvation, 1942–1944, by refusing to allow food bought by governments-in-exile to be sent to their starving countries; impeding our agricultural production in so many ways that we could not fulfill our promises to the United Nations; giving Russia dominion over helpless countries and a large part of Berlin.

Less than three weeks after Roosevelt's death, Hitler died, lifting a curse from the world but leaving it in shambles.

On August 2 President Truman called on Japan to surrender or else cities would be destroyed by atomic bombs. On August 6 Hiroshima and, a few days later, Nagasaki, were destroyed. Japan agreed to surrender on August 14, 1945. The news was too shocking to comprehend. The war was over. People were too stunned to celebrate.

Marion Holman brought her two small children to the ranch to wait for Cranston, who would soon be coming home. Our ranch chore was harvesting broccoli, which we cut with heavy knives. Having no farm labor help, Chuck and I and the boys were harvesting as much as we could salvage ourselves. Not being used to heavy work with big knives, my hands protested. The tendons knotted in cherry-sized, buzzing lumps on the back of my hands. Dr. Amby Cowden put them both in splints. Poor Marion, for several days, while I was helpless, she did all the cooking for the eight of us. My hands soon recovered, but I did not ask them to cut any more broccoli.

Our friends were coming back from war. George Keffer came and told us that Loraine was divorcing him. "For reasons I deem sufficient," she wrote us. "At least I have salvaged a mother-in-law," George said and made his home temporarily in Loraine's mother's garage apartment. Loraine's mother was feisty Agnes Cleaveland, author of *No Life for a Lady* and Stanford friend of Mummie and Daddy. Cranston arrived, gathered up Marion and his family, and went back to his medical practice in New York.

Louise arrived, resplendent in uniform with ribbons, her five battle stars, and a Good Conduct medal, which she handed to Daddy. It was a joy to have her with us again. Soon she divorced Ken; we missed his quiet presence. She settled into the family, enjoyed the children, the household routine, and our projects—for a little while. Then she was off to San Francisco and a new job. In the course of time, we were invited to her wedding to Bill, a dour young man. She looked beautiful in a blue dress, carrying a bouquet of red roses woven into a heart which I had made to her specifications.

She and Bill spent weekends and vacations with us. Bill seemed to enjoy the ranch but stayed apart from the children and guests and only occasionally joined in our projects or work. Daddy gave them our little house-trailer, the one he had given us and we had used in Pasadena for weekends at the beach or in the mountains, to live in while they attended the University of California, College of Agriculture, at Davis.

When rationing finally ended in 1945 and gasoline was at last available for civilians, I was able to find interesting activities and friends in Santa Cruz. No Quaker Meeting being available, we joined the Congregational Church. The American Association of University Women offered stimulating programs and friends. The Daughters of the American Revolution, whose interest in researching and preserving history had so involved Mummie, now interested me. Our lives became a better balance of friends, jobs, and our commitment to Daddy and the ranch.

The Seasons

In the Waddell Valley, seasons come gently, merging into each other in small increments.

Spring. Spring brings us a mounting chorus of bird songs. They sing to their mates and to warn off encroachers and, seemingly, just for the joy of spring. Their dawn chorus is joy incarnate. Meadowlarks, who have been silently with us all winter, leave to make their music in distant pastures. Red-winged blackbirds build nests in the reeds, telling about it in sweet shrill chaos. Swallows return and build their untidy nests of mud under the eaves. At night, frogs raise their voices, a din from the marsh.

In meadows, fresh green grass pushes through gray litter. Wildflowers open in the woods and meadows. Puddles along the road are edged with pollen, blown in yellow clouds from pine trees. We are out on the roads with shovels and trucks, repairing winter road damage, draining ditches and filling potholes from quarry gravel. Fern fronds uncurl, nettles spring up with poison-filled hairlets, fresh green leaves shine on poison oak vines.

Spring wind blows up the valley and whips us as we prepare garden beds for fresh planting. It carries the smell of the ocean and emerging green things. Calves, lambs, baby chicks, barn kittens, and bobcat kittens emerge into the sunshine or take shelter from spring rain.

Occasionally, on clear bright evenings, one can catch on the sea's horizon the green flash from the setting sun. Other times of the year there is apt to be too much mist or dust in the air to see this miracle.

Summer. Flowers are in full bloom and scent the air. Green meadows turn to pale gold. Trees along the creek make a deep canopy of bright leaves, drinking so deeply that the creek shrinks in early summer, later to return to its deeper flow.

Fawns follow their mothers in the fields, and flocks of quail, fluffy scampering balls, and their parents skitter across the road. Raccoon kits follow their chirring mothers to our table of scraps for them.

Out at sea, a river of fog clouds the horizon and moves in to cool our nights. Sand, washed out by winter storms, piles up in drifts again. Trade winds blow every afternoon and die down at sunset.

The valley echoes the voices of summer children. Fragrant smoke comes from barbecues and picnic fires. Roads grow dusty and show tracks of deer, raccoons, bobcats, and other valley residents.

Autumn. The smell of autumn is shale dust and sagey plants, bay trees and eucalyptus. There is the sound of hammering as repairs are made for the winter. At night coyotes echo down the valley. Distant chainsaws tell of getting in our wood supply for stove and fireplace.

Deer come to the orchard for fallen apples. Short-tempered yellow-jackets protect their well-populated nests. It is a time of harvest. Huge trucks come to transport our produce. Walnuts are gathered, and our vegetable gardens overflow with their gifts to us.

Poplars turn to gold. Poison oak justifies its existence in patches of scarlet and crimson. Autumn skies are showered with Leonid shooting stars.

Winter. At the first snapping cold, unwelcomed flies and field mice seek shelter inside houses and barns. First rain brings up mushrooms, delicious chanterelles and all the others of fascinating shapes and sizes. Little green-eyed newts leave homes under damp logs to wander the woods and trails, making their gradual way down to the creek to lay their greenish egg clumps.

A flooded creek wreaks havoc upstream but brings steelhead and salmon into the creek to spawn. It washes logs and flotsam down to the beach and builds logjams across the creek.

Winter perfume is wet woods and leaf mold and seaweed piled high on the beach, where gulls gather for refuge from storms far out at sea. Harsh waves scour the beach of sand. Winter sounds are wind and rain and the roar of surf.

Fields are beaten down to gray litter. Even the trees look tired. Roads are cut by gullies and turned into mud and potholes. Bare alders shine stark against a dark background of evergreens.

Deep into winter, curled fern fronds poke through the litter. Pale pink milkmaid wildflowers light dark corners of the forest. Rainbows span the valley: they tell us of coming spring.

Teaching, 1945–1946

Mary Vickery had come to live alone on Last Chance Ranch on top of the mountain which was our northeast boundary. We called on this new neighbor and found a delightful gentlewoman, busy writing a book and farming with enthusiasm and ignorance. There were chickens, turkeys, geese, goats, sheep, a cow, and a bull all wandering around her yet unfenced property. Chuck was horrified at the loose bull and explained bovine facts

Rob, Allan and Tooke
by the Brown House fish pond; 1946

of life to Mary, persuading her to get rid of him. Subsequently, distance and gasoline rationing being what they were, we saw Mary only occasionally.

One day, in 1945, while climbing a fence with a turkey under each arm, Mary fell, breaking her back. She lay there for three days, until a woodcutter came by. Chuck and I visited her several times in the hospital. As the time approached when she could be released, we talked it over with Dr. Amby Cowden and suggested that she come and convalesce in one of our guestrooms. She was a dear guest. In a few days she was up and helping us as well as she could. She had been emaciated when her body cast was put on; now that she was eating well again, it was getting very uncomfortable. It seemed forever until it could be cut off and replaced with a brace.

I was teaching in the Swanton Valley at Seaside School because the teacher had been in an automobile accident and had broken her leg. Although the war was over, there was still a teacher shortage and no substitute teachers were available. I was drafted, given a teacher's certificate, teaching schedules for the six grades, a pile of workbooks, and set to work. I had never taught before and had never taken an education course at Stanford. But I had typed a lot of education themes for other students. I tried to remember them. Since they were not helpful, I devised my own teaching program.

I divided the workbooks into weekly chunks and told the children that, if their chunks were done by Friday noon, we would spend the afternoon playing with their village. Chuck made a big four-by-eight-foot table on the front porch. The children, according to their skills, built a village with matchboxes, clay, paint, and odds and ends. It was a fine village with (using a little bit of imagination) houses, shops, railway station, post office, library, service station, and a school. We bought goods at our village store and made change; we sent cement and farm produce to other cities by railway. We mailed letters at the post office and found out about the countries we mailed to. We pretended that our schoolbook supply and some I brought from the Casa were the village library, and we talked about taking care of books and returning them when they were due. The children used their already extensive knowledge of cars and trucks at the service station and figured out mileage and gas amounts. At the village school were students of several nationalities. The children each chose a country and studied about it to tell the rest of us. Fridays were fun.

I especially remember a little first-grader. He knew very little English and I could not speak Italian. But we communicated. When he got stuck on a problem, I told him that it was like when his father's tractor got stuck in a mud hole—the engine just had to work harder to get out. He was a determined child and made good progress. Sometimes, when I was working with children in another grade, I would hear him, in his corner, softly making tractor sounds, "Grr, grrrr, grr grr grr." Years later, he was executed for a murder.

Winter in the Swanton Valley could be cold. I'd stoke up the round woodstove, but by noon, often the temperature in our schoolroom was only up to the fifties. Outside, the pale winter sun was not much help. I took extra sweaters to school for children whose coats did not seem warm enough.

My admiration for teachers, already high, increased exponentially. Teaching is very hard work. I was relieved when after three months the teacher returned to her job. The county office wanted to assign me to another school. No way!!!

Tooke graduated from Seaside School and started high school in Santa Cruz in 1945. He drove our old green Model A Ford truck to Davenport and there took the school bus with the Wilson twins, Dolores Viviani, and other neighborhood children. He decided that he didn't like the name Alex and changed it to his first name, Charles. This worked fine for everyone else but me, to whom he would always be Alex, or Tooke, as he remained to his family.

Robbie started Seaside School in 1945. From his first day he had a difficult time with letters. He just couldn't learn to read. I tried to help him. We'd struggle through a paragraph, but when we tried to repeat, his mind was blocked again. Nowadays this is recognized as dyslexia and is overcome with special programs. Then it was not recognized. Some children were "just dumb." Finally, the mother of a new young teacher at Seaside School, herself a teacher, tackled Robbie's problem with her patience, skill, and phonetics. Phonetics was not the approved method of reading at that time: children were supposed to learn by "word recognition." She taught him how to read.

Allan and Tooke read a lot, wrote well and imaginatively, and received good grades, but not as good as they would have been without over-active social lives.

Chuck took the job of manager of the Santa Cruz County Farm Bureau office and, later, with the California Farm Bureau Federation as their representative in the central coast counties. It was work he enjoyed. He visited the farmers, helping with their problems. He met with legislators, many of whom he knew from League of Women Voters days, giving them agricultural information. He represented farm interests to groups and meetings and organizations.

Members of the Republican Central Committee asked him to run for Congress. The idea did not appeal to him. It would mean an upheaval which did not fit into his plans. The farm bureau position was interesting work. It left him time to manage the ranch and to enjoy his family. Chuck's life plan had never included power and riches. His program was, instead, a flourishing family, friends, and fulfilling our commitment to the care of Daddy and to the ranch.

Lumbering, 1946–

Waddell Valley hills were almost clearcut in the 1860s and 1870s by William Waddell. There was a small amount of cutting occasionally after that. In 1946 Daddy told us that he was working out a timbering agreement for the ranch with a young timberman. We persuaded him first to talk to neighbor Frank McCrary before he signed a contract. Frank and his two teenage sons had come home from being Seabees in World War II. They had put together lumbering machinery from war surplus sales and with brother-in-law Homer Trumbo started Big Creek Lumber Company. Frank had done timbering in Alaska as a youth. Homer was a skilled woodsman whose family had settled near Swanton at the turn of the century, his mother having crossed the plains in a covered wagon.

With Daddy, a naturalist and conservationist, they worked out a plan for the ranch which would keep its ecological (a word that had not yet joined our vocabulary) integrity and the unique beauty of its redwood forest. The McCrarys established a small mill along the creek. They made a road up the canyon where there had only been trails. They built sturdy bridges. They ran their business from here for a number of years and then built more extensively at the junction of Swanton Road and Cabrillo Highway. As our boys grew older, they each had summer jobs at Big Creek mill.

As years went by, the McCrary family developed a policy of sustainable lumbering to protect and improve redwood forests. They have received many awards for their activities. They also have been good neighbors. Their men and equipment are first on the scene in an emergency or disaster. They make and maintain trails for all of us. They make ocean rescues. They are helpful wherever and whenever needed. Three generations—Frank McCrary, his sons Frank and Homer (Lud and Bud), and their children—of good people and good neighbors.

First Campaign, 1946

Alvin Gregory, ex–naval captain and owner of the filling station in Davenport, was our district representative on the Santa Cruz County Board of Supervisors. In 1946, he was tired of the job and decided not to file for re-election.

There were a number of things I had been trying to get the board to do, including raising county civil service salaries (our personnel turnover rate was 40 percent), getting an adequate building for juvenile hall, and moving indigent elderly patients out of the frame county poorhouses, horrifying firetraps. When I was urged to take Alvin's place, it seemed a chance to get things done. I filed to be a candidate. It was an enlightening experience.

The other board members were horrified at the prospect of a woman on the board. They voted to raise their salaries from $150 to $250 a month (which had been one of Alvin's projects) and persuaded him to change his mind about not filing for a new term. He didn't have an easy time defeating me, although there were voters who agreed with the board. One told me, "I'd rather vote for a dog than a woman."

Republican Ladies, 1946

I was crawling up and down seedling broccoli rows, weeding them with a teaspoon, when Robbie came running down to tell me that there was a "portink phone call" waiting for me. It was from members of the nominating committee of the California Republican Women's Clubs, Federated, asking me to be their candidate for state president. It seems that there was a north-south split and that I was the only compromise candidate they could agree upon. Déjà vu.

Impossible. Transportation costs were too high. Clothing required would necessarily be elegant. No one was available to replace my ranch roles as cook, housemaid, chauffeur, shopper, tutor, baby-sitter, nurse, gardener, crop weeder, and substitute tractor driver. No. Sorry. I'd love to, but NO! However, no matter how firmly, decisively, and finally I had told myself that my destiny was domestic, I couldn't help yearning for a wider stage.

Three weeks later, the Republican Women's convention was held in San Francisco. The two factions had not been able to agree on a candidate and sat glaring at each other, with a third group going around saying, "Girls, girls, we must have harmony." The nominations had been held just before lunch, but one of the candidates got angry and walked out. The meeting chairman, who was the opposing candidate, declared the nominations closed and during luncheon had ballots printed. However, there was such an uproar about closing the nominations irregularly that she said a motion had been made to reopen them.

The chairman took a voice vote that sounded about even and declared the motion lost. As there was another uproar, she asked the "ayes" to rise. She then declared the motion lost because there were more seated than standing. Along with these seated potential "no" votes were the visitors and abstainers.

The resigned candidate, who had returned by this time, marched onto the platform and demanded the microphone, but the chairman wouldn't give it to her. She dug the chairman with an elbow and got in front of her and said that the vote was not legal. The chairman said for all the "aye" voters to go into the next room, which they did with much confusion. Then the chairman said, "Well, we're rid of them" and introduced the speaker, Congressman Jack Anderson, who had been sitting on the platform with his mouth open.

The ladies in the next room, who had been waiting for their votes to be counted, boiled out. The congressman sat down. The chairman declared a recess. People came to me and said it was all my fault for not being willing to take on the situation. I don't know what happened during the recess, but when the meeting reconvened, the chairman was elected president. Congressman Anderson had left.

A large blond woman got up and waved her arms, trying to get the ladies to sing. They were not in the mood for singing, so it was a solo. She had a high squeaky voice. But she deserved an "A" for courage.

The *Seaside Reporter,* 1947–1952

In 1947, when Allan was eleven, his heart's desire was to get a gun, a single-shot, bolt-action .22 rifle. On western ranches, boys usually had guns for hunting. All our boys were excellent target shots with Daddy's guns. Chuck and I were not enthusiastic about Allan owning a gun; we sought to postpone it by telling him that he would have to earn the money to buy it.

Allan publishing the *Seaside Reporter,* 1947

He decided to earn the money by publishing a newspaper. He called it the *Seaside Reporter* because it covered the news of the county's Seaside District, in which the ranch, Davenport, and neighbors' ranches were located. On my way to a Parent-Teacher Association meeting in Santa Cruz,

I dropped him off in Davenport to collect news and advertising for his first edition. He was successful. He collected news from Myrtle, the postmistress, from the store, and from Charlie Bella's bar. Mother at PTA meeting, small son in Davenport saloon! He got advertising from the store and hotel. Subscribers would come later.

In addition to news and society items, there was a sports column, a nature column, recipes, and jokes. I typed the stencils for him; he did the mimeographing and then peddled them in Davenport and mailed them to the many subscribers. The *Seaside Reporter* evidently filled a community need. Soon news items were no problem; they were left in our mailbox. Subscribers increased. Allan wrote up school and ranch and party news. I wrote an occasional feature story.

He soon became "independently wealthy." He bought his gun. He was allowed to shoot rabbits, gophers, who sometimes poked their heads out their holes, woodrats, and, jays when they became so numerous they were a threat to songbirds by destroying their nests. He bought a trumpet and joined the school band. We arranged that he practice in a remote room, where he struggled with "Pomp and Circumstance." We attended junior high school band concerts, which were apt to be excruciating.

Because I did the typing, I could do discrete editing. Not much, because a boy's view of life was interesting: "It was a good party, but Mom made us leave before the fights started" or "The trouble with the engine was a dead mouse." But I edited out that a neighbor's "new wife is not as pretty as the old one."

The file of his *Seaside Reporter* is a record of the Davenport area from 1947 to 1952. He ended his newspaper career when football practice and a job at Linda Vista Market preempted his leisure time.

Peg's Wedding, 1947

In March 1947 Chuck's sister, Peg, was married to Bob Crowell in our Casa living room. Allan, in his *Seaside Reporter,* described this event:

". . .The altar was beautiful, there was an arch of white Choisia which Mr. McLean and Mrs. McLean Sr. had poked into a wire frame, and banks of ferns which Ted and Beryl Willis had dug up . . . During the ceremony, the Siamese cats, wearing blue ribbons, walked in and meowed, Anne Willis forgot to put them in the closet . . . Everyone said they had never seen such a pretty wedding cake . . . there were silver doves holding wedding rings and on the top was a Dresden shoe filled with orange blossoms

Mindy had brought from their orange grove in Sierra Madre, instead of little statues because Peg said she didn't like little men on wedding cakes . . . People threw a lot of rice at them which made the floor slippery.

" . . . The weather wasn't sunny so it made it crowded inside. More people came than had been expected. There were about a hundred people. We wished that a lot of people that didn't come had been there too, but then it would have been even worse . . . There were a lot of McLean relatives, but not many of Crowells because they live in the East."

Martha, their daughter, was born in March of the following year. She was an adorable baby and a perky little girl. Her grandmother McLean doted on her even though she was too deaf to hear Martha's baby voice. Like Daddy, Mother McLean would not wear a hearing aid. Daddy said that all he heard with one was his suspenders creaking. One afternoon when they were all visiting the ranch, we were having tea in the living room. Martha, about three, was playing on the floor beside me and Mother McLean. I don't know what her grandmother had done to displease her, but she looked up and said in her little voice, "I'm going to cut you into little pieces and frow you out the window." Mother McLean patted her on the head and replied, "Such a dear, good little girl."

Horses, 1945–1952

When I was young on the ranch, we always had riding horses. Now, in our farming, horses were still important. They were used for herding cattle, for transportation, and, especially in muddy weather, were important as workhorses in the fields. The boys wanted riding horses. Chuck did not care for riding horses. He said he'd had enough of them in Oregon, when he worked on a cattle drive from Klamath Falls to Pendleton. On that drive a horse had stepped on his foot, and sometimes it still hurt. He said horses were an expense and a nuisance. True.

We bought three—Capri, a beautiful racehorse whose ankles had proved too weak for the racecourse; Teddy, a good-natured herding horse; and Jolly, who was old and turned out to be practically useless, except for rides for small children.

Tooke was disappointed that Capri threw him and was not as understanding and affectionate as the horses in children's stories. Allan, on Teddy, thoroughly explored ranch hills and valleys. Rob rode sometimes but not with enthusiasm. The boys all rode in Santa Cruz fiesta parades. When a movie crew came to Swanton to make scenes for *Romance of Rosy*

Ridge, starring Van Johnson and Janet Leigh, we watched our horses acting as part of the cast of that picture. The boys and our guests rode when we rounded up cattle for dipping, inoculating, or castrating, aided by our jeep and by people running around waving their arms.

I very much enjoyed riding, but there was scant time for it. Occasionally I would entice Chuck to ride with me. My favorite time was in the evening on the beach when there was a low tide. We rode with sunset radiance on the waves and shining sand. We let the horses run unchecked along the miles of firm tideline. I can still feel the wind in my face, the taste of salt from the spray, the scent of seaweed, and the roar of the breaking surf.

Trespassers, 1914–1976

Poachers and trespassers have always been a problem for us and our neighbors. Sportsmen in Santa Cruz and San Francisco had considered these streams and hills as their special fishing and hunting grounds. When there were only a few of them, landowners were not very concerned. But, in time, it became a serious problem for many reasons, fire being the principal one. A large proportion of forest fires are set by careless campers and smokers. Farmers are also concerned about trespassers who trample fields, help themselves to crops, and release or disturb livestock and spread livestock diseases. Families are concerned about the safety of children when there are strangers in the woods.

When we came, in 1914, the first day of fishing season was a shock. We had seen practically no strangers for months, and suddenly hundreds of men arrived in trucks and Model T Fords. Some came the night before and camped on the Brown House lawn. Many came at dawn. It rained and several, not entirely sober, wanted shelter in the Brown House. Mummie and the English girls were frightened. They locked the doors and kept us children safely inside.

When Daddy learned of it, he was furious. For a few years he hired burly ex-policemen from San Francisco to patrol the front during fishing season. This made him unpopular in Santa Cruz, a situation we had to cope with when we came to live here in 1943. By that time, the trespasser situation was much less acute, but it was still worrisome, especially in autumn when the valley was dry and flammable.

Some of the trespassers' actions defied common sense. There was a family who had a picnic in the middle of a ripe grainfield. They had trampled a flat place to build their campfire. They did not react courteously when I explained the danger of their situation, nor when I mentioned they were on private property without permission. There was a young camper who, seeing the charred interior of a hollow redwood tree, thought it was a fireplace and built his fire there. We saw the smoke and caught the forest fire before it had spread far, but he had killed a venerable redwood. There were numerous other fires started from neglected campfires, some extensive, all sad and expensive.

During the 1960s hippie era, we would often be told that there was no private property because it all belongs to God. Yes, but isn't it nice that He found someone to take care of it and to pay the taxes. People do not understand why property owners do not welcome hunters, fishermen, poachers, who do not ask permission before coming onto private property. There are nurserymen poachers who strip banks of five-finger ferns and swamps of Woodwardia ferns or hillsides of huckleberry greens, who saw redwood burls from trees, who pull up tiger-lily clumps. Poaching hunters are a danger as their bullets whiz across the valley. Sadly there seem to be some people who are just natural-born vandals, who enjoy tearing up fences, stealing signs, ruining crops, or using cows or dogs for target practice.

It is painful to have to be so unfriendly to strangers. Most of the trespassers are probably not vandals or idiots, but just nice people wanting to enjoy the wilderness, people who would not light a careless fire or pull up wildflowers. The trouble was, we had no way of knowing which ones they were.

Forest Fire, 1948

Early in September 1948, a forest fire started at Pine Mountain, about five miles northeast of us. It spread explosively, reaching our border the next day and then raging behind Swanton and Davenport. At night the sky was red. We watched sparks blowing down the valley, but fire, miraculously, did not follow into the ranch. The California Division of Forestry and the army were fighting its advance. The McCrarys and neighbors mobilized to help with their equipment and knowledge of the terrain, but their volunteer assistance was refused.

Then we found out that only state parks were to be protected, other than that, the official policy was to let the fire "burn to the ocean." Unfortunately, this meant that our neighbors' property and homes in the path of the fire were unprotected. Our ranch, being adjacent to Big Basin Park, shared its protection. Our community organized, under McCrary family direction. Every man and boy, including Chuck, Tooke, and Allan, took to the fireline. Robbie and I joined the women and youngsters organized to feed the firefighters, including Forestry and Army, when they came in, exhausted and sooty, for brief respite.

Our community fought the firestorm for two weeks before its blaze was conquered. Thousands of acres had been burned, but no homes had been lost and no one had been seriously injured. Allan's *Seaside Reporter* published a blow by blow description of our battle with the flames and with bureaucracy.

Accident on Gianone Hill, 1949

One day, returning from Santa Cruz to the ranch, with Tooke and Robbie in the station wagon, we had just started down winding precipitous Gianone Hill when a gravel truck hit us. The driver had sun in her eyes and had not seen us. I had seen her and had pulled as far as I could off the road and had stopped there. Just before she hit, she saw us and jerked the steering wheel—it came off. The truck rolled down the mountainside, breaking into three pieces. Tooke had cracked the windshield with his head but seemed okay. I told him to go back to the Gianones' and phone to report the accident. I felt sure the driver must have been killed. Robbie appeared unhurt, so I left him in the station wagon, scrambled downhill, and met the driver scrambling up, unhurt except for cuts and bruises. Another gravel truck came by, rescued her, and took Robbie and me up to the Gianones'. Robbie promptly went into shock. Remembering first-aid courses in Home Department, we rushed around getting hot blankets and sugared tea for him.

While the station wagon was being repaired, I had no transportation. Our pupil-chauffeuring job fell entirely on Betty Bradley. We had been sharing it. The carload of Betty's three children, Allan and Rob, and the farm children had been my responsibility mornings and hers at the end of the school day.

With their recent return home to nearby Coastways Ranch, Betty and Hank Bradley had become welcome neighbors. They were University of California graduates. Hank was a mining engineer with interests in the California gold country east of Sacramento. He had contracted TB and was bedridden. Fortunately, it was not long before antibiotics became available, and after a long battle, he eventually regained his health.

Betty, one of six Atkins children, neighbors in my childhood, was an acquaintance. At that time the four miles to their ranch was a long separation. They would come to our events, and Mummie would persuade us to give them parts in our theatricals. Mindy usually cast them as brownies and hid them behind ferns, because, she said, they had red faces and peeling noses and had not rehearsed.

Betty now was a lovely friend. We were partners in child-raising, ranch problems, household challenges. Her home, like the Casa, was full of nice but shabby furniture. With the crafts I had learned from farm bureau home department meetings, we set to work to remedy this. For several years, each Wednesday was given to this furniture project. In the Casa garden-room, we refinished, upholstered, and re-caned two households of furniture.

Daddy noticed me refinishing a table and asked if I'd like some new furniture. Heavens, no! I liked what we had. It just needed a little loving care. He said that I was running the household very inexpensively and that he couldn't imagine a better living arrangement. Praise made the work seem lighter. We were often joined by other neighbors with similar projects. We were happy to share our skills. Ten-year-old Robbie would join us sometimes and upholster small projects. He was good at it. Sometimes our only companions were Tika and Boo.

Tika was our large Siamese cat. His chore was to catch an early morning mouse or gopher, which he brought each day to show me, then he was free to live a leisurely life. Once, I came back from a short trip to find several gophers in the sewing room closet. Daddy said that Tika had put them there for me. Tika knew how beautiful he was and would pose artistically to be admired. He had a charming personality. He was also father of innumerable purebred kittens by Mia and Sasha. They were a prolific source of a small income to us.

Boo was our beagle, a loving and not very bright friend.

Real Estate, 1945

We had started our real estate activities in Santa Cruz by buying a small lot with the money I earned while teaching for three months at Seaside School. We cleared it and leveled it and sold it for a profit and bought a small shabby cottage. We cleaned it, repaired and painted it, planted a pretty garden, and sold it for a profit. Then we bought a larger shabby house and did the same, again and again and again. We eventually owned the handsome home at 410 Walnut, opposite Santa Cruz High School (near the Victorian home that Allan and I later shared at 512 Walnut).

Buying and selling property was then much easier than it is now. We looked at advertised property, came to an agreement with the owner, wrote a check, and went to the Recorder's Office to record the new deed. No agent. No escrow. With a little hard work it was easy to make a profit.

Health Council, 1948–1949

Mary Jane Neal came to Santa Cruz as a public health nurse. She asked me to do a volunteer survey of public health services in the county. It sounded interesting but was a subject of my deep ignorance. Library research revealed that the American Medical Association had a pamphlet about evaluating community health services; this document was incomprehensible, its structure convoluted, and its vocabulary arcane. After Dr. Amby Cowden explained it to me, sentence by sentence, I translated it into plain language and simplified it into a list of research questions. A little study of the community revealed deplorable situations, most of which I have long forgotten. But I remember that a restaurant in Felton got its water supply from a hose next door, that there was a waitress working only half-time because she was ill with tuberculosis, that our health officer was hired part-time and was also director of the county hospital, and that our elderly indigent patients were housed in two very old frame houses with no fire protection. The health officer said he had nightmares about those houses.

Public health nurse Mary Jane and I decided that a Citizens Health Council might be the answer. Between us, we enlisted a group of prominent Santa Cruz citizens to study the health problems of the county. I was elected chairman of the council. At our first meeting, Mary Jane and the health officer told them about the conditions I had found, and then each member took some questions to investigate. The council turned out to be a great implement of change. The weight of its information and its collective prestige produced significant improvements. The county made the health officer a full time position and employed a full time hospital director. A rat control program was instigated. There was a restaurant inspection service and health examinations for food handlers—and other innovations my memory does not reveal.

Our success was a matter of interest to the medical community. In

November 1949 I was invited to talk on "Rural Health Evaluation" at the National Health Council's convention at Princeton. I assumed that it would be financially impossible, but the local council decided otherwise and raised $200 towards my trip. George Keffer, who was then manager of a San Francisco bank, said that he could get me free air passage both ways. First class! Bill and Jean Shockley invited me to stay with them in New Jersey whenever I didn't have to be in Princeton.

I had told Uncle Bert about it all and had said that the idea of flying terrified me. When Aunt Lou died, I had begun to write to him frequently, believing that, famous and busy as he was, he was still a grieving, lonely old man and that cheery letters about family matters and adventures might amuse him. He told me, later, that sometimes my letters were his anchor to sanity. He wired, "Take a tranquilizer and a plane and come. Visit us if you can."

Chuck persuaded me that Daddy and he and the boys (now seventeen, fourteen, and ten) could survive without me for a few days. So I went. The speech was a very great success and published later in their bulletin. I told them that the basis of the study was their own association's community evaluation translated into English. I had a wonderful time, slightly flawed by getting a rusty iron splinter imbedded in my eye. The surgeon said that I was "entitled to a good deal of pain for the next few days." So I went to stay with Bill and Jean Shockley, and their children, who had been at the ranch for my free summer camps. Bill had just invented the transistor, which eventually gave us computers and transformed the world. It amused us that the children were more impressed with what I was doing than with their father's accomplishment.

I visited Mary Jane Neal, the former public health nurse who was now married and lived on a farm in upper New York. In New York I visited Marion and Cranston Holman, and their children, who had forgotten their two-week visit to the ranch during the broccoli debacle. They had a handsome apartment, but I wondered about the problems of raising small children in that city. And I had a good visit with Uncle Bert and Bunny. Bunny had been a Stanford friend of ours. She became Aunt Lou's social secretary and now took care of Uncle Bert's social engagements and his domestic affairs. In New York I also indulged in a longtime yearning for portraits by the Bachrach photo studio.

On the way home, the handsome captain of the plane walked down the aisle and I recognized the man with whom I had been wildly in love when we were both sixteen. "Alexis!" I said. He was delighted and took me up to the front with him. Three other officers were there, facing a battery of buttons, lights, and levers. All swiveled their chairs around when Alexis explained our history, and we reminisced about teen adventures.

"Who is driving this airplane?" I asked nervously, realizing that no one except myself seemed conscious of the buttons and lights. When they explained that the airplane took care of itself, I asked what they were all there for then; they said it was to look as though they were earning their pay.

Alexis gave me a copy of his book *My Three Years in the Air,* an engaging story of himself and the early years of flying. He was one of the first air-mail pilots. As an adventurous teenager he had flown the early Western Air Express mail planes, and he regaled me with tales of harrowing narrow escapes, probably true.

How Do Teenage Boys Live to Grow Up? 1949

Tooke got his letters in track and football and graduated from high school. During the summer he worked for the McCrarys at Big Creek mill. In the fall of 1949, he registered at Stanford as a freshman.

That summer Allan had a job bagging for Linda Vista Market, always a good advertiser in the *Seaside Reporter.* He brought them a number of customers, *Seaside Reporter* readers.

The whole Davenport area, helped to a community awareness by Allan's newspaper, gave dance parties. They were family affairs: babies slept on blankets in corners, children learned to dance from older children, teenagers showed off the latest steps, farmers and cement plant workers danced or watched the dancing. Music was provided by local talent. Refreshments were cakes, brought by the women, and coffee and punch. If a few of the men escaped to Charlie Bella's Bar, they were not missed.

Robbie was in Seaside School with an excellent teacher, Helme Smith, who was a nature enthusiast. She gave the children an appreciation of more than book learning. Her husband puttered around keeping things in repair and order. He built a sandbox for the small children, and he made the garden bloom with roses and morning glories and sweetpeas on the fences. The Swanton community organized to improve the one-room school. Under McCrary direction, we installed an inside bathroom and built a stage. I helped reshingle the roof. At noon we had a picnic. This project took us several weekends of hard work.

Our boys had guns, as did most boys on ranches. They were for hunting and for protection of stock. Chuck taught them gun safety and hunting conventions and manners, which, too, are designed for safety. The boys handled their guns responsibly and became very good shots. Allan was East Coast sharpshooting champion in the army and was invited to participate in the Olympics. But guns are always dangerous, and scary things would happen. Allan had his front teeth broken by a recoiling

Seaside School, where my sons attended elementary school,
and where I taught briefly; 1950

shotgun, and he has a small scar between his eyes where he was hit by a bullet exploding in a bonfire. Rob, hunting rabbits with Wright Randolph, came around a corner unexpectedly as Wright was shooting a rabbit. Robbie has the scar of the bullet along his cheek and through his earlobe.

As the boys became old enough to have their own "wheels" for school transportation and social life, we were adaptable parents. One of our few rules was that, if they were not going to be home at the agreed upon hour, they must phone to keep us from worrying. With very few exceptions, this plan worked well.

Tooke was taking friends home from a party, and he phoned us to say he would be later than planned. We relaxed and went to sleep, to be awakened at three in the morning by a police call, "Do you have a son Charles?" "Yes." "We have him here. He was in an accident and is a little confused." We dressed and drove to the police station in Santa Cruz. On his way home on San Jose Road, Tooke had missed a curve and shot down a small cliff into an orchard. Knocked unconscious, he lay there. The owner, a friend of ours, had heard the crash and looked out his door but could see nothing. When Tooke regained consciousness, he climbed the cliff and made his way to the house, but he was confused and gave no coherent explanation. Our friend, not knowing who Tooke was, called the police, who called us. He seemed okay by the time we arrived to get him, but we took him to Amby the next day. His young brothers were delighted when we were told that "he has nothing in his head." "We always knew that," they said.

A somewhat similar accident happened to Allan later. Driving home on San Jose Road with his pal Paul, Sheriff Tara's son, he swerved to avoid hitting a cat. The car turned over. The boys were hurt, but when they remembered the beer in the car, illegal at their age, they crawled out with it and hid it behind a bush and then waited to be rescued.

There were undoubtedly other harrowing adventures prudently kept from our knowledge. I sometimes wonder not only how teenage boys live to grow up but also how parents survive their sons' teen years.

Perhaps

Perhaps some human characteristics can be explained by what must have been imprinted on our psyches throughout human evolution. Humans have been on earth for millions of years, modern man—with essentially the same mental and physical attributes as at present—for thousands. What we are now is based on what happened to us in the distant past.

Consider the illogical adventuring and defiance of so many of our adolescent males. In caveman days, at this age they were probably kicked out of the family group by alpha males. Most of them may have been eaten by tigers, but a few survived, those who were wily, inventive, and lucky. These were the ones whose characteristics were passed on to emerge today as longings for freedom and adventure, not appropriate to today's economic and social requirements. Now civilization requires them to stay in the family group throughout adolescence, although their atavistic yearnings chafe for independence. Our modern tigers are gangs, guns, drugs, and criminal temptations.

Another scenario. Sitting around the campfire, men of the tribe are sharpening their spears, stringing their bows. They talk of past exploits as they plan for the coming hunt. Tomorrow there will be glory and meat for each of them.

Early in the morning, the men take off in great panoply. When they are gone, the women take the children and set out to check rabbit snares, dig roots, and gather seeds and greens. They build up the fire and make a great pot of rabbit stew.

The men straggle home, weary and empty-handed. As they eat the rabbit stew they tell of their brave feats and narrow escapes and about the spirits that arranged the escape of their prey from well-planned traps. They arrange to propitiate the spirits and await the next approach of game worthy of male attention.

The veneer of civilization has only been with us a short time in our human history. Such civilized qualities as restraint, consideration for others, and courtesy are virtues which can be shed in episodes of greed or fury. We all know of situations, individuals, instances, when this veneer has cracked, revealing a dark legacy of our racial past.

The Early, Busy 1950s

In the early 1950s we were busy in our jobs. We also did much entertaining, which Daddy encouraged. He enjoyed his friends and was entertained by ours. When he tired or there were too many people around, he would retreat to his haven in the library.

The boys were all in their teens and moved in social circles apart from ours. They brought their friends for self-organized events. I remember one weekend when there were nine teenage house guests, three of Tooke's, one of Allan's, and five of Robbie's.

Daddy's friends were especially welcome. Remembered is a visit from a mining engineer who brought his nine-year-old grandson along. The little boy followed Robbie around. During their visit there was an earthquake, 3.5 I would guess, which rattled dishes. In the garden, Rusty's special bark told us he had found a rattlesnake. And a forest fire started. We saw smoke above Mirey Spring. We gathered spades, hoes, and sacks and rushed up there—Robbie, Chuck, I and the little boy. A trespasser had built his campfire under the pine trees. We could see that he must have thought he had doused the fire, but it had crept along in pine needles below the surface and burst into flames in dry grass. It was still in a small area, not more than fifty feet in diameter. We beat it, spaded the hot coals, and kept it back. Soon the McCrarys, who had seen the smoke, arrived from the lumber mill with their equipment, and everything was under control. Next morning, when the guests left, the little boy thanked us for a wonderful visit. "An earthquake, a rattlesnake, and a forest fire," he said rapturously.

Now we were blessed with the arrival of Mrs. Cleaves. At last a housekeeper who was competent, hard-working, and caring. But even she could not entirely cope with the twenty-room house and a teenage social milieu. There were plenty of jobs left over to absorb our spare time.

On rare weekends when we were not too busy with chores or guests, Chuck and I might go exploring. There was so much of the ranch that we had never seen and places where no one had ever been. We followed deer paths and found unknown majestic redwood circles, or huge madronas and nutmeg trees, tiny fern-lined springs that disappeared into the hillside, patches of impenetrable lilac, bare rock outcroppings, and hidden dales. " . . . and Thou beside me singing in the wilderness—oh, wilderness were happiness enow!"

Our twenty-fifth wedding anniversary came in December 1950. Our wedding had been without any trimmings. Now I wanted a wedding cake and a party. There were more than two hundred guests, neighbors and friends from Santa Cruz and some from Palo Alto, San Francisco, and Pasadena. There was also a pleasant elderly lady who had not been invited but who had heard about the party and decided to attend. She came by bus to Davenport and phoned for us to pick her up. She had worked hard on my unsuccessful supervisor campaign and had been desolated when I didn't win. Perhaps the party cheered her up. She bustled around in the dining room and kitchen and seemed to enjoy herself. There was a champagne and buffet supper. With Soozie's help, I had made five gallons of turkey a la king, twenty dozen patty shells, and twenty tomato crab aspics. When the five gallons of turkey ran out, we sliced a ham (Betty Bradley had brought us one) and made a big salad.

When we left Pasadena, I did not foresee that we would ever fill that dreadful emptiness, but now our lives were rich with new friends and interests. The only sadness of this party was that Louise had not been there.

After Louise and Bill graduated from agricultural college in 1959 they had taken over Johnny's lease and started raising turkeys, thousands of them. At first these not very bright birds ran free and got themselves caught in fences and drowned in the creek. They were a treat for bobcats and coyotes and eagles. Bill trapped coyotes and bobcats and he shot our last nesting pair of golden eagles. He then, sensibly, confined the turkeys.

Bill was not friendly. He rejected the neighbors' sociable advances. He was discourteous to our friends. He intensely disliked me, Chuck, and our children. He ordered us to keep away from the farmyard and Louise and did not allow her to visit us. He was angry that, although he had a lease on farmyard and fields, Daddy did not turn Rancho del Oso management over to him. This was still our responsibility. It was a sad situation. Its miasma clouded these 1950s years.

A very special occasion was Daddy's eightieth birthday on January 28, 1951. We felt that he should have a party and that it would give him pleasure if the three of us, Mindy, Louise, and I, were the hostesses. He had been saddened (as was I) at the barriers that had been built between the three of us. My sisters declined to be hostesses and did not come to the party. We asked Daddy if we could invite a few of his friends in to celebrate his birthday with us. He said that he thought that would be nice. He changed his mind several times, having avoided parties all his life, but we went ahead with plans.

We solved the next two problems, the fact of Daddy's aversion to crowds and that his diet did not include party food. We held a big party upstairs in the living room with party food and beverages, while guests, a few at a time, visited with Daddy in his library, where there would be angel food birthday cake and fruit juice. His friends came from all over to honor him in this celebration. It was a great success. Afterwards he said, "It was a nice party. I'm glad we had it. It is the first party I ever had."

There was a good story about the party in the *Santa Cruz Sentinel,* which surprised and pleased him. For years, starting when Daddy closed the ranch to poachers, the newspaper editor had been actively unfriendly. One of our friends was also a friend of the current editor (the son of the former editor). Our friend talked to him and they decided it was time to stop "baiting the old man" and asked me to write a suitable story. So it told about the party and a bit about Daddy's accomplishments. Daddy commented, pleased but not exactly graciously, about the article, "That snipe must be getting some sense. Nothing but facts in the story. Not a snickersnee sticking out of it anywhere."

In 1953 Tooke was in the marines, Allan was entering Stanford, and Rob, a self-sufficient fourteen-year-old, was finishing Mission Hill Junior High. Chuck was enjoying his work on the staff of the California Farm Bureau and on the board of the Boys' Club.

I managed the farm bureau insurance business in Santa Cruz and was involved in a number of other projects. I finished writing and illustrating a collection of ranch stories, *Tomorrow Is the First Day,* which I'd been working on off and on for a number of years, and gave it to Daddy to read. He

Uncle Bert, Hulda, Daddy and Allan; 1953

didn't like it. At the time I thought that was because the book was no good so I put it away. Forty years later I ran across it and realized that his negative reaction was not to the quality of the book, but the fact that he was the main character in it. I had it printed. People liked it.

I was asked to raise money to keep the undercapitalized Santa Cruz County Farm Bureau Farm Supply business afloat. An onerous job. The business was important to local farmers; before the competition it offered, farm supplies in this area had been unconscionably overpriced. I persuaded the farmers who benefited from it to keep it going for them.

Another job that wasn't fun at all was when I was appointed chairman of the Citizens' Committee for High School Reconstruction. Santa Cruz High School had been condemned as earthquake unsafe. The committee discovered a bunch of dangerous conditions, such as hollow bearing-columns filled with trash, main crossbeams that did not meet, and crumbling concrete. We found that it would cost much more to repair than it would to build a new school. A local builder claimed he could repair everything for $35,000. An outlandish underestimate by more than a million dollars. But many people believed him. An election was held. People loved their impressive pseudo-Greco building and voted to fix it up. It cost even more than we had feared. Teachers now complain that it is badly designed for teaching. But it is handsome.

My insurance business flourished, not an inspiring activity but helpful to people and never dull. What is now called "sexual harassment" was then an accepted part of the workplace. It was a common hazard and we developed defenses against it. When I made home calls it amused me that the same men who were a problem in the office or field were quiet and respectful under the view of their wives.

Every once in a while, a headquarters insurance supervisor would spend the day in the field with me. My sales methods irked him. I would start by telling a farmer that I was not going to sell him a life insurance policy today; this visit was to tell him what was available and what it would do for his family. So that is what I did. When we left the farm the supervisor might begin spluttering. "You should have signed him up right there!" No, I wanted the farmer to think it through himself, not just succumb to my words. I won none of the company's silly sales competitions, but at the end of the year my sales were ahead of many who had.

There were no cancellations of my policies. What I sold stayed sold.

When we could find time for short vacations we liked to go rock-hunting. Daddy, as a mining engineer, had accumulated a museum-quality collection. When I was a child, he had given me pieces from his supply and had taught me about them. I had enthusiastically added to them whenever I could. Chuck and I had some fine trips, including one to find benitoite sapphire gems in the New Idria quicksilver mine tailings. Several times we went to Jade Cove in Monterey County for bits of translucent green jade. We found garnet "rubies" in Ruby Creek in Idaho, pink and green tourmaline crystals in San Diego county backlands, amethyst crystals in geodes from the desert, and turquoise in New Mexico mine tailings. Eventually I gave my collection to Tooke, our mining engineer son. He would have inherited his grandfather's collection, but that had been stolen.

Daddy Goes to the Hospital, 1954

Daddy's cold got very bad. His doctor came and said he was afraid it might go into pneumonia and that Daddy belonged in the hospital. He must have felt awful, because he did not protest the trip, as he usually did any sortie from the ranch. The nurses were dear in their care of him but upset by his refusal to conform to hospital ritual. No hospital gown—he had his own long nightshirt. No sponge bath—he could wash himself, thank you. No temperature—the thermometer probably had hospital germs on it. And, certainly no hospital food, although we persuaded him to eat hospital oatmeal for breakfast. I brought his other two diet meals in to him every day. "Where in damnation is my pipe!" No pipe, sorry.

His throat was too painful for conversation, but I brought my mending in and sat by him and talked about such things as Robbie making a surprise for him when he got home and Rusty missing him and the albino robin coming back, and, especially, about the bobcat kitten.

Driving home one afternoon from Santa Cruz, Chuck and the children had found a tiny bobcat kitten beside the road. Covered with mud and bone-thin, it had offered no protest when they put him in a cardboard carton—groceries dumped on the back seat. We put him in one of the covered wire dog cages with a heated house. He greedily ate milk-soaked dog food and went to sleep. As he grew stronger, he expressed a great disinclination to be friendly. "Sorta like Bill," said Robbie. He grew clean and strong and beautiful, but he never stopped spitting and snarling when we came near. Not in the least afraid of us, he would try to attack us through the wire. We had to poke his food in with a stick. Our intention had been to release him as soon as he was old enough to take care of himself, but we realized that, not being afraid of humans, he could be a real danger. Daddy had a friend who managed the Oakland Zoo, and he suggested that might be his best home.

Daddy came home after a week, much to the relief of the nurses, but he wasn't responding to medication as well as hoped. I promised to make sure he took his pills—no problem, he was meticulous when it came to pills and diet. But he did not feel strong enough to get out to his beloved vegetable garden. Chuck and Robbie took care of it for him and gave him detailed reports. When Chuck was away, I did it. Rob reassured his grandfather, "Mom is a good weeder." In a few days Daddy came and sat in the sun to supervise us. And, then, to our intense relief, he was well enough to pick the beans and hoe the zinnias himself. Zinnias? I had discovered that the best way to keep a supply of cut flowers for the house was to plant annuals in rows between his vegetables.

In his second year, the bobcat was a gorgeous animal, big and fierce, fluffy, with black rosettes along his sides. We gave him to Daddy's friend at the Oakland Zoo, not an ideal life for a bobcat, but better than no life at all.

Waddell Beach

Early summer mornings, at sunrise, was a magical time when the world sparkled and sang. Sometimes, when problems overwhelmed me, I would seek the solace and solitude of the beach—where sun and sand and the ocean's infinity would shrink human sadness back to manageable size—before I had to return home to prepare breakfast for everyone. At daybreak, the beach was fresh and still. In afternoons, fierce trade winds flung stinging sand and did not subside until evening. I'd watch the waves, lost in the sound and sight of their power. Or, I'd walk the shining tideline, picking up an occasional shell for our collection.

In childhood I had been captivated by the beauty of shells. I had collected them and drawn pictures of them, amazed at their mathematical perfection. I made up names for them (there were no field identification books then)—smiling clam (a bent-nose macoma), rainbow oyster (jingle shell), fat fan (broadwing scallop), graceful fan (spear scallop).

In 1943 when we came back to the ranch from our life in Pasadena, there were still no identification books available. We went to see the West Coast mollusk expert professor Myra Keen of the Stanford Biology Department. She was friendly and helpful. Later, when her book on West Coast shells was published, it became my beach bible. Dr. Keen 's office was lined with shallow shelves filled with shells. I pored over them until I found the identifications needed. Years later, in 1975, it was with her encouragement that I published my book *Tide-drift Shells of the Waddell Beaches*. In the preface to that book I wrote:

> During my childhood, remote Santa Cruz beaches were wild, lovely, lonely places far from the path of picnickers and tourists. Wheeling gulls and racing sanderlings were my companions on daylong carnivals of wind and sun and sand and waves.
>
> The dunes, untracked except by beach creatures, bloomed with beach asters, pink morning glory, and heliotrope-scented sand verbena. In early summer one walked the dunes carefully watching out for plovers' nests. On autumn evenings one met little spotted skunks foraging for tidbits among the drifts.
>
> The tidepools were thriving communities of tiny fish, sea flowers, scuttling crabs, brilliant nudibranchs, and lacy seaweed in shades of red and green and purple and brown. I would lie on the slippery rocks, wet from seaweed, chilled by the wind, watching tidepool pageants, too fascinated to leave, and so still that the shy shorebirds paid no heed to me.
>
> Today, the easily accessible rock ledges, alas, are no longer rich in life. Too many yellow busloads of children have carried off the pools' helpless residents, to die and be discarded as malodorous mementos of a day on the beach. Nevertheless, the tides continue to wash in and out, bringing shells, seaweed, flotsam and small creatures trying to reestablish their eco-systems.
>
> The dunes are stripped of flowers. Now only during winter storms are Santa Cruz beaches the wild lovely places where one can share the waves and dunes with wheeling gulls and racing sanderlings.

In addition to the joy of tidepools, shells, and birds, beach excursions often included a glimpse of the ocean's larger inhabitants. Dolphins played in the furthest waves, California sea lions kept pace, in the near waves, with our progress along the beach. Little harbor seals, from their low rock at Buena Point, watched us with curiosity and occasionally came closer for a better look. Several times, pilot whales "spy-hopped," seemingly standing on their tails in the breakers to look at us.

Majestic gray whales, in autumn, went by from Alaska to their calving grounds in the bays of Baja California. In the spring they passed again on their return trips. One at a time, or in small pods, they revealed themselves through their misty fountains and the occasional sight of a barnacle encrusted back or tail. Sometimes one, dead, would wash ashore with wounds from an orca or shark attack. Pods of orcas were sometimes visible, and sharks could sometimes be seen silhouetted in a towering wave.

At Rocky Point, if I turned over enough rocks, I would occasionally find a small octopus. Once a very big one, tentacles six feet long, washed up on the beach.

During my childhood, otters and elephant seals were considered to be extinct, eliminated by fur and blubber hunters. However, both had lived in hidden places. By 1943, they had made their way back north up the coast. In the following years, elephant seals took over Año Nuevo Island and then the peninsula. On occasion one would hunch himself out of the waves and up Waddell Beach. He was usually bloody from territorial battles on Año Nuevo and came to recover in a peaceful spot. People's reaction to these monsters during my childhood varied. Most, sensibly, kept a prudent distance from them. Some threw rocks at them, ignored by these well-blubbered beasts. One man, sorry for the bloodied, sleeping elephant seal, ran back and forth to the waves, bringing water to splash on him. He did not realize that if the seal wanted to get wet he would have hunched back into the waves. It would have been wiser to keep a safe distance from these mostly indifferent but potentially dangerous giants.

Tooke (Charles Alexander), 1950

In 1950, during the Korean War, Tooke left Stanford and enlisted, with a friend, in the marines. The captain wrote me, "He is a fine personable young man and I feel sure he will be a credit to the Marine Corps." I wondered if it was a form letter. As long as he was in boot camp, he was required to write a weekly letter home. A lovely idea.

He was sent to Korea, where his job was to teach Korean soldiers how to cope with their equipment. He repaired tanks, landing craft, and electronic equipment. I sent one of my guardian angels to take care of him. (Chuck had said that God must have appointed a committee to watch over me, because one couldn't do the job alone.) It is strange how you can believe in something you rationally know is not true: there is no such thing as an angel. But I nevertheless rely on my guardian angels. When Tooke got an R & R leave, he went to Japan and visited Takeo Matsumoto, our former foreign student Christmas guest on the ranch. Takeo wrote us, "Sgt. Charles A. McLean in a snappy uniform and a moustache showed up in my office today . . . I was very, very glad to see him and we drank sukoshi together." The friend Tooke had enlisted with was killed in action. When his body was sent home, we went to his military funeral.

Tooke, a boy of nineteen when he enlisted, came home a man of twenty-two. He got a summer job digging ditches in the desert. Thin and tanned, he registered at Stanford in the fall. His university career was now aimed at becoming a mining engineer like his grandfather. He said he'd had enough of barracks living, so we bought a tiny, two-room cottage in an apricot grove in Los Altos.

He came to the ranch often. His grandfather enjoyed him. Our housekeeper, Mrs. Cleaves, adored him. He seemed to enjoy being involved in our work projects or wandering by himself along the beach or in the woods, which long ago used to so annoy his cousin Anne, who wanted him to be more sociable. He said, "It's a fine place to come home to."

Being Teenage Robbie's Mother, 1952–1955

Children on a ranch learn to drive equipment and cars early. They are experienced drivers before it is legal for them to drive on public roads. And they are frustrated. Until they were twenty-one (the law later changed to eighteen), they had to have a parent's permission to get a driving license.

Tooke had been a trifle irked when, as a veteran marine staff sergeant, he was told in a loud voice by a license clerk that he had to bring written permission from his mother before he could renew his license.

At thirteen and fourteen it was irritating to Robbie, who was very social, that he couldn't legally drive a car. It was embarrassing that his mother had to drive him on dates! When his current girl interest lived in La Honda, twenty miles from the ranch, I would drive him to see her, but I parked well out of sight and worked on reports in the car until he was ready to come home. When he went to teen dances, held Friday nights in the Scotts Valley Barn, I took him and then stayed in the basement playing cards with the other unwanted parents. One evening the dance was invaded by tipsy older boys. The young ones had a fine time in the ensuing battle, being the numerically superior force, until someone spoiled the fun by calling the police. Youngsters without parents to sign for them were taken to juvenile hall. For once my motherly presence was appreciated.

Life on the ranch had become rather dismal for Robbie; Tooke and Allan were gone, Bill a menace, Granddaddy failing. Rob did not object when we decided to send him to Robert Louis Stevenson boarding school in Monterey. He found congenial friends and got good grades, having "nothing else to do." His only complaint—"no girls." He had frequent long weekends at the ranch. We watched him grow up. I missed our little-boy-Robbie, but the teenage Rob was nice, too. He had the same good manners and consideration for others that they all had learned from Chuck. He still had a great curiosity about everything. He understood mechanical things much better than the rest of us. He liked to be lazy but could work hard when necessary. The world was a more serious place for him than for his brothers. He had an admirable earnestness but lacked their light-hearted sense of humor. We did not doubt that he would live a sensible and successful life.

Allan in 1954

For Allan, 1954 was a bad year. He flunked out of Stanford in his first freshman quarter, talked his way back in, and flunked out again. He got arrested for having beer in his car. His girl broke up with him; he was devastated until he fell in love again. He and this love, with another couple, went to San Francisco and didn't get home that night. We and the girls' parents were frantic. The young people showed up, having changed their minds about a double elopement.

Allan was drafted into the army. Then he fell in love with Hazel Bassett, the pretty impulsive young daughter of our rancher helper. They eloped and were married in Reno, October 9. I loved both of them but was heartbroken by the tragedy I saw ahead of them. Apart from their youth, sixteen and eighteen, the marriage was a mistake for both of them. They were conspicuously unsuited for each other, young love notwithstanding.

The army sent Allan to camp in Maryland. His childhood shooting practice with gophers and bluejays paid off; he won honors as top marks-man of his division.

John David, first of their six children, was born in November 1955.

Giraffe, 1954

In 1954, the Third District representative on the Santa Cruz County Board of Supervisors died. Some people believed that Governor Earl Warren, who had previously appointed me to the California Citizens Tax Committee, should appoint me for the unexpired term. My supporters formed a committee and wrote letters and talked to influential people. The political reality was that the governor would appoint whomever the Santa Cruz County Republican Central Committee recommended. The central committee recommended a person who had no qualifications ex-cept that he was male. He was appointed and did a dismal job.

It was interesting that almost every member of the Republican central committee came to me, one at a time, and told me that he had voted for me, but that sentiment against a woman on the board had been too much. Most of the members of the central committee had voted for me? But the vote was against me! Ah, politics.

It reminded me of the time when I was a very little girl and had wanted a giraffe for Christmas. I made all the right contacts (Santa Claus and his elves) and was qualified (had been a very good girl) and made the right preparations (a bed for him near the rabbit hutch). But I didn't get the giraffe.

"I Don't Know This Place!" 1955

As 1954 progressed, Daddy was not well and was occasionally confused. He'd ask me what day it was, or if he'd had lunch yet, or if Mindy was here. He became overly worried about theft and locked and relocked cupboards and doors. He got frightened. One evening we came home to find him sitting with all the doors locked, shades drawn and tied down, a loaded gun in his lap. He said the radio had reported two boys had es-caped from a detention center in San Francisco. Another night he woke us up and said there were two men in the house. We made an intensive search to re-assure him. I phoned Mindy for advice. She said, "Don't make up stories about our father."

During the day he spent most of his time sleeping in a comfortable chair in the warm kitchen, Tika's great-great-grandkittens nestled in his lap. He removed my power-of-attorney. He replaced me as executor of his estate, naming Mindy instead. He questioned bills; I think he had a return of the fear of poverty of his youth. It was sometimes just too difficult and distressing to guide him in figuring out maintenance and repair and other ranch bills, so we paid an increasing number of them ourselves. After all, although the agreement had been that we would care for the ranch and he pay the bills, he had been generous about them for a long time. Perhaps it was now our turn. Chuck had an excellent job and I was getting commissions from insurance. Our commitment had been to take care of Daddy. This now seemed the way to do it.

Chuck and I were supposed to go to a farm bureau meeting that evening, February 5, 1955, but Daddy hadn't been feeling well in the afternoon so we decided to stay home. It would also be a chance to catch up on news of Tooke, who was home briefly from Stanford, and Robbie, who had a weekend free from boarding school.

After an early dinner we all spent time together in the library. Tooke and Robbie had been dreaming of making scads of money by skin-diving off Año Nuevo and finding old shipwrecks. Daddy appeared to be feeling better. He was cheerful, interested and, clear-minded. He told us about his experiences hunting treasure and lost mines. Tooke left to return to Stanford, and he would drop Robbie off to go to a movie in Santa Cruz. Chuck and I sat talking to Daddy in front of the fire. Then Chuck went to bed and I went up to the kitchen to spread my insurance notebooks on the table and work until time to pick up Robbie from the midnight bus in Davenport.

A little after eleven I heard a racket on the stairs to the library, and I ran down and found Daddy clinging to the banister and pounding the steps with a rock. He said, "I can't move and my head roars." I helped him to a chair and dashed upstairs to wake up Chuck. He carried him up to bed, where he sat and held him. I clasped his cold hands. Daddy said, "Charles, Charles, I don't know this place!" and died.

Sunday there was a graveside service on Grateful Mountain just as he had planned, with Mindy and Neal, Louise and Bill, Tooke and Robbie, and Chuck and me. He rests beside Mummie in that quiet spot overlooking the valley to the ocean.

Tuesday afternoon, there was a service in the Stanford Memorial Church. Allan had obtained emergency leave and had flown from his post in Maryland. Daddy's good friend Professor Tickell gave the memorial address to friends who filled the flower-massed church.

We drove Robbie back to school in Monterey and returned to the Casa. Uncle Bert had phoned us twice, but there was a telegram from him. It said ". . . your complete devotion to him has always had my greatest admiration."

After twelve years, our commitment was completed.

Seaside School
Watercolor by Hulda

4
Santa Cruz
1955–1971

We Carry On—For a Time, 1955

LIFE WAS DIFFICULT AT THE RANCH after Daddy's death. The Bassetts were furious at Allan for marrying their daughter, and their anger included us, so there was no help from them. We paid them an extra month's wages and told them to go back to their home in town as soon as their tenants moved out. We talked to Mrs. Cleaves and told her we had no idea what would happen and that we could only pay her for a short time. She said that she had plenty of money, that we should not worry, and that she would like to stay as long as possible.

There was much that had to be done at the ranch. Weekdays we worked at our jobs, often staying overnight in Santa Cruz in the little cottage we had bought on High Street. Weekends we worked on maintaining the ranch.

We looked for a new farm tenant and found a Pescadero dairyman, Willis Brown, who was looking for a location. Mindy approved and the ranch became a dairy again. The Browns were a good family, and they were excellent tenants for several years, until Willis' health made him retire from business.

Daddy had left the ranch jointly to his daughters, naming Mindy as executor. Though conscientious, Mindy lacked the knowledge or temperment for that task. She made some poor decisions which created problems both for us and the ranch operations. Louise, or probably Bill, did not want her share of the ranch, just the little Wilson Gulch and a lot of cash. Mindy and I bought them out. My assets were $70,000 short of enough. Neal said he'd lend us the money, as a business arrangement with my interest in the ranch as collateral. However, our friend George Keffer, who was now manager of a San Francisco bank, arranged a bank loan.

The 1955 Flood

Shortly before Christmas 1955, there were terrific storms and flooding. It had been raining when Chuck and Tooke and I went Christmas shopping in San Francisco. Late in the afternoon we turned the radio to weather and heard there were slides on the Coast Road. If we hadn't left Robbie at the ranch painting the kitchen, we would have stayed in the City, but we wanted to get back to him.

We decided to drive home by way of Palo Alto. The rain was bucketing down and we went through some shallow lakes on the road. Cars were stuck; but there was always someone at hand to pull them out, so we did not have to stop and be Samaritans. We went along Bayshore to Sunny-vale and got to Saratoga Road safely. From there it was a struggle—deep lakes and a detour at Cupertino. The highway at Los Gatos was a flowing stream. At Linden Hotel there was an official, standing in the water turning people back because the Coast Highway was closed. We went to the police station to find out if Hecker Pass road was open, but there was no one there. Back at the hotel, the official was gone, and two cars and a Santa Cruz County truck were planning to go through. We joined the convoy. Tooke remarked that we had nothing to worry about except submarines. The men got out several times to move rocks and trees off the road, but we made it to Santa Cruz.

Opposite the Santa Cruz post office we almost got stuck when the river in the street came over our running board and seeped in the doors. We pulled out of that and made our way slowly twenty miles up the coast. Just inside the ranch gate we finally got stuck. We got out of the car in our San Francisco clothes, in the pitch dark and rain: sky, mountains, fields, and road were a uniform dead black. Mud and goo were over our ankles (I lost my shoes on my second step). Here and there the road had been washed away. I was in the middle and Chuck kept falling off the road on one side and Tooke on the other. It was a long mile to the Casa. When we arrived home, of course the power was off. But Robbie had a kerosene lantern and there was plenty of hot water, which we certainly needed. And there was first aid and sympathy for my muddy, bloody feet.

Early in the afternoon, Robbie had taken the pickup onto the high-way to see what was going on. He got stuck in a deep lake in a dip in the road. A large truck came along and, needing to get by, had pushed Robbie out of the way onto the highway. He drove home carefully.

In the morning we saw devastation. A deep canyon was across the road by the Casa gate. The road to the Green Cottage was washed out. There was a tremendous slide between the Farmhouse and the front gate. The lower pastures were a lake, acres of fields had been washed down the creek. But we were lucky. Above Swanton a dam had broken. Houses were washed away. Harold Gianone was swept off his front porch and carried three hundred feet before he struggled free. Helme and Thornton Smith were flooded in their bedroom. Thornton got up to investigate and his pajamas filled with sand and gravel. Helme reached out of bed and held his head above water until Dick West and Harold, although painfully injured in his ordeal, carried them to the next house. Gladys West was swept from her living room and drowned; her body was later found resting on a mudbank.

Next morning Tooke made our road barely passable. We went to town for supplies. What a mess! Ladies' coats in show windows had six inches of mud on their hems. Benny Mock's drugstore storage basement was full of water. Palomar Garage cars all floated away. Plate glass windows had been smashed by flood-driven logs.

The Casa roof had not been resealed before winter, so ceiling plaster was falling off in goopy glops. We decided to move into town to a nice small house we had just bought on Laurel Street from Judge Scoppetone. Chuck and Tooke and Robbie and the neighbor Bradleys moved our furniture, and Soozie and I arranged it. On the way to town, we had stopped at the Davenport post office and picked up a present from Uncle Bert, a five-pound box of chocolate. It was damp and broken into and looked as if it had been sat on. After settling in, we all ate squashed chocolates and enjoyed them mightily.

We decided we would stay in town during the week and go to the Casa weekends to attend to the ranch. With our jobs and Robbie's high school life and the awful roads, it was the logical thing to do.

County Supervisor, 1956–1963

I had been elected to the Board of Supervisors of Santa Cruz County and was very busy in this job for the next six years. Its activities were quite apart from the ongoing "Real Life" of family and ranch.

California counties are governed by elected boards of supervisors. In Santa Cruz County there are five members, each elected from a district. I was the supervisor from the Third District, which was half of the city of Santa Cruz, along with Bonny Doon and Davenport. In 1954 I had tried for the office unsuccessfully. In 1956 I was successful, and I was re-elected in 1958. It was a challenging job and fun in a sort of frustrating way.

As when I had been president of the California League of Women Voters fifteen years before, I felt that I was leading a double life—in two separate worlds, the world of politics and the world of family.

In 1956, I ran against the man who had been appointed in 1954 to replace a supervisor who had died. The new appointee had not been a great success in office. His nickname in the county courthouse was "Stupid Smith." My 1954 sponsors and supporters, along with new recruits, rallied as we worked out an effective campaign plan. It cost $1,500 for printing, newspaper publicity, and radio time. Television had not yet be-

Santa Cruz County Board of Supervisors, 1956:
Lewis Nelson, Hulda, Vince Locatelli, Francis Silliman, Walter Merrill

come a factor. There were a few donations from supporters, but I did not ask for money. I paid most of the expenses myself.

There was an imposing group of official sponsors, community leaders who were brave enough to support a woman. And there were many enthusiastic workers, my friends and others enlisted during our campaigning. However, there were other people, especially doctors, who assured me that I had their full support, "but don't tell anyone." We called them our "rabbit committee."

Campaigning is a strange occupation, with frequent paranoiac overtones. It was sometimes difficult to tether my helpers to reality. The hardest work of the campaign was door-to-door precinct calling. I did most of it, but helpers did a lot, too. We talked to voters if they were at home. If not, we left a flyer. My opponent also did precinct calling; he went up and down the streets, ringing every doorbell. We rang only the doorbells of houses that had registered voters living in them. Helme Smith, retired from teaching at Seaside School, got precinct lists from the county clerk and made block-by-block calling lists for us. It saved much effort.

Most people who answered the door were not really interested, so I just told them who I was, left a pamphlet that had a nice picture of me and told of my qualifying background, and reminded them of the importance, in our form of government, of voting. I skipped houses with dogs on the front porch, but one dog came out and bit me anyway. Fortunately it was a chilly day and I was wearing a heavy coat. When he snuck up behind and jumped on my back, all he got was a mouthful of wool. At one house the front door was open, with a latched screen door. Inside was a crawling-aged baby sitting on the floor playing with his mother's sewing basket and sticking the needles and pins into his shirt and diapers. I rang and rang and shouted and shouted and eventually a cross and sleepy woman appeared. She gave a shriek and grabbed the baby. I stuck my flyer in the door and fled. Another time I was met by an unshaven man holding a gun. He told me that all politicians were going to hell. Some people were just against women on general principles. One or two told me that poor old "Stupid Smith" needed the job more than I did. One woman answered the door nude. I wondered whom she was expecting.

Two of the three things I had always wanted the board to do were easily accomplished—bringing the county wage scale up to standard and getting rid of the firetrap old-people's home. The third, an adequate juvenile hall, was slow in coming. Several other needed procedural changes were made with only one negative vote. We persuaded the county treasurer to invest county funds instead of keeping them all in savings accounts. We abolished the industrial zoning then existing for a hundred feet in depth back from all county roads. We codified county ordinances, which had not been gathered together but left in minutes and reports. Reviewing these ordinances, we rescinded many of them, such as the one that required horse troughs every mile along county roads.

Three major projects of the board while I was on it were:

1. Preparing for, and cooperating with the state in establishing, the University of California at Santa Cruz.
2. Drawing up a Santa Cruz County Master Plan.
3. Building a new Santa Cruz County courthouse.

The chamber of commerce had been a powerful opponent in my campaigns, although several of the members were among my sponsors. My first difference of opinion with the chamber when I was on the board concerned advertising. Along California highways were billboards "Come to Santa Cruz," with pictures of underclad bathing beauties. I convinced the board that tax money should be spent on advertising projects with higher standards.

Knowing something about insurance, I reviewed our county insurance program. Some policies were unsuitable, and many were overpriced. New specifications were drawn up and the business put to bid. We obtained better and less expensive coverage, some from the same carriers.

Two battles I lost because of pressure on other board members. I was not subject to pressure because I had no job or business that could be threatened, and Chuck's interests were beyond the reach of local powers. The first defeat was my attempt to make highway Route One go along the edge of the city instead of bisecting the town along Mission Street. The second one was to control dust emission from the Davenport cement plant, which devastated a section of the coast. I had researched this problem and knew that the savings from reclaiming cement dust would make the cost of control negligible, but the plant manager said that the plant would be forced to close and all the jobs would be lost. This was a powerful threat. Families felt fearful and unions opposed me. The dust situation was not remedied until the state passed control laws.

Another thing I felt was wrong, but could never put my finger on, was overpriced bids. We obeyed the law that required us to put county business to bid, but often the bids came in too high. A couple of times I persuaded the board to call for new bids, but there was little improvement. Explanations were made that seemed to make sense to the rest of the board but not to me. My questions related to things I knew something about, like office supplies, furniture, hospital and household items. Often we could have bought them more reasonably at stationery or hardware stores.

I included board of supervisor news in my letters written to Uncle

Bert. Occasionally he'd write me advice, terse and to the point. I was troubled the first Christmas by all the gifts which came to each of us from the people and firms the county did business with. His comment was "take no gifts from anyone." I talked it over with the other members of the board before the next Christmas came around. They made a policy that no gift would be accepted that could not be consumed within twenty-four hours. Glug. Glug. Well, better than no policy at all.

One of the most difficult things I and another supervisor did was to fire the director of the county hospital. A delegation of nurses had come to us to tell about the problem, including drunkenness on duty, mistakes in prescriptions, failure to search for an elderly patient who had wandered off and was found dead in a vacant lot a couple of days later, and sexual harassment of the nurses. It is not easy to fire a civil service employee. The ensuing personnel hearing was very unpleasant. I was accused of a personal vendetta and conspiring with a nurse (I'd never heard of her before) to get rid of the doctor. A team of lawyers defended him and local doctors spoke in his favor. Some of these *same* doctors privately phoned me and urged me to get rid of him! Rabbits.

Being a woman on the board at this time, when almost no women were ever elected to anything, had its special problems. For instance, if I asked the sheriff about a budget item, the newspapers reported "Mrs. McLean attacks sheriff." If another board member asked the same question, it was just considered a request for information. Some department heads flatly refused to work with a woman. One of the reporters assigned to the board, a friend, told me that he had been instructed by his editor to leave me out of pictures (fine, I hated to see my picture in the paper) and to write about me only when it could be a negative or humorous story. Vulgar jokes were made about me. State meetings were held in men's clubs which did not admit women on the premises. I was left out of meetings and conferences. Meeting rooms were thick with cigar smoke and spittoons. Something I soon learned to avoid was being late to meetings; when I came in late, all the men would rise with a great scraping back of chairs. I probably shouldn't have been so annoyed about compliments on my personal appearance, but they sounded so patronizing. I would reply, in the same tone of voice "and yours is very nice, too".

Most of these gender inconveniences lessened as respect increased for my knowledge of government and the county and for the practicality of my proposals. Young women today complain about sex prejudice and harassment shown in the workplace, and they are right about it. But progress has been made. It is not nearly as bad now as it was when I was pioneering the territory.

Most board work was not interesting. It was hard and repetitive, made more difficult because we had no staff (except a secretary to take minutes and type documents) and no office space in that crowded old building. It was a full-time job and paid $250 a month—it cost more than that to *do* the job. Our office at home was a comfortable place to work but far from the county departments.

As the workload grew, I suggested to Shep Quate, who had succeeded me in the farm bureau office, that he take some insurance courses and get a license. When he'd done that, I turned over the farm bureau insurance program to him, because I needed more time for the supervisor chores.

At Tuesday board meetings, time was always set aside for public comments. These comments too often showed an abysmal ignorance of county problems and board powers. I decided to try to get more information to my constituents and so instituted two programs: the first was a radio news broadcast every Sunday evening and the second was to hold public meetings monthly in our home to discuss problems and answer questions. Neither had ever been done in the county. These were popular and somewhat effective. Subsequent members of the board have held public meetings. There have been no radio programs. With the advent of television, communication became expensive.

General public ignorance of county government agencies and responsibilities continued to bother me. I decided to write and distribute a small book about it. With the enthusiastic support of the department heads, I wrote up each department of the county—its legal responsibility, its problems, and what should be done to improve its public service. The Grand Jury took a dim view of the project, and summoned me and scolded me for wasting county time and resources on the endeavor. The Grand Jury may have been irritated because I had not made a secret of how incompetent I thought they were. Grand juries vary in value; some do a great service to the county and some are entirely useless or worse. Future grand juries, for several years, used my book as a reliable source of information and, as a result, most of its recommendations were carried out.

My second term expired in 1963. Should I file for re-election? I was tired of the responsibility, but there were unfinished projects that needed my help. I ran for re-election but was defeated. My opponent was a young businessman who had been a war hero. He campaigned on the issue "It's no job for a woman." He also campaigned against things I was supporting. He was against the new juvenile hall, "Stop pampering delinquents." He was against controlling dust pollution from the cement plant, "Leave our employers alone." He pointed out that it would be cheaper to use the existing Mission Street for our through highway than routing it around the city as I had pointed out should be done.

My feelings at losing the election were mixed, annoyance that the students and faculty at the university had voted as a bloc against me, hurt at being rejected, relief that the job was over. The other supervisors organized an appreciation dinner for me. I was pleased and very surprised when more than three hundred people came to it and told of their support for the things I had been doing.

I was also surprised by the flood of mail. Perhaps the letter that pleased me most was from the general manager of the California County Supervisors' Association. He wrote "No supervisor has shown such a wide knowledge of county government and its problems. I hope that you will find a way to use your wonderful talents." He also wrote that, if I changed my registration to Democrat, I could have my choice of several fine jobs. I didn't want that kind of a job. To tell the truth, I don't think much of either party—self-aggrandizing machines. But philosophically, I am with the Republican principles of limited government and individual responsibility.

The new supervisor did a good job. Within a few months he realized that a new juvenile hall was necessary and he also carried on most of my other projects. However, the highway was routed along Mission Street and, as I had prophesied, has caused endless problems ever since.

"Real Life" Goes On, 1955–1962

The flood damage of 1955 made the daily drive from the ranch to our jobs in Santa Cruz impractical. We moved into the small comfortable house on Laurel Street. We stayed there during the week; weekends we spent working on the ranch.

Rob, living with us, was busy in high school and then at Monterey Peninsula Junior College. We had thought that, like Tooke and Allan, he would be anxious to be on his own at college, but he chose to stay at home, which pleased me very much. He was charming company even if he did like loud rock music while he was studying. I got up at three in the morning to get his breakfast and make his lunch before he caught the bus to Monterey. Rob was a good cook and could have done this himself, but I doubted that he would take the time. Some of the high-school friends were on the bus, including his special interest and future wife, Jean Branstetter.

By 1956, Allan had finished his army enlistment and returned to Santa Cruz to work for PG&E and Big Creek Timber until he joined Lockheed. One of his initial jobs at Lockheed was to rout rattlesnakes out of the newly built test complex located above the old Mill Creek Dam. (As he progressed in degrees and abilities he held various positions with the organization during the years. When he retired in 1998, it was from the position of Proposal Manager for Strategic Programs and Technologies for Lockheed Martin Missiles and Space Program.) The reason that there were rattlesnakes in the buildings is that the doorway had no sills because the machinery had to be rolled in and out of them. Allan was accustomed to rattlesnakes on the ranch. He had respect but little fear of them; most of the other employees felt more strongly.

Tooke attended Stanford, living in the small cottage in Los Altos. When it was no longer needed, we sold it, making his housing cost negligible. In 1957 he had a paper to write about gold dredging. George Keffer arranged for him to dine with Norman Cleaveland, who was visiting from Malaya, where he was president of Pacific Tin, a gold dredging enterprise. Tooke obtained good information for his paper. Norman got to know him and told him to get in touch when he graduated. Tooke did, and he worked for Norman in Malaya for seventeen years.

On weekends we did the work which accumulated at the ranch. Since Mrs. Cleaves had the Casa under control, I was able to work with Chuck on repairing flood damage, on roads and fences, garden and orchards, water supply, poacher patrol, maintenance of Brown House and Green Cottage, and all the other ranch needs. Daddy would have been pleased with the way we kept it up.

Our schedule was to work hard on Saturdays and on Sunday mornings and then to have a noon picnic, often under the grape arbor on the terrace above the Casa. There would usually be guests with us, neighbors, friends from Santa Cruz and Palo Alto. Daddy's peacocks joined us there. They seemed to miss him. We fed them tidbits and admired their splendor, all except one who liked to attack us. We ate him for Thanksgiving.

Betty Bradley and I worked on the flood-ruined furniture from the Shaw and West homes and gradually got it restored, refinished, reupholstered. Until their houses were rebuilt, we stored it at the Casa where it helped fill the empty spaces left when Louise and Mindy took their share of Casa furniture.

The seasons came and went, each with its own magic. One spring, when I was afraid I had lost my share of the ranch, I wrote "No Other Spring."

No other spring has ever been so fair,
The fields so green—the sky so deeply blue.
The field lark's song pours through the sunlit air;
The spider's lace is starred with dew.

The trees have caught some wisps of morning mist,
The seagulls wheel above the gleaming sea
Whose crashing chords the killdeers' cries enlist
To counterpoint a symphony.

No other land could ever be so dear.
Drink deep the song, and every lovely thing.
Lock in your heart the picture, close and clear,
For there may be no other spring.

In 1957 we sold the Laurel Street house to Shep and Barbara Quate and bought one we had wanted for a long time, across from the high school and a few blocks from downtown. At last, we had a perfect home of our own, in Santa Cruz. We shared a wide driveway with good neighbors. We had always had good neighbors, beginning with dear Mr. Wilson and his gooey sandwiches in our Cornell Avenue house in Pasadena so long ago.

Our new home had a pretty garden with a blooming jacaranda tree and masses of blue scilla and, best of all, a mockingbird who had learned canary songs and added his own rich tones. There was a sunny breakfast room so we could turn the dining room into our office with desks and files and a typewriter and adding machine. There was a cheerful downstairs bedroom, with a door to the patio, and bath. We had hoped Chuck's parents would soon come to live here. We moved in and gave a gala housewarming party with our new and longtime friends.

Chuck wanted to see the world. However, our responsibilities still prevented that. Anyway, we couldn't afford expensive trips. Instead, we took brief, inexpensive trips to Southern California, Mexico, and Hawaii—when we could escape from other commitments.

In January 1958, Chuck's father, eighty-three, had died of a heart attack in Boise. He was a good man, friendly, with courtly manners. Born on Prince Edward Island, Canada, he came west to join his banker brother. Dad became vice-president of a Portland bank until it, along with thousands of other banks, failed in the 1929 depression. Moving to Boise, he became Idaho's Controller of Welfare. Through the years, Dad and Mother McLean had spent many vacations with us at the ranch, and we had often visited them in their Warm Springs Avenue home in Boise. They were generous with encouragement and love. They were, perhaps, too over-impressed with my virtues and forgiving of my faults. They were dear to us.

When Dad died, Mother Lillian, tiny and fluttery, was helpless. She had no idea how to cope with anything. Someone had to do something immediately. Chuck flew to Boise to be with her, but his job would not let him stay long. I could not leave my board of supervisor job and my insurance responsibilities. Capable Mrs. Cleaves went to Boise to take care of her and to move her to Santa Cruz to be with us. Tearing her away from her home and friends was cruel, but there was no alternative. She could not take care of herself or plan her life. Dad had always done all the family planning and management. Living with us, she would have a loving family, and her daughter, Peggy Crowell, and family nearby. She came to the pleasant apartment downstairs where we had hoped she and Dad, too, would live in his retirement. Because she could not be left alone (she was prone to forget she had left the iron on, or water running), we found a companion housekeeper to live with us.

Mother missed her Boise friends but gradually made new ones. She was a "people person" with a talent for friendship. If she was on a train, she made friends with the porter; if she was in a taxi, she soon knew the driver's name and ages of his children and remembered to ask after them next time she saw him. She seemed happy with us, enjoyed her family, and, especially, Allan's little ones. But she was desperately lonely for her husband. She would pray, "Lord, please take me to be with Charlie again."

Casa Fire and Other Traumas, 1959–1962

The year 1959 was eventful. In February, Rob went into the army. He was stationed at Fort Ord, in California. He and Jean Branstetter were going through an off-again, on-again engagement. In April, the Casa burned down. In May, Chuck had emergency surgery and again in September. Allan had a good job and was also registered at San Jose State University.

Chuck and Allan clearing the road
after a winter storm, 1967

Tooke wrote fascinating letters about his adventures in Malaya.

The Casa fire was a shock. We were having dinner in our Santa Cruz home when a phone call told us that news of the Casa fire was on the radio. We rushed to the ranch. The house was engulfed in flames. Neighbors and people who had seen it from the highway were watching. The Davenport Fire Department was aiming an ineffective stream of water into the heat. Some rescued furniture and tools were piled across the road under an oak tree.

I sat on the terrace, paralyzed. I was not fond of the Casa and perhaps could have watched its fiery finish with pleasure if it had not been full of Daddy's library and Mrs. Cleaves's things and ours. I thought of the irony of having the day before searched for Daddy's set of diary volumes. Mrs. Cleaves was away for the weekend and I couldn't ask her where she had put them in her flurry of cleaning and rearranging the library. These diaries, the library, and some of the paintings were a terrible loss. Everything else was just *things*—furniture, silver, rugs, clothing. I was glad that the furniture we had restored for our neighbors had already been reclaimed by them. When it became obvious that the Casa was going to burn to the ground, we left and went home. The last thing we saw was Goober, Daddy's cat, jump into the inferno of the basement.

The next day we returned. Goober was there, singed and miserable but otherwise unharmed. All the things that had been saved and piled under the oak tree were gone, all but a large (twenty-four-by-thirty-five-inch), ornately framed picture of Uncle Bert. The picture had a strange history. In about 1941 it had been found on the back seat of a stolen car, abandoned, out of gas, near the front gate of the ranch. It was a dreadful picture. Evidently a highly enlarged photo of Uncle Bert had been un-skillfully painted over in oils. Daddy had adopted it and hung it in the Casa living room. I had not been able to live with it there and had taken it down. Daddy hung it in his garage. Now it was the only survivor of the fire. Evidently no one thought it worth stealing. I propped it up behind a bush out of sight. In a few days it disappeared, too.

The insurance ad-juster came. Cause of the fire had not been deter-mined beyond the fact that it had started in the library. A wire defect was the general verdict. I thought of Mrs. Cleaves's chain smoking, which had always worried me. There was no indication

Chuck and Tooke getting our firewood supply, 1969

that the fire was arson. The adjuster and I went over the claim. I'd taken pictures of the Casa interior for the executor, and they helped a bit. But "Two hundred tied dry flies!" said the adjuster. I hadn't given them a thought over the years; they'd just been there in Daddy's desk drawer. But, two hundred! He must have bought out a surplus stock some time. A $2,500 rug? "No rug is worth $2,500," he said. Yes, $2,500, a moderate depreciated value for an Oriental rug that covered the twenty-by-thirty-foot library floor. A stuffed cormorant. "I'm sure every family has a stuffed cormorant," he said. The adjuster threw up his hands and allowed the full insured amount.

Watching one's home burn is a traumatic experience. For years after-

Tooke and Mary, 1962

wards I could not bear to read about or watch TV news of fires. Loss of possessions was sad but not disastrous. We had a furnished home in Santa Cruz. Mindy and Louise had already taken their share of Mummie's lovely things. It was a comfort in later years to see something I thought might have been destroyed safe in one of their homes—sets of dishes, first editions, paintings, and especially the exquisite antique silk embroidery of waves.

In May, Chuck had emergency surgery in the Santa Cruz Hospital for a perforated ulcer. He was a terrible patient and slow in healing. He called a taxi and came home from the hospital in his pajamas while he still needed more skilled care than I could give. The Visiting Nurses Association helped me, and he survived. In September, he needed more surgery and went to Stanford Lane hospital in San Francisco, one of their last patients before it moved to the Stanford campus. This time he was a cooperative patient and made a good recovery.

We camped in the Green Cottage on weekends when it had not been promised to guests. We painted and refreshed it again and planted geraniums and nasturtiums for quick color in the garden. Cousin Van Ness used his skills to upgrade the plumbing and electricity. Steve and Margery Stevens brought us a carload of welcome bedding, dishes, and household equipment that they knew were in short supply in the cottage.

Mrs. Cleaves moved into the Brown House. She took a dim view of it but preferred it to the Green Cottage. She was a perfectionist and the Brown House did not respond to soap and water as had the Casa. However, she and Goober and hound Sam lived there happily. Mindy adopted the Brown House as Willis territory, and we were happy when she relieved us of its expenses and Mrs. Cleaves's salary.

In October 1959 Tooke arrived home from Malaya on a convalescent leave. He had been in a hospital in Singapore with amoebic hepatitis and assorted Asiatic ills. He registered again at Stanford to work for a master's degree in mining engineering. It was lovely to have him nearby again. Afterwards he would return to his job with Norman Cleaveland in Malaya.

In February 1960, Rob and Jean were married in a splendid ceremony at the Santa Cruz Christian Church, a reception at the Women's Club after-

Jean, Rob and Chuck,
with Bill and baby Judy, 1966

wards. Gen, Jean's mother, and I had made both church and clubhouse lovely with white plum blossoms and other flowers from the ranch and Catherine Steele's garden. We had not known for sure that the groom would be present, which made me a bit nervous. He was stationed at Fort Lewis, Washington, and had somewhat overused his brief, restricted leaves with flying visits to Santa Cruz and Jean. A leave for his wedding was in doubt until the last minute, and then he barely escaped camp as an alert was called. Henry Bradley, best man, took him in hand and delivered him to the church. Everything went off beautifully. Even, Joe, the bride's father, was happy. "That was fun, let's do it over again."

Tooke had written us about Mary, sister of Norman's wife. He told us that he had landed her on a mudbank while water-skiing and that she had thrown rocks at him. Evidently she forgave him. In April 1962 they had a big wedding in Kuala Lumpur at St. Mary's Episcopal Church. Chuck and I could not go—a fact we always regretted—but it had been impossible. Our finances were at their nadir because of interest on the $70,000 loan needed to save the ranch. (It didn't seem a practical idea to ask Tooke to postpone their wedding a couple of years until our finances were in better shape.) Norman wrote us about it and told us of the ambassadors, commissioners, nobility, ranking officers, and about a hundred other guests who were at the wedding and that "all dresses, hats, flowers, etc., were just dandy but beyond my power of description." Tooke sent pictures.

Broken Back and Other Problems, 1963

Busy as I was with county affairs during these years, there were other things of more importance. We had our pretty and comfortable home in Santa Cruz, our increasing family, and the work of ranch maintenance. Although it was Mindy's responsibility as executor of Daddy's estate to protect its assets, she had no idea of the amount of work and expense necessary to keep up the ranch. We continued our work of maintenance there and paid any of the bills that she, as executor, refused.

We worked hard but enjoyed other interests. I was doing flower paintings which were selling well. Chuck was busy with his interest in the Boys' Club. He also enjoyed playing poker with a group of old friends, including Leavitt McQueston, a retired entomology professor who was a poker expert. He taught Chuck an expert's game.

In October 1963 Chuck broke his back. I found out about it from a reporter friend while I was on an errand in the courthouse. "He's going to be okay," he told me. I said "Who?" He told me that Chuck had been in an accident and was in the Dominican Hospital. I raced down there and found that he was in "stable condition" in intensive care, with crushed vertebrae, woozy from pain medication but remarkably cheerful. He had been driving just beyond the fishhook overpass in Santa Cruz when the car brakes locked. The car skidded on wet pavement, turned all the way around, went down the embankment, turned over and landed right side up in the deep ditch. A passing motorist scrambled down the bank, checked for leaking gas, turned off the ignition, and told Chuck not to move, action that undoubtedly prevented further injury. An ambulance arrived, extricated him carefully, and took him to the hospital.

Mother McLean was woeful and fluttery about it. She kept telling me to keep my strength up and plying me with beef broth. Chuck's hospital stay was long. He felt fine, except for his back and being immobilized. He was a popular patient. Doctors and nurses spent their off-time in his room. Evening visiting hours were social parties. He gradually mended but was never afterwards completely well. We were glad the accident had been covered by workmen's compensation insurance because of the care he needed through future years.

When he was convalescent, we drove to Baja and camped on a warm, tranquil beach. I searched for shells while he sat in the sun and regained his strength. I was fascinated by shells and had collected them ever since I was a little girl. When we came back to live at the ranch, we went to the Golden Gate Park Academy of Sciences to look up identifications of Waddell Beach shells. At that time there were no identifying field books about shells. The director told us that the Baja California beaches were some of the best collecting sites in the world. Beginning in about 1957, we went collecting

Catherine Steele and Soozie McMahon
with their godchildren:
Teddy, Scott, Cheryln and John
(Allan's children); 1961

there. Days of joy and sunshine. Glorious. And so began our love affair with Baja California, which resulted in many Baja trips during the next years. Now this is no longer possible, and I am almost homesick for it.

While we were in Baja we heard over our little radio of President Kennedy's assassination in November 1963. Camelot ended. It had been a flawed paradise—this time it was the king who betrayed his vows. It was the beginning of the less glamorous, but more capable, Johnson administration. Widowed, beautiful Jacqueline seemed more angry than sad. She was determined to keep her children from being absorbed into the Kennedy clan. When she married little, kind, ugly Greek Ari Onassis, I felt that it was probably so that she would not be dependent on Kennedy money—Jack had left her little.

In 1963, too, Soozie died. Dear Soozie. She left her life insurance to her godchildren, John and Cheryln. I hope that there is a Heaven so she could rejoin her Bill and perhaps help out my guardian angels now and then.

Allan's children were born: John David, 1955; Cheryln, 1957; Skyelar (Scott), 1959; Theodore (Ted), 1961; and Allison, 1963. One at a time they spent every weekend with us at the ranch. We loved having them: John, a dreamer; Cheri, full of gayety; Scott, quiet and observant; Ted, unpredictable; and Allison, adorable and affectionate. In fact, they were all, except Scott, clingingly affectionate and all, with the exception of Ted, well-behaved. They looked forward to their turns to visit us—Cheri, "because it is a happy house," Scott, "because of the deer and little things and a clean bed."

One night a small feverish grandson and four teddy bears crawled into bed with me. In the morning he looked like a chipmunk storing nuts. Mumps. Pretty soon I looked like a chipmunk, too. It wasn't bad, and I'd chosen a fine time for it, Christmas season. No one argued when I told why I canceled three speeches, got substitutes to chair two meetings, and shed my responsibilities for two bazaars. I rested in bed, mumps-resistant people waiting on me. Lovely.

Uncle Bert

Uncle Bert and Aunt Lou had been a part of my life forever. When I was a little girl, Uncle Bert was someone who fixed toys, answered questions, and smoked fragrant cigars. Aunt Lou was sort of a second mother, a gentle authority figure. In my teens, Uncle Bert was a hero who saved millions of people from starving and was very important. Aunt Lou was a role model of gracious behavior and courage and a source of good advice.

As I grew up, I gradually began to appreciate them for what they actually were, extraordinary people. Uncle Bert was compassionate on a worldwide stage. He had a superior mind, encyclopedic knowledge, and the ability to make things happen. Aunt Lou, a gracious, sensible, loving woman, was equally at ease with royalty and small children; she was my special friend. During the years 1929–1933, when he was president of the United States, Uncle Bert was lost to the family. He was much too busy and besieged for any of us to dream of bothering him. If a family problem urgently needed his attention, Aunt Lou coped with it. We all mourned that the crises of the worldwide great depression denied opportunity for him to use his genius for organization and efficiency that our government so badly needed and still needs. We were sad that politics defeated the measures he designed to ameliorate the disasters of the depression in our country. All this I wrote about and documented in my biography of him.

After Aunt Lou died in 1944, I became closer to Uncle Bert in his loneliness. He was interested and, I think, somewhat amused by my political life, and he gave good advice.

When he was ninety-two years old he failed in health and mind. Toward the middle of September 1964 we received a phone call from an Army general telling us that Uncle Bert was dying and that we would be notified when it happened. Word came, and we were sad, although we knew it had been inevitable and timely. The Army told us about the arrangements for the Iowa funeral and that we would be met in Cedar Rapids and driven to West Branch. In Cedar Rapids were cousin Herb and Peg and their family, cousin Allan and Coby and theirs, Bunny, Barry Goldwater, and many others. We were all driven to West

Uncle Bert and Hulda
in his Waldorf Hotel
apartment;
New York, 1962

Branch for the funeral, which was conducted by Elton Trueblood, our Quaker minister friend.

Then about twenty of us who had come from California were flown home in the *Columbia*, which had been President Eisenhower's plane. On the way home I made a somewhat abstract painting of the funeral—of us wending our way up the hill. The best part of the trip home was learning that cousin Herb's hearing (lost in childhood) had been restored by surgery. It was wonderful to see him, buoyant with freedom from his burden.

YWCA, 1964–1966

In 1964 I was asked to take the position of YWCA executive director to replace the retiring director until another could be found. This sounded like a pleasant job, no long-term commitment, and a fine chance to strengthen a limping but worthwhile organization. I enlisted volunteers to improve the board and to lead youth groups, expanded classes. I organized support groups. We cleaned out closets and drawers, replanted the garden, and made the dingy lounge bright and inviting. I straightened out the files and finances. I inherited the capable and cheerful office secretary, who was happy to share my enthusiasms. She had a hitherto undiscovered talent for developing attractive promotional material for our projects.

It was rewarding work with good people. Our projects were challenging. One was a pioneer demonstration of Head Start, the new idea in getting underprivileged children better prepared to start school. We proved the idea's practicality for local children, and it was adopted by the school system here. I was later surprised at how much more it cost when done by tax funds than when we had done it.

Another new program was helping welfare women into jobs. We took two women at a time to learn skills in our office. We outfitted them from our thrift shop (and from donations) and found "real" jobs for them. Most of them worked out very well. It took me back to my days with the Pasadena SERA Project, when I had organized a similar program.

We gave a Christmas party, encouraging Head Start families to come. There was a Christmas tree, small gifts for everyone, and cookies. I had Allan's three-year-old Teddy at the party with me. He came to me in great excitement, "Granmother, come and hear angels." We went out on the porch. Far in the distance carolers were singing "The First Noël."

Mother McLean, 1965

Mother McLean, who had been living with us in Santa Cruz, had always been tiny and slim. Now she was getting frailer, until she looked as though a breeze would blow her away. She wanted to get to Heaven to join Charlie. She needed a lot of love and care and encouragement. Margaret Burns, the housekeeper-companion, was kind and affectionate.

Mother loved the children and had always enjoyed playing with the littler ones, but now they quickly tired her. Margaret said that she seemed to especially enjoy the quiet weekends when we were working at the ranch and the two of them were alone in Santa Cruz. Mother spent most of those days in bed.

One day in 1965, she told Chuck that she'd like to be nearer to his sister, Peggy Crowell, who lived in Sausalito. She asked if he and Peggy would look for a nice rest home there. They spent a while looking, while I was frantically busy with Allan's children who had just come to stay with us in the Farmhouse. Mother moved into an attractive home nearer to Peggy.

We went to see her often. She told us she was pleased and happy with her care and surroundings. She was always asleep when we arrived but roused and asked eagerly about our activities and about the children. She was getting frailer and frailer, until one morning she just didn't wake up.

In Loco Parentis, 1965–1966

In 1965, when Hazel, not for the first time, left Allan and the children, we sold our Santa Cruz home and moved to the Farmhouse so that we could care for the children there. John and Cheri could go to the little Davenport elementary school. The Farmhouse was a blessing, but it was not designed exactly to fit our needs. We wished that our long dream of a home of our own on the ranch was not still only a dream. The ranch belonged to Mindy and me in undivided ownership. It would not be wise for us to build on land half-owned by Mindy, and she had not been willing to make a trade that would make each of us sole owner of a few acres.

The Farmhouse was a handsome stucco hillside home. The main floor had three bedrooms and two baths. There was the living room with a large rock fireplace flanked by gun racks. There was a dining room, kitchen, pantry, and a terrace. Downstairs there was a small apartment, a large storeroom, and a very big dining room, all used when there was a crew of farmworkers.

Mindy and Neal Willis, 1963

Cousin Roy Heald had designed and built it and the farm buildings for us in 1917. Roy and his family moved into the Farmhouse, and he worked as farm manager in the early years. There was a dumbwaiter to take food from the kitchen down to the farmworker's dining room below. The first time Cousin Kate used it she loaded it with dishes and food. Cousin Roy, who was explaining it to her, said, "Let 'er go." Kate let go of the guide rope instead of letting it out slowly. The dumbwaiter and its load crashed on the dining-room floor below.

Chipmunks somehow made their way into the downstairs bathroom and drowned themselves in the toilet. I didn't think this was premeditated suicide; I kept a branch in the toilet so they could climb out. It sometimes puzzled guests.

One afternoon soon after they had moved to the ranch, Allan's five children, John David, Cheri, Scott, Teddy, and little Allison, sat on the Farmhouse back steps watching a huge, eight-wheel truck pull a machine through the irrigation pipes with a heavy steel cable. Catherine Steele had sold her ranch, and the new owner was relining with cement the pipes that took water from the Waddell to Green Oaks Ranch.

The children became bored and went down to the beach. Just after they left, the cable broke and sent the truck hurtling through the steps where the children had been, into the house, crashing through the bedroom wall and shattering table, chair, and bed, cracking glass windows in the kitchen, knocking plates off the shelves, and generally creating a shambles. The man in the truck was thrown out, unhurt. A miracle.

The pipe men did not seem concerned about our house. Their worry was the machine left in the pipe with setting cement. They worked until two-thirty in the morning clearing out the pipe. As there was no place for them to eat, I took them coffee and sandwiches, for which they were grateful. We had been alerted about a severe storm, and the wind had already started. When Chuck got home, we nailed plastic over the hole in the house and lived that way for two weeks. This had all happened three days before Christmas. Storm after storm descended on us. Carpenters would not come out to make repairs. Of course, the light and power and telephones were also knocked out. We felt like pioneers—five children and nothing to use for heat or for making hot water or cooking food except the fireplace.

Again, a few months later, repairs continued on the pipeline, in the field by the Farmhouse. The pipe men were working with torches. I went out and reminded them that the grass was dry and so please be careful. Soon I heard a noise in the garden and saw the pipe men running back and forth with buckets of water. The field was on fire! One of the men jumped on his tractor and drove it back and forth making a fine ditch where the fire had already been. I called the forestry department, then got some wet sacks and told the men to beat out the flames. They did not listen to me. I finally planted myself in the path of the man running back and forth with pails of water and said, "You *idiot,* listen to me," shoved a wet sack at him, and started beating with mine at the edge of the fire. He finally caught on, but by then was gasping with exhaustion and had to lie down and throw up. There was a brisk wind and it blew the fire up into the clump of pines. I expected them to explode, but the fire just raced through the grass. So we still had a chance to beat it out before it reached the brush if we worked hard enough.

Then Lud McCrary arrived, having seen the smoke from the mill. He used his walkie-talkie to tell Bud to bring the tanker and then went to work with the wet sacks. The idiot on the tractor came up and saw that if a male was using wet sacks it was probably a good idea and went to work with us. We had the fire surrounded by the time Bud arrived with the tanker, and it was all out by the time Forestry arrived with three fire engines. Insurance paid for my scorched shoes and suit but wouldn't pay for my ruined hair styling, which had to be redone because of smoke and soot.

Allan was offered an attractive opportunity by Lockheed in Georgia. Hazel came back, and the filed divorce was called off. January 1966 the family left for Georgia. I missed the children. They all wrote or sent me picture messages, often. I wrote to them and sent them the stories that were later collected into *When I Was a Little Girl.* Five-year-old Teddy printed, laboriously, "If I promise to be good please can I come home."

During the winters we had the ranch to ourselves most of the time. There was no one else living there, and we were still leading our double lives—weekdays in Santa Cruz working at our jobs, weekends on the ranch doing maintenance. When Chuck had to be away weekends, I was alone in the Farmhouse. I did not like this. People stranded on the highway or in trouble on the beach would come there for help. Escapees from the work camp in Big Basin would make their way down the Waddell valleys. We had never had any trouble and there was really nothing to fear, but reason has little to do with fear. It was not possible to lock up the Farmhouse securely, so I put a bar across my bedroom door. If something tried to get in, I would drop out a window and melt into the brush. Silly? Yes, but that was the way it was. Daytimes were okay. I was not afraid to be alone then and I did what I could without Chuck's help. If it was wet, I took a hoe and drained mud puddles to protect the road. In spring, with a hoe again, I chopped up emerging thistles, or I tidied, patched, and painted the houses.

Winter, spring, summer. There were cattle in the meadows again. Instead of dairy cows there were polled Herefords, beef cattle that Chuck

Hulda collecting shells, 1968

and Lud McCrary were raising. The McCrarys had resumed logging in the valley once more.

On the way home from one of our trips, we visited Allan's family in Georgia. John told me that it had taken two weeks to clean the house to get ready for us. It was a nice place with a large lot sloping down to a creek and a Civil War battle site where the children dug for bullets.

Ten-year-old Cheri came from Georgia and spent most of the summer of 1967 with us, to my delight. She was fond of me, too, and told me that I was worth a dozen teddy bears. She and I were on the beach one day watching surfers ride the waves when we heard shots coming from a group of young men on the road above us. Bullets were hitting the waves all around the surfers. I sat Cheri safely behind a log and ran to our car to get back to a phone, but the shooters took off, too far away for me to get a license number.

In these flower children years, there were usually hippies camped on the beach. One group made sure that the beach was kept clean. They picked up trash left by picnickers (paper, cans, old Levi's, mattresses, magazines), and they gathered up the broken glass from bottles that had been used as targets. Cheri suggested that we might say thank-you by taking them some food. We cooked up a big pot of spaghetti and took it to them. They were surprised.

To make a definitive collection of Waddell Beach shells replacing the one that had burned with the Casa, I went to the beach for each special low tide, usually early in the morning when the air was cold and still.

Cheri went with me. We would look at tracks in the wet sand—raccoon, skunk, opossum. Shorebirds would run with the waves. On the horizon far to our left, dawn painted the beach with a rose glow.

Shell collecting was always my occupation of choice for rare beautiful unfilled hours. Helme Smith, long retired from teaching and no longer busy as my volunteer secretary for board of supervisor work, went with me as we combed the beaches. When she wanted some owl limpets, those three-inch tortoise-shell-like rarities, I knew we could find them on a nudist beach just north of Santa Cruz. It was a cold windy day when Helme and I and a fellow sheller went looking for them. I remarked that I thought the nudists would be clothed in such weather. "I should hope so," sniffed Helme.

However, with eyesight better than Helme's, I noticed their pink forms on distant sand dunes. We were walking slowly, studying the tidelines, when a young man wearing only a cap and a tan tipped his cap to us, "Good morning, ladies." Helme looked up and gasped. When we came to the rocks, I climbed them to look in the cracks. Helme, too heavy to clamber around, stayed at the bottom looking into the crevices there. A slow wave's froth crept up and she stepped back to avoid it. She fell over a low rock behind her and the water foamed around her. Helme, chubby, with short arms and legs, was having difficulty turning over. She looked like a stranded turtle. I started down to assist when a concerned young nudist ran over and helped her up. I quietly went back to my quest. We were nearly back to the car, satisfied with several shells, when Helme started to laugh. "You'll never guess what happened to me," she said. "Cross your heart to keep a secret," and then she told me about the gallant nudist.

Shells are not the only treasures we have found on the beach. For a while we found a great many useful boards lost from large lumber barges, and during World War II, huge shell casings came up with storm waves. In the spring of 1969, hundreds of blue and green glass Japanese fishnet floats washed up on local beaches. I gathered forty of them, with diameters of from two to twelve inches. Some changed ocean current had brought them then and never before, or afterwards.

Political Action Consultant, 1968

Summer 1968 on the ranch was as busy and sociable as ever, interrupted by a forest fire started near the site of the big fire twenty years earlier. At night the sky was red behind Grateful Mountain. This new one grew from a neglected campfire left by a Sierra Club officer. Fortunately, the wind blew it away from us. Borate, from planes, and three hundred firefighters put it out before it became a wide disaster.

Allan's family moved back from Georgia, ecstatic to be home. Until they could find a house in Santa Cruz, they lived in the Green Cottage. We'd fixed up a big tent nearby for the overflow of children. There were now six children; little blond Robanne had been born in 1967 in Marietta. Allan found a large old home on the corner of Mission and Walnut in Santa Cruz, shaded by a towering gingko tree. The house had been lived in by a group of young men and it needed considerable repairs. Allan bought it and fixed it up. It was a good home for the family. John and Cheri went to nearby Mission Hill Elementary School. They all, again, one at a time, spent weekends at the Farmhouse with us and the many friends who came to visit.

From March to the November elections in 1968, I worked at a well-paid job for the California Farm Bureau Federation as their political action consultant. The project was to advise the county farm bureaus' boards of directors on working effectively to elect candidates who understood the problems of agriculture in their districts. First I wrote a handbook of procedures and suggestions and a program, and then I visited and revisited the county farm bureaus throughout California. For someone who is not happy on airplanes, I spent a great deal of time on them, going up and down the state and crisscrossing it.

We started by interviewing candidates. Then the local farm bureau board decided whether there was one candidate who would represent the problems of agriculture intelligently. If so, did the farm bureau want to invest its time and resources in this candidate's campaign? Some farm bureau boards were already politically sophisticated and knew how to work effectively in a campaign. Others were complete political novices or had naïve ideas of methods. Some did not feel that they had the resources to invest in political activity. Others were enthusiastic. It was my job to assess their capabilities and to show them how to use them to the best effect.

By the end of the eight months, on election day, farm bureaus in California were a much stronger voice in the election than they had ever been before. There were happy successes, and there were dismal failures. But farm bureau members knew their candidates and understood political realities as they never had before. Political parties and candidates had a better realization of farm problems and of farmers as an active force to be recognized.

There was great satisfaction in working with so many dedicated men and women. However, for me, the very best part of the job was this opportunity to see our beautiful state of California through spring, summer, and fall, from the deserts of the south to the dark forests in the north, from the ocean to the high Sierras. I got to know the people who loved it, each small corner of it, and who were determined to protect and nourish it.

In springtime there were the myriad shades of green, with wildflowers like great splashes of paint, orange and blue, yellow and purple. In summer, dark forests contrasted with gold fields and hills, deserts glowing in the lights of dawn or sunset, and always, there were the bright threads of rivers and jeweled mountain lakes.

The part I didn't like was the many hours I spent in airplanes, which seemed determined to scare me to death. Landing in Reno once, there was a wall of flame outside the window. "Just burning off fuel," comforted the pilot. Just! I was not comforted until it died down. Another time I was in a small, three-passenger plane when it started to buck and wobble. The pilot said he thought that he'd better turn back. A passenger protested that he had an important meeting to get to, so we wobbled on. In another plane I could see the trees below through cracks in the floor. I decided that the California Farm Bureau Federation considered me expendable.

Astronauts—a word we would get very familiar with—had just made their first flight. How could anyone make himself get into that little shell, have himself shot in a fiery arc to space, then come crashing back into the ocean? It was beyond my comprehension.

Vietnam War, c. 1965–1975

These were the years of our long escalating war in Vietnam. The country had been drawn gradually into it, trying to honor our commitment to protect South Vietnam from the Communists in the north. We withdrew our troops in 1975, when it became obvious that this crusade was a bloody, costly failure.

The war was opposed by a large and vociferous part of the American public. The cause of this opposition was never generally recognized. I believe it was because, for the first time, the blood and dirt and horror of war had been seen and heard by everyone. Television. Sitting in our living rooms, we saw our young men die gruesomely, fighting for a faraway country many of us had never heard of. Myths of war, patriotic chivalry, and triumphs were forever destroyed by reality. All of us were horrified, seeing and hearing terrors we had only imagined. Young men in our country wanted none of it. Protests and marches against it (egged on and exploited by Communist sympathizers) and draft evaders were a natural result.

TV shows us what a sad and dangerous world we live in. Perhaps we were happier before we knew this. Television also shows us how beautiful our world is. Life before television? I was in my teens when I heard a recently invented radio, squeaky and full of buzzing. I was in my thirties before I saw a fuzzy pictured television set.

With all our developing knowledge and communication can we find understanding and perhaps a way to build a better future for humankind?

Insect Project, 1969

Beginning in March 1969, Chuck had a particularly rough time. He had surgery to remove a lung lobe, then got pneumonia and TB. It was "atypical tuberculosis," an uncommon strain with a low level of contagion. We all tested negative to it. He took a leave from his job, but I did Farm Bureau things for him that he said had to be done, leave or no leave. I spent most of my time at the hospital with him and then at home in the Farmhouse. I wished we had not sold our more comfortable home in Santa Cruz.

Chuck was a heavy smoker. Dr. Amby told him that there was extensive damage to his lungs. If he'd stop smoking, the condition could be stabilized; if he didn't, it would get worse. He gave up cigarettes for only a short time.

Chuck said that he really wanted very much to build a home for me on the ranch. Again, I took up the subject of land exchange with the Willises. Mindy and I owned all ranch land together. The logical thing to do was for us to exchange our part interests so that each of us would have a building site with sole ownership. Mindy was unwilling to make the exchange.

Not wanting to leave Chuck, I kept busy at home. There was always plenty to do. And we watched television. Cousin Van Ness had installed one for us. The antenna was on top of a fir tree on top of the mountain, which made it hard to repair after a storm. Tooke said it was sticky with resin and was full of ants. In July 1969, we saw on TV the astronauts walking on the moon! Chuck said it didn't look like a place he'd want to spend a vacation.

I also drew hundreds of portraits of insects. Chuck's poker friend Leavitt McQueston, the retired entomology professor, had dreamed up a project which would make us all rich. It didn't. But it was fun and more than paid for itself. Briefly, it was an insect collecting project for school classes that could be used as an introduction to entomology, biology, and general science. We furnished the collecting supplies, teaching materials, and illustrated plates. We lectured and gave field trips. But first, I had to draw pictures of about eight hundred insects to make the plates identifying the insects in the school collections the students would make. Dr. McQueston furnished insects from his collection, for me to draw. It took me longer to do this than for Chuck to get well again.

The insect project was ready to start; everything had been printed, and the supplies were attractively packaged. Dr. McQueston and I met with science teachers and sold the project to school districts, ten of them. The price was $500 for supplies and $500 for services. There were a couple of additional districts which bought only the supplies, having personnel capable of directing the project.

At the end of the year, the classes that we were directing had an insect collecting field trip to the ranch. I enlisted Chuck and friends to help. He'd take the uncooperative boys—there were always a few who took a dim view of chasing butterflies and catching bugs—and this group would go scorpion hunting. That interested them; it had an element of adventure. They always got enough for everyone. Chuck knew where the scorpions lived, under rocks by the old county road. There would be a picnic and an identification period. Then, tired and cheerful, they loaded onto their yellow busses.

We received some wonderful thank-you letters. "Mom won't let me grow the green fuzzy ones." "It was super, especially when we fell in the creek." "Thank you for the yucky bugs."

The insect project occupied a large part of my time for the next few years, until it became so very time-consuming that I had to phase it out. The schools had the material, and they could continue to make their collections more and more extensive without my help.

5
The Casita
1971–1985

Our Casita At Last, 1971

IN 1970 CHUCK RETIRED from the farm bureau position because of his health. He had two dreams for the few remaining years of his life, he wanted to see the world and he wanted to build me our home on the ranch.

In 1971 Mindy decided she wanted to build a house on the ranch, too. The land exchange that made this possible was arranged. To end Mindy's fear that this could mean fragmenting the ranch, we agreed that there would continue to be family right of way over all the ranch, with no locked gates or boundary fences. Papers were quickly signed and our home, the Casita, started. Our house plans had been drawn for years. (I had even made a model of them, and, in our imaginations, we had lived there.) It was built of natural redwood, which would, in time, silver and melt into the landscape. It was built around an enclosed courtyard. Our home was one side, the other sides were made up of the guest cottage, bunkhouse, tractor shed, garage, tool room, and storerooms. I was ecstatic, and somewhat surprised, when it turned out just as we had dreamed. It was perfect for us, for our guests, and for the children, who held their parties in the bunkhouse.

We had fun doing as much as we could ourselves, with a very patient contractor. We copied the huge rock fireplace that had been in Daddy's Casa library. One weekend when we had a lot of visitors, we had a picnic on the beach and then carried back fossil rocks for it. Bud McCrary handplaned the thick redwood mantle. We planted hundreds of daffodil bulbs lining the driveway circling the Casita. We paved the court with redwood rounds. Inside it were the barbecue and many plants kept safe from deer.

Starting to build the Casita, 1971

Outside the protection of the courtyard would be planted the flowers that deer don't like: rhododendrons, camellias, wild lilac, fremontia, bird-of-paradise, montbretia, and well-protected fruit trees.

Big windows in the living room framed a view of meadows and hills. The huge bedroom windows overlooked the marsh and, beyond that, the ocean. We made the place secure so that I would not be afraid, as I had been in the Farmhouse when Chuck had to be away. The splendid solid oak, paneled door that John Lisher designed and made for us had hidden hinges. Because our house had the only lights visible in ten miles of dark highway, people in distress came, not infrequently, to our door. Now I could open a hidden panel and talk to them without unlocking the door. If they were out of gas, I could tell them where a two-gallon can was kept under the steps for the purpose. If they needed a telephone, I could hand it out through the open panel. If, as had happened twice, they were lost children, I would take them in and find help for them.

The Casita was finished in March 1971. Chuck moved us in while I was in the hospital for cervical cancer surgery and radiation. I arrived home to a beautiful bedroom where I could lie and watch the waves. Catherine Wilson, the twins' mother and our friend, came and cared for me for the few days until I was up and able to do the simple housekeeping of a well-planned house.

It was Eden.

Casita front entrance

Graduations and Other Events, 1972

While we were building the Casita and coping with illness, the rest of the family was also busy. Family life and projects were going on around us.

Rob and Jean owned a home on San Juan Avenue in Santa Cruz. Rob was working hard at his job at General Telephone and Electronics, and they were both devoted parents of Bill and Judy, intelligent and beautiful children.

Allan and his family were living in the attractive old house, shaded by a huge gingko tree, on the corner of Mission and Walnut in Santa Cruz. Allan worked for Lockheed and was studying for his master's degree.

Tooke and Mary on leave from his job in Malaya were at Stanford, where he was taking a double course towards master's degrees and Mary had a job arranging foreign car purchases by travelers.

All of them spent their spare time at the ranch. Tooke and Mary cleared out a delightful area by the creek. We named it Alder Grove Camp. It was a green, sunny, flat place shaded by alders and poplars, where the thrushes sang in the evenings. It was a favorite summer camp-site for the young McLeans and their friends. In winter, the Casita's bunkhouse and guest house were welcome shelters when weather did not cooperate for picnics and camping.

View from the Casita

At the end of the 1972 school year, Allan received his master's degree from the University of Southern California in Systems Management, and Tooke got his advanced degrees, Master of Science in Mining Engineering and Master of Business Management, from the Stanford Business School. These all were truly prodigious accomplishments. The amount of determination and hard work involved was mind-boggling. We went to the graduation ceremonies and were exceedingly proud of our sons' accomplishments.

Mindy built her vacation home on the site where the Casa had burned, surrounded by its garden. Her grandson, Danny, named it the Deck House because of the wide deck overlooking the valley.

Louise, long divorced from Bill, still lived in Alameda alone in her bungalow next to a garden apartment building she owned. As always, her garden was fabulous with flowers and fruit trees, and there was a swimming pool where she swam daily laps. It comforted me to see her happy among her beautiful things.

Fine additions to our ranch family were Ted and Eleanor Gregory. Ted, principal of the Davenport school, had phoned us one day and

The McLean family, 1972

Rob   Cheryln   John   Tooke   Mary   Allan   Peg and Bob Crowell

Hazel   Jean   Hulda   Chuck   Scott

Teddy   Bill   Allison   Judy   Robanne

asked if there was a house he might rent at the ranch. We told him that nothing was for rent, but the Green Cottage was empty, somewhat in disarray because Clarice, the Seaside School teacher, had just moved out. Ted brought Eleanor, his new bride, to look at it. I doubted that she would be charmed by the untidy, shabby, small but beloved Green Cottage. Eleanor looked at it and at the neglected garden and said, "It's just what I've always longed for!"

We invited them to settle in—no rent, but cautioning that maintenance would be their problem. If the roof blew off, they'd have to nail it back on. It did, and they did—along with making numerous other improvements. First, they had to strengthen the floor so it would hold up the piano and organ that they put in the living room. Eleanor planted a prolific vegetable garden. They became a cherished part of our extended family.

Friends and children on the ranch again reminded me of those first years when we came from Pasadena. But now, they were the children of the children who had been here then, and without Casa guestrooms, most of the families camped.

Allan's Family, 1973 —

Hazel left again with her latest romantic interest and Allan's family fell apart. In May of 1973 there was the divorce, and later I was assigned custody of the four younger children: at age sixty-seven my life returned to parenting. The two older ones, John David, eighteen, and Cheri, sixteen, knew that they would be welcome with us at the Farmhouse but chose to be on their own. There was nothing we could do for them except keep our home and hearts open to them.

All the children were desperately unhappy. I don't know what Hazel told them to make them so afraid of us. Scott, fourteen, and Teddy, twelve, would not, at first, come to us but stayed with Hazel. We did not want to force anything on them. Allison, ten, came to protect Robanne, six—little Robanne, confused, sad, and puzzled. Allison, with her caring, nurturing heart and her take-charge talent, gave and needed infinite love. Their pain wracked me. And it was heartbreaking to watch, bright, beautiful Hazel make her tragic choices into a world of alcohol.

Loraine, in New Mexico, phoned and said she thought I needed assistance. She spent two weeks helping me with the work and reorganization and giving much appreciated encouragement.

Chuck and I, realizing how very difficult Christmas would be for the children, decided to change the environment by taking them on a cruise to Panama. This turned out to be an excellent idea. The cruise ship's program for children was excellent and the four of them had a festive and wonderful time. On the way home we went to Disneyland.

We arrived home exhausted but hopeful. Things gradually got better. The children became happy and affectionate. One day I especially remember. Chuck was away. A cold had left me with an inner-ear infection. The room rocked, dipped, and spun around. I couldn't stand up. My longest excursion, hanging on to the bouncing wall, was to make my way to the bathroom. Competent ten-year-old Allison took charge. She served cold cereal for breakfast and peanut butter sandwiches for lunch. Much as they wanted to, the little girls could do nothing to make me feel better. They bounced sympathetically on my bed and comforted me with pats and kisses. Teddy was having a tantrum and kicked the side door out. I asked Allison to tell him please be quiet. He went into the garden and pulled up the dahlias. By dinner time the world was spinning more slowly around me. Allison made toast and opened a can of soup for the children and then they put themselves to bed. Next morning I felt fine.

In a few months Allan got his life reorganized and gathered his family together again. He bought a large home in Scotts Valley, and as single father of six children, settled down to his years of herculean responsibility and work. Chuck and I stood ready to help when we could.

Writing and Painting

Margaret Koch was writing a book in 1974 about historic homes in Santa Cruz, *They Called It Home*. I made a series of illustrations for it—pen-and-ink drawings of the homes she wrote about. All the houses were fascinating. It was an enjoyable task. The book was well received—an important documentation of early Santa Cruz and bygone architectural styles.

Margaret was a reporter for the *Santa Cruz Sentinel*. I sometimes suspected that whenever she ran out of other news features she'd turn to me. Although I didn't usually like to be in the news, I didn't mind her stories. However, whenever she wrote about me, she'd usually say that I was writing a book about local shells. I remonstrated that I was doing no such thing, that I didn't know enough about conchology to write about shells. Dr. Myra Keen read one of Margaret's stories and said, "You really should write about your shells, about the shells on your beach. Why don't you?"

So I did. *Tide-drift Shells of the Waddell Beaches*. Over the years my collection had become definitive for the area. I made sure that the identifications were correct and I did pen and ink portraits of each one. It was a pleasure to work with their mathematical and beautiful intricacies. Then I wrote a paragraph about each one. I did not look for a publisher, knowing that the book was useful only locally, but it was important because at that time there was no other reference book of this area. I had it printed in 1975 and it was very popular. In 1992, it was expanded and revised to encompass the wider area Monterey Bay and republished by the Santa Cruz Natural History Museum as *Tide-drift Shells of the Monterey Bay Region*.

I had written a book, *Uncle Bert*, about Daddy's brother Herbert Hoover and had copies made. It was hard to keep up with the demand of people who wanted a copy, so I was delighted when, in 1974, the Hoover Institution at Stanford University decided to publish it. (In 1998 the Herbert Hoover Presidential Library Association in Iowa published a second printing.) My reasons for writing it are given in the preface: "This biographical portrait is written as an introduction to a great man and a beloved uncle. I want to tell our children and grandchildren about what kind of man he was and about his life and what it means to us. I want others, too, to understand his life and accomplishments, and to be armed with facts against the slanders still told about him."

I found great joy in both writing and painting. Time and space vanish as one is caught in the spell of creating beauty. I preferred working in watercolors. I never painted an oil that I didn't think would have been better in watercolors. I liked painting landscapes, to catch the soul of a place. I did many of the ranch scenes that I loved. I also painted when we were on trips. The mood—ambience—of a place is more surely caught in a painting than in most photographs. When we got home I was often asked to talk to groups about the trip, and I enjoyed having them illustrated by paintings. It felt more comfortable than sitting in the dark explaining travel slides, although I did some of that, too.

I participated in art shows now and then. They were much work, but Chuck helped with transportation and hanging. Other than that, I made little attempt to sell the paintings. Enough sold themselves to pay for paints, paper, and brushes, expensive items. The ranch pictures were not for sale; they were kept for myself and our family. Selling any painting was painful. Heavens knows why. Certainly it makes more sense to have them hanging on a wall where they can be appreciated than to stack them messily in my closet as I would like to have done. So I sold them to be enjoyed. On my birthdays, I sometimes gave paintings as gifts to friends who wanted them. It has always seemed more sensible to me for the birthday person to give gifts than to receive them.

The California State Parks Department, 1975

It became obvious that we could not continue to carry the major part of the labor and cost of caring for the ranch. Farm buildings needed extensive repairs; taxes were going up; illness had reduced our stamina; and the necessity of making our living outside the ranch took most of our time.

Rancho del Oso is unique in that it is protected on two sides by mountains, at the north by Big Basin Park and on the south by the ocean. It is something like an island with its protected ecosystem of plants and animals. We were determined that this land, so long defended by Daddy, should be preserved, not developed. For this reason we were not interested in the high prices offered by developers. We wanted it appraised and sold at or below that figure.

Years ago, Daddy had offered as a gift to the state the land above the forks for an extension of Big Basin Park. The state had not been interested. In recent years, however, there had been talk of the need for a "corridor to the sea" down Waddell Creek from Big Basin. With the help of Sempervirens Fund staff, we talked to interested state officials about this.

Mindy was understandably opposed to its sale to the state. However, after some difficult California State Park Commission hearings, the final agreement, announced in March 1976, was that the state acquired from the Willises and McLeans, for park purposes, approximately 1,600 acres in a gift-purchase agreement. We made a gift of the mile of Waddell Beach and sold most of the property northwest of the creek to as far upstream as Long Pool and all the property above that. We retained the land on the southeast side of the creek approximately to Long Pool. We kept the Brown House and the Green Cottage fields area, not quite a thousand acres. In addition, Louise's daughters, Dellalou and Judy, still owned the adjoining Wilson Gulch.

We were satisfied that this was the best solution (protection of the ranch and retention of an affordable share) to an inherently insoluble problem (the cost of holding together Daddy's legacy). We determined to work with state officials to make Rancho del Oso State Park a success and to work with the family to keep our jointly owned property a source of pride and pleasure to all of us.

Bureaucracy, 1975 —

The gift-purchase of most of the ranch for a state park assured us that its natural assets would be protected, that its beauty would be available to anyone who wished to experience it. Chuck and I were freed of the crushing work, expense, and responsibility we had struggled with for so long.

There is, necessarily, close association of the park and ourselves because of shared roads and creek and common problems in the valley. Park personnel—supervisors, rangers, park aides—assigned to Rancho del Oso Park have almost all been capable and cooperative as we work together.

Nevertheless, coping with bureaucracy at any government level can be frustrating. Our aggravation was mitigated somewhat when we remembered our experiences with bureaucracy in other countries where it is complicated by the fact that in many of them bribery was an expected part of every step. The basic problems of bureaucracy are red tape, uncertainties of budget appropriations, job security for the incompetent, and over-abundance of rules and legalese. In the park department, a policy of frequent personnel transfers added to the confusion. A few examples:

1. One of the first irritations also amused me. I asked to be allowed to continue to collect insects to extend the ranch collection. After several months I received permission to collect two of each species. Two mosquitoes? Male and female, I presume. Two ants? Larva, worker, soldier, queen? Difficult choices!

2. A ranger asked if he could take some logs washed up on our property to mark a parking area. Chuck suggested we trade them for a small redwood, suitable for rounds, which had fallen across the creek. No, against park policy.

3. We had always kept the roads in good condition as Daddy had showed us, shallow ditches on each side and a rounded crown so that rain water would run off. State maintenance crews scraped the canyon road flat and piled scrapings on both sides. It made a fine runway for floods when it rained, and it left huge mudholes.

4. Hikers did not enjoy meeting our cows on the road and that annoyed the rangers. Part of the sales negotiations had been for the state to fence their property line. No fence. So we had a big roundup—fun for all—and sold the cattle, fortunately profitably.

These and many other incidents were annoying, but then we remembered that we no longer stayed up on hot nights watching the skyline for forest fires, that ranch taxes and maintenance expense were reduced to a manageable level, and that the ranch was protected forever. Frustrations were a small price to pay.

Fiftieth Wedding Anniversary, 1975

December 5, 1975 was our fiftieth wedding anniversary. Good heavens, we'd been at the ranch for thirty-two years since leaving Pasadena! Pasadena before smog, smelling of orange blossoms; Pasadena with three babies; Pasadena full of friends and interesting projects, forever a radiant time and place in my memory!

Time for another party. December, a rainy season, is not exactly a good time to hold a large party at the ranch, but I depended on my

Chuck and Hulda on their fiftieth wedding anniversary, 1975

guardian angel commit-
tee to take care of the
weather for me. And it
did; it was a brilliant day,
crisp and sunny.

Tooke, Allan, and
Rob were hosts. Orga-
nizing and running the
party was a group of fam-
ily and friends. They all
worked hard. Mary had
brought me from Malaya
a gold and cherry bro-
cade, which Annie Bach-
ar made into a dress with
a bolero top; it felt festive.
Jan Wilson did the cater-
ing. The wedding cake
was an edifice of layers,
iced with yellow sugar
roses. The new Casita
was bright with yellow
chrysanthemums, with a

Chuck and great-grandson Dom, 1977

special gold and yellow flower table arrangement, a gift from the Mc-
Crary family.

We had invited scads of our friends from all over the world, knowing
that distant ones could not come, but wanting all to know that we cherished their friendship. More than two hundred people attended. And
there were piles of letters and telegrams and phone calls from all over. It
was a really lovely party, lasting all afternoon and far into the night, when
the paths were lit with luminarias.

It was a gathering of people dear to us. How blessed we felt!

Hidden Redwoods Camp and Other Events, 1975–1978

Life at the ranch and what Loraine called "the soap opera of Allan's family" (Loraine had been Allan's godmother) went on. Hazel was in Alaska,
married to a soldier stationed there. Cheri and her baby, Dom, lived with
her for a while. Then Hazel's current husband vanished with her bank ac-

count and money and Cheri's legacy from Soozie. John, twenty years old, was at the University of Alaska and was learning to be an airplane pilot. He had delighted us by flying down from Anchorage for our fiftieth anniversary party.

Allan bought a house on a big lot on Lockwood Lane in Scotts Valley. His children one by one became disillusioned in Alaska, and soon he had them all with him again. The children came to us at the ranch on weekends. They shared our love for it. Allison chose it as the subject of the ode she wrote for a school assignment.

Ode to Morning
Allison McLean

When I awake the world is gray—
No early light to promise day.
But sun will come and bring the light
And I await the end of night.
Now, on the hills—a lighted frieze,
The rising sun gold-tips the trees.

As creeping gold descends the hill,
Dispelling slumber, gloom, and chill,
A bird in song awakes the dawn,
And cheerful notes proclaim the morn.
With blessing from the sun above
I start my day with joy and love.

Summers at the ranch were, as usual, sociable, with guests who were camping or in the Casita guest house. Tooke and Mary came home in January 1976 from a demanding job in Bolivia. They stayed with us for a short while before leaving for a job in New York. Mindy's son, Ted Willis, and capable dear Aggie were married in Mindy's summer house at the ranch.

We built the Cabaña, a small house on the hill above the Casita. Nino and Annie Bachar moved from their trailer to live there with their babies and help us on the ranch now and then.

Cheri's fiance, David Taylor, a good-looking young soldier, came down from Alaska on leave in March. They planned their wedding to be held under a nutmeg tree on the edge of Twin Redwoods field. A few days before the planned wedding, David ran his motorcycle into a tree on the ranch road and was injured. In the hospital he died of a heart attack. We were devastated. The hardest thing I have ever done was to telephone his mother. Cheri bore their daughter, Lillian Brooke Taylor, in August 1976.

Because our popular Alder Grove camp, Twin Redwoods camp, and Herbert camp were now in the state park, Chuck and I explored for a new family camping site on our remaining property. We decided on a grove of several redwood circles just above Twin Redwoods field; Allison named it "Hidden Redwoods." Allan declared a work day. His family, and the Saylors, Bachars, Willis's, and Briggs all worked with us clearing brush.

Cherlyn with her children
Dom and Lili, 1977

Gene Saylor made a fine large rock barbecue. No one realized it should have a drainage hole at the bottom; in winters it is a pool. Our "Hidden Redwoods" campsite has been used extensively as the years go by.

Meantime, I worked on a number of projects. I published an addendum to the Hoover genealogy book. So many additions and clarifications had come in that it was necessary. Another job was to make a report for the Santa Cruz County Probation Department. Being chronically understaffed, they had neglected to produce records required by state law. I went through their activities and records of the past few years and organized the information so that it could be published to meet requirements. Another activity got its start, pen-and-ink sketches of the Santa Cruz area made into notecards which I then hand-watercolored. They were sold in Santa Cruz shops, until they became so popular I couldn't keep up with orders. Then I withdrew them from shops and only sold as many orders as I could manage.

Our Charlie Brown Christmas Tree, 1977

We had planned to take Rob, Jean, and their children to Hawaii with us in July 1977. On a recent trip we had discovered a small delightful hotel on

Nawiliwili Harbor on Kauai and had made reservations for all of us. But, just before we left, Chuck became ill again; the young people went without us. They had a fine time. Remembering ourselves at their age, I didn't think that the absence of parents was a hardship.

I decided that the doctors didn't have a foggy idea of what was wrong with Chuck. They were treating symptoms one by one with little success. Of course, a lot of it was because of his heavy smoking. He had made many attempts to stop, including weeklong hospital nonsmoking programs—all failures. When I got impatient, Dr. Amby told me that nicotine addiction is the most difficult of all addictions to overcome. Chuck spent a while at the Stanford Hospital. Doctors unanimously told him that unless he stopped smoking, there was little they could do for him. But smoking did not alone explain the recurring collapses with pneumonia, high fever, chills, and delirium. At first he went to the hospital each time, but Amby decided he would do better at home. So we suffered through them together.

One time while Chuck was recovering from a collapse, I had to have an emergency gallstone operation. He did not need a nurse, what he needed was food and cheer. Rob and Jean had their jobs and family keeping them more than busy. I phoned Tooke and Mary in desperation. Mary flew out from New York to be with us for a few days until I could cope again. I was cross with everybody for not warning me how much the surgery would hurt—it was before the small-incision gallstone operation method was invented. Mary was a lifesaver and I am forever grateful to her.

By Christmas time we were well again, but not sufficiently ambitious to get down the box of decorations and decorate the rather lopsided fir tree. Decorations gradually accumulated—four folded birds that Mindy made for us, one small Santa Claus who looked as though he were being hanged, and the bows from our Christmas gifts. It was a cartoon-type Charlie Brown Christmas tree.

A Calm Interlude, 1978

Although we were making many exciting trips to foreign lands in these years, we were always happy to return to the ranch and our Casita.

In 1978 Chuck was feeling better and was enthusiastically riding the tractor and repairing roads and working with Anne's Bob Briggs, who was taking on ranch responsibility.

I took our granddaughters, Allan's Allison, fourteen, and Robanne, eleven, separately to San Francisco as birthday presents. We stayed a few days and had fun at the zoo, in parks, Chinatown, the aquarium, theatre, Fisherman's Wharf, enjoyed chocolate sundaes at Ghirardelli Square and shopped. Across Golden Gate Bridge we visited the Crowells. We crossed the Richmond Bridge and went to see Louise in Alameda in her bungalow. We sat under the arbor in her lovely garden and talked about gardens, old friends, and happy times. She was not well. Her childhood friend, Elizabeth Hyde (now Betty White) came and took care of her. I went to see her often, taking a child with me for company on the drive and so they would get to know their legendary great-aunt Louise. The drive was a long and dreary one, through heavy traffic on the East Side of the bay.

At the ranch I worked on the insect collections—one of ranch insects and one a general collection. The ranch collection was a valuable museum-type with twenty frames. I figured that each frame represented a hundred hours of work. I also worked on shells. I also made a bird list of ranch birds which the ranger had asked for. I checked Daddy's notes and my lists and the lists of the bird clubs who had been here. I had not realized how many people would be interested, as time went on, in this list of ranch birds; I had thought that Daddy and I were lone bird nuts.

In early summer evenings, Chuck and I often went to the beach and watched the sunset. Very occasionally we would see the dreamlike "green flash." It is a sudden flash of intense green, like the sparkle from a diamond, in the instant after the sun has set. There must be a perfectly clear sky such as one sometimes sees over the ocean or a desert. There can be no mist nor dust in the air. The Scottish say that to see the green flash is to "heal a wounded heart." It has been called "a split second of paradise." Cousin Allan wrote me "I have seen it many times. In Hawaii, if you are at an elevation above the sea on an absolutely clear evening, it occurs without fail. It has something to do with the bending of disappearing rays of the sun which has just gone beyond the horizon." In the arctic night, I am told that it is watched for both when the sun disappears for its long night and when it is just about to arise for the long day.

Eleanor Gregory and I decided to make a cookbook of favorite ranch recipes. One that the farm bureau women had compiled of Davenport recipes years before was still asked for but there were no copies left. We collected recipes from the ranch families. Eleanor typed them up and I illustrated it and printed it. It was a great success, and very useful.

My continuing project was putting together the biography of my grandmother, Hulda Minthorn Hoover, 1848–1884. I had researched her life in letters and records and interviews, and once Chuck and I had gone to West Branch, Iowa, where she had lived, to read newspapers of the mid–nineteenth century. She had been an impressive individual—"gifted girl," teacher, wife, mother, and talented, eloquent Quaker minister.

The sport of hang-gliding reached Santa Cruz. The first hang-glider we saw took off from Last Chance Road on top of the mountain and landed in a patch of poison oak halfway down. The next one landed in a field among our startled cows. After that, the cliff at Buena Point above the beach became the favorite launching point. Gliders could catch air currents and rise to sail above Waddell Valley among the red-tailed hawks.

We gave a party honoring Myrtle Garaventa, retired from forty-four years as Davenport postmaster (and central community news source). Jan Wilson was a cohost. Rob barbecued chicken; Annie Bachar made the bread. Neighbors brought salads and we made ice cream. A good party, well deserved.

A Christmas to Remember, 1979

In November 1979, Chuck's doctor checkup showed an expanding aneurysm which would require surgery. It was set for about a month away, soon after Christmas. To clear my calendar for that time I moved dates ahead into early December—speeches and committee meetings and report deadlines. It was a bit frantic. Guests who were visiting in the guest house were a great help in the Casita and in entertaining Chuck, who was not happily anticipating the operation.

Soroptimists correspond with Soroptimists in other countries. A member from our sister-city, Salisbury, Rhodesia, wrote that she and her husband were making a leisurely trip around the world and planned to be in California for Christmas—was there a Soroptimist they could stay with? I thought that their presence at Christmas might divert Chuck from his worries, so volunteered that they could come and stay in our guest house.

The best laid plans . . . Chuck's next doctor visit showed that surgery could not wait. We went immediately to the Stanford Hospital in Palo Alto, December 4, 1979. The operation was a success, but he was in intensive care for two weeks. For a day or two I stayed in a nearby motel; but the empty evenings and nights there were so awful, I went home and drove to the hospital every day. I was allowed to see him for ten minutes of every hour.

The future was problematic, but there was no way to reach the Rhodesians on their world tour. Visiting friends made the guest house ready for them and, with Teddy, decorated the Casita and put up the Christmas tree.

Chuck's recovery problems came when a lung collapsed, but he pulled out of it and the doctors told me that, because of the very intensive and painful treatments they'd had to give him, his lungs were in better shape than they'd been for a very long time. He was moved to a ward until the doctor decided he'd be better off at home. Then I made plans for the next day. That evening on my way home from the hospital, my car was attacked by a truck which hadn't made the stop onto Sandhill Road. I had to climb a high divider curb to avoid collision. It popped the left hub caps off and shattered a headlight, but the car still drove, so I went home.

The next day, December 18, I got Chuck happily settled—as glad to be home as I was to have him. After lunch, Jill and Norman, the Rhodesian guests, arrived, just as a storm moved in on us. They were tired from their travelling and said they'd like to sleep for a couple of days. Me, too!

I had errands in Santa Cruz—bank and get the car fixed. I asked the garage mechanic to replace the hubcaps and the headlight. He said "Hubcaps, hell, you need new wheels. You haven't been driving this thing have you?" Just a hundred and fifty miles! "God, you're lucky to be alive!"

The storm took out the power line, leaving us and twenty-four thousand other homes in Santa Cruz without power two days before Christmas. The phone didn't go out until the next day.

The Rhodesians were delightful guests. I was worried that I couldn't entertain them properly, but they took my mind away from other problems and I was glad they were there. Chuck was not yet strong enough to meet them. The Soroptimists were a great help, especially John and Juleen Lisher, who, each morning, came and picked up our guests and took them on excursions in the storm—Santa Cruz, Monterey, San Francisco. I was glad they were well fed for lunch, for without power, I fed them cold cereal for breakfast and salad and cold meat for dinner.

Rob and Jean came to see if they could help. Power had been restored in Santa Cruz but not yet on the ranch. They decided to have Christmas dinner with us, to cook it and bring it out in their camper. Daughter Judy, eleven, was recovering from pneumonia and would stay in bed in the camper.

On Christmas afternoon, Chuck felt well enough to get dressed and meet our guests. He sat by the fire with us—Rob, Jean and son Bill, Jill and Norman, Ted and Eleanor Gregory from the Green Cottage. In the early stormy darkness we lit candles and kerosene lanterns to help the firelight. Chuck had his Christmas dinner on a tray by the fire. The rest of us sat down to Jean and Rob's dinner. I sighed blissfully "This is nice. But if anything else goes wrong I shall lie down and scream." At that point there was a loud explosion. A gallon of wine had exploded on the bar behind us. Glass and wine all over the kitchen and dining area. We cleaned it up as well as we could in the dark. The wine had been a gift, brought that afternoon, from an Italian farmer who gathered mushrooms on the ranch. "Very fine wine"—he'd made it himself.

I rose early the next morning to clean up. Guest Jill was up ahead of me and was busy with soapsuds on the sticky mess. This day after Christmas was bright with sunshine. For the first time, our guests could see the valley. We went for a walk in the damp woods and picked chanterelle mushrooms for lunch. Everything was lush and green and smelled wonderful. During lunch there was a small earthquake which knocked the Christmas tree over.

Our guests left soon after lunch to continue their world travels. "This," said Jill, "is a Christmas I'll never forget."

Finis, 1981

Before Christmas, I often helped the younger grandchildren make their gifts. Christmas 1980, Robanne, thirteen, and Allison, seventeen, decided to give Christmas cookies to everyone (Robanne's list had twenty-nine names). We mixed and rolled and cut, with my collection of cookie cutters, dozens and dozens and dozens of angels, Santa Clauses, Christmas trees, stars, snowmen, teddy bears, wreaths, and bells. Chuck and Tooke (home briefly from Connecticut), Allison and Robanne and I all cut and cut. Then they were baked and iced and sprinkled and decorated, arranged on Christmas paper plates, and tied with cellophane bows. All of us decided we never wanted to see another cookie!

Christmas is party time, and Chuck wanted to go to the parties. I watched him with apprehension as he sometimes struggled to breathe. Consulted, Dr. Amby said for him to do whatever he had strength for. Each party exhausted him. He slept at night breathing with tubes from an oxygen tank beside the bed. In the morning he was ready for the next party. It was a festive Christmas season. Christmas day we joined grandchildren for their celebrations. And then we went home to the quiet of our blessed Casita.

The first months of 1981 are hazy in my memory. Chuck spent most of his time in his comfortable chair in front of our bedroom window, overlooking trees to the ocean. I stayed home with him except for a morning walk to get the mail and hike a mile along the beach. Through the window Chuck could see me most of the way. Friends came to visit him. His granddaughters put their arms around him. He was snappish with his grandsons who were sometimes trying; they left tools out in the rain and were careless with the truck.

As winter turned into spring, the daffodils we had planted while the Casita was turning from a dream to a home were blooming along the driveway. Hemlock and wild morning glory shone white against the dark willows. Wrens nested in the hollowed-out gourds nailed above the window. When their eggs hatched, the parents made more than a hundred flights a day (Chuck counted them) to feed their brood. Then the nestlings tumbled out and flew, wobbling, away. "As ours had done," he said.

Rabbits and deer nibbled on the lawn. The bobcat who was so frustrated by our protected chicken pen came and sat on the porch. In early mornings there was the spring bird-chorus. At night, coyotes sang under a red moon, colored by atmospheric ash from Mount St. Helen's explosion.

He felt better by early April. We went to the elegant Octagon Museum dinner on April 3. The evening of April 6 Chuck was up for dinner, and we sat together on the couch in the living room by the fire, listening to a TV concert. I was coloring note-cards to catch up on orders. Concert over, we talked until the fire died down.

I woke up in the middle of the night; Chuck was not in bed. I got up to look for him. He was lying in the hall. He had died, while I slept.

The thought of living the rest of my life without Chuck was frightening. I woke each morning with a sense of unfocused despair. But life has a way of pushing one into a morass of details which deaden thought. There was the imminent income tax deadline; the constantly ringing telephone and stream of heartwarming friends; the Casita to keep clean and tidy with all that coming and going; answering letters and paying bills. Our eccentric power line gave out, leaving me with primitive heat and light. The water pump burned out. Ah, the joys of living in the country.

There was preparation for a memorial service, a celebration of

Chuck surveying a field of wildflowers,
Prince Edward Island, 1963

Chuck's life, in the ancient redwood grove of Hidden Redwoods Camp. June 7 was a perfect day in sun-dappled Hidden Redwoods for the memorial service. Ted Gregory furnished the music; Allan introduced friends. The minister spoke of Chuck as a "gentle, wise and loving man." Back at the Casita the children complained that she had said only good things about him and hadn't mentioned how grumpy he was sometimes. I reminded them that he was only grumpy when misbehaving grandchildren brought out his grouches.

We Saw the World, 1963–1981

Chuck long wanted to "see the world." In the 1960s and 1970s we had set about accomplishing this and saw a large part of it, at first by ourselves and then, usually by going on Cabrillo College study/travel trips. Often our friends Margaret and Ed Koch and Dr. Ed Halley were with us. It would take a very large volume to tell all that we saw and learned. We were richly rewarded. Here I give only a brief account of the travel adventures of these years.

Prince Edward Island, 1963 was the place Chuck first wanted us to visit. This Canadian Province in the Gulf of St. Lawrence had been the home of the McLeans from the time they left their ancestral home in the Hebrides until Chuck's father came West in 1898. Now that I was free of Board of Supervisors responsibilities, we decided it was time for the PEI trip. "The Island" that summer was an enchanting place. Red dirt roads ran between fields of pink clover and wildflowers, white shasta daisies, buttercups, and many flowers I did not know. Tiny villages of white houses clustered around steepled churches. We went to Keppoch by the sea and stayed at an inn, white with green trim and covered by vines, that had once been the home of Chuck's grandmother Robertson. We visited a variety of relatives and the places that were in the story of his family.

Alaska, 1965. We did not know exactly what we wanted to see in Alaska so we just flew to Prince Rupert and took a ferry up the Inside Passage. We got off when we saw something interesting. Because we had no reservations, of course all the hotels were already booked up; but we'd go back in the evening and there would always be a "no-show" place for us. There was spectacular scenery and a strange palette, grayed colors with a basic milky green of glacier water. I tried to catch it in watercolors. Twenty-four hours of daylight is confusing. When Chuck was having breakfast, I might be coming in from painting to have lunch.

Sociologically, Alaska was interesting: Indian culture being eliminated

Dogsledding in Alaska, 1965

Chuck at the Prince Rupert harbor, Alaska, 1965

by our welfare system and alcohol, a pioneer society financed by federal government handouts, self-conscious adventurers with tourists looking over their shoulders, shack-type architecture and high-rise apartments. It is a fine place for the young and vigorous to make a life, but not for me.

England and Scotland, 1966, 1974, 1986. Christmas, 1966, we flew to England to spend Christmas with the Thrings, Tooke's in-laws. They lived on a farm, part of the ancestral estate which had been long sold and divided. Admiral Thring had bought back the farm and retired there. We had a fine Christmas, like those of my childhood. And we had walks in the damp woods and afternoon tea in front of the fireplace. We watched a fox hunt. Participants were dressed appropriately. The horses were handsome, bugles were sounded, and we had a fine afternoon. The dogs lost the fox: the hunters lost the dogs. They found them enjoying garbage cans behind a pub.

Alford House is huge—four stories and a keep (tower) and a large haunted cellar divided by brick arches. There is a small, ancient, stone chapel on the farm with marvelously carved, uncomfortable dark oak pews. Admiral Thring gave the Christmas service, and Mary played Christmas carols on the small organ. The neighboring village, Castle Cary, was, a long time ago, part of the estate. It has some thatched cottages, a shopping street, and a round stonewalled jail.

We left Alford and went to Scotland. On the way we visited Tooke's godmother, Winnie Kydd, Dame Winifred, our good friend from McGill days. She lived in Castle Duchray near Aberfoyle. She and a friend had restored it—a small exquisite castle where Rob Roy had once hidden. Winnie had been knighted for her work with displaced populations.

On the Isle of Mull we called on Sir Charles McLean, Chief of Clan McLean. He wasn't home, but Lady McLean invited us to tea and served Scotch whisky.

We went back to England in 1974 with an "Art in England" study/travel tour organized by Cabrillo College and led by Artist David McGuire. It was a ten-day trip costing $800 for airfare, hotel, and tickets to plays. Our hotel in London was near Addison Road, where I had lived as a child. The neighborhood had been heavily bombed in World War II. These craters where mansions had once stood were replaced by apartment houses. Our elegant 65 Addison Road home had been turned into flats and was a bit shabby. We rode the red double-decker busses. The red-nosed, whiskered conductors I remembered had been replaced by dark Pakistanis.

There had been recent IRA terrorist attacks—along the streets broken windows were shuttered. Our purses and packages were inspected at each door. We were hurriedly evacuated from the British Museum because of a bomb threat. On the way out I evaded guards and dashed into the checkroom to grab our parcels. London statuary was happily familiar: heroic men on horses, lumpy angels, Queen Victoria surrounded by garlands and fat cherubs, and lions—many lovely London lions.

Then we, with the Kochs and Dr. Halley, went to Scotland—to Edinburgh, Inverness, and the Hebrides. Our destination was the Isle of Skye, where I wanted to follow up on some genealogy clues. When Chuck had bought the tickets the agent said, "Why do you want to go to Skye? Nobody goes to Skye this time of year." We were, of course, the only visitors in the small hotel.

The friendly young man who brought our luggage up from the ferry was also the desk clerk and the dining room waiter. The Isle was beautiful under its snowy mantle. Chuck said, "Brrr, I see why they left!" The records I'd hoped to find in the church had been sent to archives in Edinburgh.

It was more than ten years, 1986, before I got to England again, this time with friend Mally. This trip was unusually enjoyable—a coach trip to country inns of England and Scotland. The trip was a fabulous birthday present from my sons, who also gave me an eightieth birthday party at elegant Chaminade. There were a hundred guests and a splendid buffet containing a contented-looking suckling pig with an apple in his mouth.

Guatemala, 1973. It was in 1973 that we drove our Ford Econoline van with the Kochs through Baja to Guatemala to visit Chuck and Sue Atlee, who were there on an agricultural project. There was no paved road down Baja, and the drive took us ten days, following little more than tracks across the desert. We had been in Guatemala once before, in 1971, but by plane. Driving was more challenging but also more fun. Chuck Atlee worked with the Indians, trying to diversify their farming. The villages were barely surviving on their corn crop, and a diversified agriculture would vastly improve their lives. Chuck would help a village learn how to grow crops successfully and then leave them with the necessary knowledge and supplies. Then he would move on to another struggling village. When a few months later he would return to the first village, however, he'd find that they had usually reverted to corn. They explained that they did not know the prayer and ceremonies necessary for success with the new crops.

Margaret and I had an adventure on Lake Atitlan on our way to the village of San Francisco. We took the shabby little ferry. Although the lake had been calm when we started, it became rough as we progressed. It was explained that the commotion was caused by a big gold crab who lived in the bottom of the lake. A little more than half way across the lake, we noticed that crew members were running around getting water by letting buckets over the side with ropes. They told us that the engine was on fire. We looked around. There were no fire extinguishers, nor any lifebelts. We looked at the rough lake and knew that our swimming abilities were not adequate for the occasion. We were very glad indeed when another boat rescued us.

We joined some of the Atlees' friends to charter a boat from Belize to explore around the cays. It was a small grimy boat with an uncooperative captain. I wanted to go ashore on one of the cays to look for shells. The captain would not take me there, but he let me off on a long shallow reef so I could wade ashore. This was fine until I thought of sharks. However, I found a supply of shells which Dr. Myra Keen was delighted to add to the Stanford collection. I was glad when Chuck commandeered the rowboat and rowed to the island to rescue me.

When we anchored at night without lights, I was worried that another boat might ram us in the dark. The captain explained that if we showed lights we'd be in danger from pirates.

New Zealand and Australia, 1976. The airplane trip was especially awful, eighteen hours. Chuck sat on one side and a large man on the other side of me. The huge man was too big for his seat and so took up half of mine. When he was awake he tried to scrunch up, but when he was asleep he was all over me, as was Chuck from the other side.

New Zealand is a happy land, with happy, tall people who are very proud of their country and look like Texans with a strange accent. They have a beautiful land. Much of the south, temperate island resembles San Mateo County, while its west coast has fjords like Norway. The tropical north island has jungles and hot mud geysers and the native Maoris with their art and culture.

On to Sidney, **Australia,** the breadth of the continent away from Perth where I had been as a child. We petted soft, fuzzy koala bears and bought black opals—which are a lovely iridescent blue. We cruised Sidney Harbor, geologically so similar to San Francisco Bay.

Then to **Tahiti.** Polynesians are a beautiful, soft-spoken, and graceful race. But on Tahiti they were unwelcoming and rude to us. I don't blame them for not liking us tourists, who overran the place.

We flew to nearby Huahine Island. As I was bending over to pick up a

Chuck and Hulda on the Pasangan River in the Philippines, 1977

shell, my jeans split up the back. I changed to a bathing suit and went swimming in the comfortable tepid water. Chuck didn't go swimming nor did he tell us he had seen a nearby shark. We had been assured that sharks inside the reef were harmless.

Southeast Asia, 1976–1977. We found Southeast Asia fascinating on trips led by Sandy Lydon, proficient and enthusiastic history professor from Cabrillo College. We made two trips there with him. We took Mally with us on the second one. They were truly superb experiences.

We went first to Japan. Japan is a nation of artists. Everything is artistically arranged: food, wall space, even garbage cans in an alley. Outside of the inner cities, it is a country of gardens, beauty to look at, distant music blending with the cicada song, the smell of flowers and new-cut grass, and the feel of damp earth.

Next was **Singapore,** self-consciously clean and modernized. High points are orchids, Tiger Balm Garden with its hideous tawdry statuary, Jade House (too dimly lit to see the intricate carving), and snake charmers. (However, it was in Bangkok where a snake handler draped a heavy but lethargic python around my neck.) In Singapore I sat on a planter and did a painting of a market street, with the usual group of small boys

Margaret Koch, Hulda and Chuck; Bali, 1977

watching me. It was a hot day—the lemonade that a nearby shop-keeper brought out to me and presented with a smile and bow was welcome.

From Singapore to **Kuala Lumpur, Korea** and to **Bangkok** with its appalling traffic and beautiful women dancers. We went to a floating market—a traffic jam of boats on a filthy canal in which children were swimming and women were brushing their teeth. Yellow robed monks were everywhere. There was a terrific thunderstorm and the undrained streets turned into dirty rivers, through which we waded. I bought a ruby and a star sapphire (which were stolen a year later). A controlled prosperous society with an aura of danger.

Hong Kong. There was conspicuous industrial development and highrise housing, festooned with laundry. The old buildings were lumpily British. There was a fantastic jade market, with jade from surrounding villages displayed on carpets in the street, which had been closed to traffic. Not being a good bargainer I probably paid twice as much as I should have, but they were bargains at that. Hong Kong was flooded with refugees from China. The people appeared terrified by the imminent Chinese takeover.

Seoul, Korea. It took three hours for the group to go through unfriendly customs. They threw away all the pills they found. Fortunately, all we had was aspirin which we could easily get along without. Seoul, the whole place, was uptight, terrified of the threat from North Korea just a short distance away. Acquaintances asked repeatedly for reassurance that American troops would not abandon them.

Bali the beautiful, warm with a cool breeze, shell-littered beach, shallow warm water, tiny pieces of red coral. The people have no words for "hello" and "thank you," a smile does instead. No word for "tourist," we are guests. But no one is permitted to stay unless he has brought a needed skill. Bali was the only place we have visited where people were not predominately dressed in western-style clothes. I wonder how much longer they can protect their unique culture from the tide of Western civilization.

Back to **Hawaii.** Throughout our trip, Mally had been pursued by phone calls from Harold Shelfelman, a lawyer in Seattle, who seemed un-necessarily worried about competition from Dr. Halley. At the end of the trip Mally flew home to marry him. Chuck and I spent a few days in Honolulu to rest. I felt like the tourist overheard saying, "I need a vacation from this vacation."

Hulda and Dr. Halley, 1981

The Caribbean. Cruising is not my favorite way to travel. It is like being in a sailing hotel without much of a chance to get to know the lands one touches. However, it suited our current need. Chuck had been very ill. The cruise would be a fine way for him to convalesce while pursuing his plan to see the world. The American Farm Bureau had chartered the Greek ship *Stella Solaris* for a trip among western Caribbean islands. Among the many shipmates were our good friends Shep and Mildred Quate. The Caribbean islands were delightful. From San Domingo I bought amber with interesting bugs in it. At Cartagena I bought an emerald.

Panama City was fascinating and dangerous. We were warned not to go exploring. One of the crew was knifed and another had been robbed and injured. The Panamanians we talked to were definitely opposed to the United States turning over the canal to their ruler—said that it would be stripped and mismanaged.

Dr. Amby had said that I must see that Chuck got exercise, so we walked about the deck for a mile every day. The rest of our time we lay on the deck chairs and watched the ocean, or the entertainment offered, and enjoyed tea time with its concert. Good company, good food, sea air, and exercise worked their magic and Chuck got stronger.

The Mediterranean world, 1978. Chuck and I, with Margaret and Ed Koch (complaining all the way that he didn't like cruises) set out on a cruise of the Mediterranean world in November 1978. We flew to Athens and then spent time in Egypt, Israel, Turkey, Russia, Romania, and Greece on this well-planned trip.

There were only a few days in Greece. I decided I'd have to come back to learn more about this font of civilization. Egypt was a contrast in the misery of poverty and the ruined magnificence of a past civilization. There is no way of comprehending the vastness of a pyramid until one has stood in its shadow. In Israel we saw the places we had heard about forever. I was impressed by the miles and miles of rocky desert that Christ and his followers walked to get from one place to another. It is easy to read "and they went to Cana" without comprehending what a journey that must have been. Jerusalem was crowded with tourists. Christ, who tossed the money-lenders out of the temple, would not be pleased with the commercialization of holy places.

There was mind-boggling Ephesus, then Istanbul and then Yalta, which is depressing. Odessa was clean and pleasant; the people there all emphasized that they were Ukrainians, not Russians. Constanta, Romania was also depressing. The children were laughing and lively; how did they change into such dour adults? We went to a winery and, after sampling twelve kinds of wine, our guide became jolly and more inclined to answer our questions.

The twenty-hour trip home from Amsterdam, including waits in airports, was the usual nightmare. Traveling is not the happiest part of trips. It was a relief when it was over and we were home.

China, 1981. We had planned this trip for a long time. When Chuck died I didn't want to go anywhere, but was persuaded that this trip would still be a good idea. It was difficult.

China's closed borders had just been opened to the rest of the world. Tourist dollars were desired, but the country was not ready for us. Our "very American" recommended hotels had tiny grimy rooms, no hot water, defective plumbing, one light bulb hanging from the ceiling, and no elevators. Our "American breakfasts" were strange. One was lemon jello, hard-boiled eggs, and orange pop. Another was sugared sliced tomatoes, powdered-egg omelet, and pound cake.

However, our lack of comfort was a minor part of our experience. The people were overwhelmingly welcoming. Wherever we went, they lined up by the dozens to get a look at us. Most had never seen "roundeyed barbarians" before. Some just stared, open mouthed, but most smiled and said welcoming things to us (or so our guide told us). Young people in the cities, practicing their English, joined us as we walked, and wanted to be taken back to America with us. Small doll-like children chattered to us. "Chinese must be an easy language," said Dr. Halley, "even the children talk it."

Museums were overwhelming in the beauty and antiquity of their treasures. The tomb at Quin, which had started to be excavated, was stupendous with its life-sized molded clay soldiers and horses.

Our excursions into the country-side were eye-opening. Rice paddies in the communes were ploughed by water buffalo; rice was being harvested with scythes. The commune hospital had dirt floors and bars on the windows. We watched a blood transfusion: the blood was poured from an open pitcher. Our cultivated and educated young guide told us that this was not a typical commune—it had been prettied up for display. But he was a loyal communist and told us that the new leaders had made a new step in communism. Now farmers and craftsmen could sell their surplus and keep the money. None of us were unkind enough to tell him that this was called capitalism.

Heat and unappetizing food and strenuous activity in China had somewhat tested my limits. Just as I was about to show my passport in Hong Kong, I fainted on the filthy floor. Somebody poured a pitcher of water on me and our guide carried me out to our waiting bus. The hotel lobby kept spinning and I was happy to get to my nice clean Hong Kong hotel room and fall into bed. That afternoon I watched Britain's Prince Charles wed Lady Diana Spencer—a fantastic spectacle of elegance and opulence.

Then Singapore, Bangkok, Penang, and Japan again. Without Chuck it had all been lonely and difficult. I was only eager to get home.

To Belgium with shingles, 1989. It had been eight years since Chuck had died. My life was beginning to sort itself out again. I signed up to go on a trip with the Hoover Presidential Library Association to Europe, retracing some of Uncle Bert's activities. And then I got shingles, severely. Mally came to take care of me. I thought I should cancel my trip, but Mally said to wait. Eventually knockout pain pills became unnecessary and I rejoined the world. Recovering from shingles would not be any more painful in Belgium than at home and considerably more fun. Mally went home to Seattle and I went to West Branch to join the travel group.

We went to London where we explored the world of Herbert Hoover—and of my childhood memories. Then on to Belgium, where he is still revered as the savior of their country. Most of the world, including the United States, appears to have forgotten his humanitarian career, which started in 1914 when he organized and ran the Belgian Relief undertaking to save the starving country of Belgium, after it had been conquered and its crops looted in World War I by the Germans. This gigantic accomplishment presaged a lifetime of lifesaving, including feeding the Russians in the famine of 1921 and the Polish nation in 1940 and organizing the Famine Emergency Commission for the countries of Eastern Europe after World War II.

In Brussels, Leuven, Bruges (breathtakingly beautiful), Ghent and Antwerp, our group were guests of honor in grateful memory of Herbert Hoover.

Travels with grandchildren, 1975–1982. In addition to these trips were the wondrous ones I made with our grandchildren. The purpose of these was to expand the horizons of their minds. We had seen too many people whose minds are crippled by provincial attitudes, preventing them from realizing or appreciating the wide world around them—its history and current news, its art and literature, and, most importantly, our place and responsibilities on this spaceship, Earth. My time, energy, and money were well spent in showing our children another part of their world.

For this reason I promised our grandchildren that as each reached the age of sixteen I would take them anywhere in the world they would like to go. Places chosen included Greece, Rome, France, England and Scotland, and Hawaii. These trips were most often study/travel trips organized for groups of high school and college young people. The trips were mind-stretching and a great deal of fun.

Grand Jury Foreman, 1981–1982

Late in June 1981, Superior Court Judge Harry Brauer phoned and asked me to be foreman of the 1981–1982 Grand Jury. He reminded me that he had asked me the same thing in 1973. Since I had just been made guardian of Allan's children, the job of grand jury foreman had been impossible. Now, he reasoned, there was nothing in my way.

"Nothing," I said, "but the fact that I am going to China in July." He said that was no problem, all I had to do was to get the grand jury organized before I left and to resume the job when I returned. There was no convincing argument against him. The day the appointment was announced there was a front-page story with a dreadful picture of me. "Looks just like you," people said. Bill, said, "But, Grandmother, does the judge know that you lose things and forget things and usually start out in the wrong direction?" To celebrate the appointment, Dr. Halley brought a bottle of champagne to our weekly dinner—the Kochs, Dr. Halley, and me. When he opened the bottle, the champagne all shot out with the cork.

Faced with the newly appointed grand jury, eighteen strangers who had never seen each other before, and making them into functioning committees took a bit of work. We identified the first problems to work on and agreed on general basic information to be studied for background—budget, last year's report, grand jury office files. There was work to be done while I was away.

Home from China ten days later, it was time to take up my job as foreman. In my experience, committees, if left on their own, are apt to go off on wild goose chases or just paddle around accomplishing nothing. Surprise! When the committees reported to me, they showed that they had been working hard on their assignments and had made substantial progress. Here was a group of uncommonly capable and dedicated men and women. Together, we had an opportunity to suggest constructive solutions to vexing county problems.

A county grand jury is selected, supposedly at random, from the list of registered voters and the owners of registered vehicles. The duty of the grand jury is to examine "every department of government" and also to decide on whether or not to indict in cases brought to it by the district attorney. It is impossible for eighteen inexperienced people in a one-year term to investigate *every* department. What the grand jury actually does is investigate problems that are evident and those brought to its notice by officials and citizens. Department heads, with good reason, distrust grand juries. A capable and responsible grand jury can accomplish a great deal by bringing to light hidden problems and by making enlightened recommendations. An irresponsible or incompetent grand jury can do a great deal of harm with inadequately researched accusations and impractical recommendations.

Although it had been seventeen years since I had served on the Board of Supervisors, some of the department heads and other employees who had been my friends then were still around. Fortunately, those who had worked with me before trusted me as grand jury foreman. They were cooperative and helpful. They added a great deal both to the factual basis of our work and to the strength of our recommendations.

It is against the law to save notes of grand jury deliberations, and time has robbed my memory of most of what we did. But I remember the skill and hard work of the committee members. I remember that a committee checking nursing homes made 3 AM surprise inspections on these facilities. I remember our frustration when threats caused a witness to disappear and a victim to withdraw charges. I remember my annoyance at threats to me: "Watch your back," "Your house is wired," "There is a bomb in your basement," threats which I would today take more seriously in this more violent age. I remember that our investigation into innumerable complaints about the planning department showed that the basic problem was an overload of state laws and rulings—sometimes contradictory—and that our suggestions untangled an administrative blockage for the over-worked department. I remember my frustration with the county administrative officer, impervious to my criticism of abrasive personnel methods. He was pleasantly but adamantly uncooperative, smug in his knowledge that grand juries come and go but that he was secure in his civil service job. I remember with satisfaction the many complaints from the public we settled without publicity and there was one quiet resignation and restitution.

We published several interim reports and our final year-end report. All were well received.

The end of our year's work came as a relief. I was tired. But there was regret at breaking up what had become a functioning family, the hard-working members of this conscientious grand jury. We all took satisfaction that a long difficult job was over and that it had been well done.

"Real Life," 1981–1982

In the meantime, "real life" went on.

Allan's John David, twenty-six, had stayed with me in the days after Chuck's death. Now, several months later, he decided to transfer to the

University of California, Santa Cruz and live with me so that I would not be alone. He and his brother Scott, twenty-two, built a bedroom above the bunkhouse, full of windows "to let the sky in." John was the dreamer of a bright future.

Allan's Ted, nineteen, had received a settlement from a crippling motorcycle accident, and he bought a tiny cottage among the redwoods in Brookdale. With physical therapy and gritty determination he had brought himself back from the helplessness of his injuries. Although his left side was permanently paralyzed, he could with great effort take care of himself. He went from Allan's home to live in his cottage, wanting independence and no hovering from us. What a hard-hearted family his neighbors must have felt we were as they saw him struggle, alone, with the challenges of daily living—simple things accomplished so easily and unthinkingly by all of us.

In the winter of 1981–1982 there was another bad flood. It was not as extensive as the flood of 1955, but it did more damage because more people had come into the area and had built on flood plains and steep mountainsides. It puzzles me why people build where there is such obvious danger. On the ranch there was, again, damage to the road and fields.

During 1982 I had increasing pain in the back of my head. Dr. Amby referred me to Santa Cruz specialists, but they gave no effective treatment or reasonable diagnosis. Mally suggested that I go to Dr. Dalessio in the La Jolla headache clinic. A friend lived in La Jolla, and I welcomed a chance to see her. I had done a painting for her. Some artists are huffy about being asked to do a painting to match interior decorating, but I considered it a challenge. In springtime, the ranch riparian corridor is pink with bud sheaths of willows, and the meadows and woods are shades of clear spring greens. Those were just the colors she wanted, so that's what I painted for her. It was a delight to see the painting looking so lovely on her living room wall.

Dr. Dalessio looked at the material I had brought with me, x-rays and diagnosis and treatments. He asked me questions and poked at my head. He put me in the hospital for a few days and cut a few nerves. When it was time to leave, the nurse was reluctant to release me when she learned that no one was meeting me and that I was going home alone on the Coast Daylight train. It was Christmas Day, 1982, and the train was almost empty. I lay back to watch the scenery go by; I'd hurt too much on the way down to enjoy scenery. Now, with no pain, the towns and fields, forests and rivers of California were a joy. It might not be the merriest way to spend Christmas, but I was certainly less sad than I would have been with our festive family without Chuck.

The Octagon Museum,
Rancho del Oso History Exhibit, 1984–1985

The Octagon Museum in Santa Cruz put on interesting exhibits of local history, and each year, it gave a formal fundraising dinner. It was an organization that was fun to work with. I was on its board of directors for several years, and its president for several terms. Before becoming a museum, this small octagonal-shaped brick building had been the County Recorder's Office.

In 1984, the curator decided to present an exhibit of Rancho del Oso history. He asked me if I had any memorabilia or pictures. Mindy had the negatives from the photographic equipment drawers in the Casa library. I suggested that he write to her in Sierra Madre and ask for the loan of them.

Mindy replied that she had the negatives. Grandson John and I went to Sierra Madre for them. We stayed with her a few days, sorting through the files. Along with family postcard-sized negatives, there were smaller ones from my Brownie camera. I was delighted to see them, for I thought they had been burned in the Casa fire. Among the Brownie negatives were dozens and dozens of pictures of bored cats. I must have liked cats— there were our cats and neighbor cats and friends' cats. I left the Brownie negatives with Mindy; they were safely stored there.

Back in Santa Cruz, I took those I had chosen to photographer George Lee. Chuck and I had taken photography courses from him. George said that it would be horribly expensive to get all these old black-and-whites printed. He suggested that he lend me the supplies and show me how to do it myself. Chuck and I, in Pasadena, had developed our own black and white negatives, so it would not be hard to renew my skill. I enlisted grandson Bill, twenty-one, to help me, and we made rough prints.

The museum director chose about a hundred of them and greatly enlarged them. These, along with some artifacts we had saved, and our collections of shells, insects, Anne's pictures of mushrooms, and earlier historic pictures of that area made up the exhibit "History of Rancho del Oso." It was the most popular of the museum's 1985 programs. Afterwards, the pictures were given to the Rancho del Oso Nature and History Center to exhibit there. The photographs include pictures of Mummie and Daddy, Miss Pickering and Jarvis, and a host of other ranch people. Pictures show me growing from a scowling little girl to a scowling big girl, and Mindy and Louise, more portrait poised. Then they show me and Chuck and our boys in the ranch years. I am not sure that they are of importance to the Nature and History Center, but they are a saga of our family.

John David, 1985

We went proudly to grandson John David's graduation from the University of California at Santa Cruz on June 11, 1985. We all knew how hard he had worked for his degree. He had a talent for friendship, and when he walked across the stage to get his diploma, a loud cheer came from young people in the amphitheatre. That night he came home very late from celebration parties. In the morning he was gone and so was my truck. He often used the truck, but he always told me or left a note, saying when it would be back. No note.

By the next day I was really worried. Allan, John's father, was away and I couldn't reach him. I phoned my friends in the sheriff's office to report John missing. His brothers and sisters became frantic. Over the next several days they phoned and searched. They had posters printed for distributing and for newspapers. My truck was the best clue. We reported it missing. We searched for it in airfields, big and little, thinking that John might have had an emergency call to pilot a charter flight. Allan returned, hired a detective, and took charge of the search.

We heard from a girl who said that, at three o'clock in the morning after graduation, she had phoned John to tell him she was stranded in Half Moon Bay. He said that he'd come to get her. He never turned up. On June 23, Allan asked Bud McCrary to fly the route looking for him. From the air they saw the truck and John's body at the bottom of a ravine near San Gregorio.

I answered the phone to weeping young people. Allan, and John's sisters and friends, planned his memorial service at Hidden Redwoods. Our minister said that, of all the memorial services he had been to in his long years in the ministry, this had been the most moving and beautiful.

One windy day I scattered John's ashes along Emeritus Trail.

John's life had been a roller coaster of adventures; he was full of energy and dreams, humor and love. His intelligence and driving force were potentials for great achievement. What a waste. What a terrible, terrible waste.

> What did your eyes see that made you hold such grief?
> My heart speaks loudly with no shadow from the tongue.
> My hand is bound by the poverty of language
> When the punch line . . . is death.
>
> *John David McLean*

Casita Sale, 1985

By 1984, I realized that I would have to sell our beloved Casita, Chuck's dream home he'd waited so long for and enjoyed for so few years. Living there without him was getting more difficult. When grandson John David had come to live in the apartment he had built, he had been a caring supportive young man. When he died, I talked various alternatives over with my sons, and they concurred that I must move to Santa Cruz.

When word of the possible sale of the Casita got out, there was the usual interest by developers. But, as in the case of the previous sale of ranch property to the state, I was only interested in a buyer who would preserve and enhance the natural treasures of the Waddell Valley.

The State Parks Department expressed an interest in buying the Casita complex, its sixty acres of land, and the Cabaña, a small house above the Casita. But remembering the problems we'd had last time we dealt with the California State General Services Department and its abrogated promises, I was reluctant to take on this bureaucracy again. In 1985, the executive director of the Sempervirens Fund suggested a solution: the Fund would buy the Casita complex, develop it according to my plans for a nature and history center, and then, as an ongoing project, sell it to the state.

My lawyer, Louis Rittenhouse, went to work protecting rights of way and other legal matters; my real estate agent went to work looking for a condo for me to live in. I started the herculean job of giving possessions away and sorting and packing for moving. How could the accumulations of a lifetime be reduced to condo proportions?

I found a condo I liked and was able to move some of my things into it. My family chose what they would like to own. And then the burden of moving was lifted; some angel organized a Casita workday. People showed up early in the morning of October 26, 1985, my sons and families,

Briggses, some Willlises, hikers, and other friends—twenty-five adults, four trucks, and uncounted children. I had made a list of everything that needed doing, and people chose their jobs. Six more loads to the dump, five loads to a bonfire in the pasture, two loads to Goodwill. Chuck's huge pile of rusty odds and ends, saved "because they might come in handy sometime," was mostly claimed joyfully by male helpers. His bottle collection in the basement was taken to the dump. I hoped that some knowledgeable collector would find the treasures in it. The courtyard was weeded, and the garden was trimmed and tidied. Windows were washed.

At noon I put out sandwich makings, beer, and lemonade. At five there was a chicken barbecue and sundae makings. Everyone went home full and happily tired. How could they ever realize how amazed I was and how much I appreciated their kindness and their hours of labor.

I sat down, alone in our stripped Eden.

6

Walnut Avenue

1985–

A Home to Live In, 1985–1987

IN OCTOBER 1985, I MOVED into the condo apartment in Capitola. It was comfortable and elegant. There were two bedrooms and baths. The living-dining room was large but dark, so I made one wall into a large mirror to reflect light. My apartment looked lovely, furnished with the beautiful things from Chuck's family and a few nice things we had brought in from the Casa before it burned. It was a pleasant place for entertaining, and it was convenient for my projects. I was as satisfied as my sad loneliness allowed.

The condo was pleasant and comfortable, but had its drawbacks. After the Casita, it was so confining! The storage space and garage space so small! The tenants' rules so restrictive! Sometimes, feeling lost, I'd revert to a solacing ruse used in the past to brighten clouded hours. I'd visit an imaginary room with many windows, each one showing a vista of a favorite remembered scene:

A field of wildflowers on Prince Edward Island in the Gulf of Saint Lawrence. A village on Samos with white walls bathed in the pink sunlight of the Greek Islands. The ocean view as one turned onto the highway from the ranch—early morning, with a pale blue sky and frothing waves beyond the wide, still lagoon. Nevada desert at dusk—sagebrush casting long purple shadows. The Isle of Skye in winter, stark black and white of rocks and snow. Warm desert-spiced air meeting the tang of the sea, as frigate birds soar above the azure water of Baja California. Hong Kong at night—gaudy neon brilliance lighting the crowded street with rainbows. The view of Waddell Valley over green pastures where Herefords graze, past pink-budded willows and dark pines to misted mountains. Stark geometric Egyptian ruins—

512 Walnut Avenue, Santa Cruz; 1999

broken columns steeped in hot sunlight, rising through rays of goldlit dust. A Japanese garden, so immaculate each leaf seems glued in place, each flower carefully positioned, and bright koi swimming in a designed parade. Pelicans in stately formation, skimming the waves of a translucent green sea. Our little boys, playing in the filtered light of the orchard. Chuck, on his tractor, disking a hillside field and followed by seagulls.

There were some things I really liked about condo living. There was a hole in the wall in the back hall where one put trash and it disappeared forever—I thought perhaps into another dimension. The Jacuzzi was a joy, hot massaging water to take away the aches after exercise class. There was also a swimming pool, which I didn't use but which the grandchildren enjoyed, not to the delight of other residents.

Then Allan suggested that he and I look for a home to buy together. A fine idea. His family had scattered: Cheri lived in the Green Cottage with her children; Scott and Carol's family lived in Santa Cruz; Ted was in his cabin in the Redwoods; Allison and Robanne were in college. Our real estate broker started looking for a suitable place. During the next ten months we saw a great many houses. One day early in 1986, the real estate agent phoned, "I think I've found it!" Walnut Avenue again, this time about halfway between our home, where Mother McLean had lived with us, and the corner home that Allan's family had lived in. (Allan's home was later torn down and replaced by doctors' offices.) It was a handsome Victorian house built in 1887, basically in good condition but needing alteration to fit our needs, some repairs, and a great deal of repainting. Scott, who had taken construction courses at Cabrillo and had been working in construction, did a major part of the work.

Allan's apartment is upstairs—two large rooms, two tiny rooms, a porch and bathroom. Later we had the attic floored and wired and he spread there, too. We remodeled the downstairs maids' quarters for me, bedroom, bath, office. We share the living rooms, dining room-kitchen, and utility rooms. We made a bunkroom with a loft for visiting children. Because the house is near the high school, street parking is sometimes impossible, so one of the first things we did was to pave an area for parking in back—accommodating five cars comfortably, eight if crowded, twelve if also parked in the driveway.

This all took several months. I moved in, January 1987, and sold the condo. Allan moved in somewhat later and rented his big house in Scotts Valley. When he had suggested this happy arrangement, I had said, "Yes, but I'm doing no cooking." All those years cooking for all those people on the ranch had gone a long way toward using up my cooking enthusiasm. Allan and I were both too busy to sit down for meals together, except Sunday dinners, which we tried to share and which Allan cooked. He is a good cook, but his menu includes too many vegetables for my taste, which runs to peanut butter sandwiches and chocolate bars. I spent long years planning and cooking balanced meals and being a good example by eating vegetables and drinking tomato juice. No more. I seldom cook anything, and I never drink tomato juice.

This old home is inhabited by ghosts, happy ghosts who give it a welcoming feeling. They rattle and thump in the evening when I am home alone, reading or watching television. The kitten, Missy, watched them as they moved about.

We have enjoyed our home—a convenient location, a beautiful house outside and an interior that people exclaim about, a garden with good basic planting, enlivened with colorful annuals when I have the energy to plant them.

Rancho del Oso Nature and History Center, 1985–

Progress at the Casita, now the Rancho del Oso Nature and History Center, went as planned. Sempervirens Fund, the new owners, worked with me to develop it as I wanted it. We enlisted members for a good volunteer board of directors who were interested in making the center into a place where people would come and learn about the area and its wealth of natural treasures. When the center was set up and functioning, Sempervirens sold it to the California State Parks Department. It official opening was in July 1986. A volunteer organization, the Waddell Creek Association, was set up to run the center in cooperation with the State Parks Department.

Diane at the Nature and History Center

The State placed Diane West-Bourke, a pretty, cheerful young woman, as resident naturalist in the Casita guesthouse. At first I did not pay much attention to her, assuming that she was just another bureaucratic cog to be dealt with tactfully and ignored politely. I pressed on, working with the cooperative board of directors to build the center into a mini-museum and learning center, where people, especially children, would have an opportunity to realize the beauty and importance of the natural world around them.

It was soon evident that Diane was not a bureaucratic cog, but was passionately dedicated to developing public realization of its responsibility to the world of nature. She was an independent spirit, a trained naturalist, an interesting teacher, full of good ideas and with energy and knowledge necessary to carry out programs and projects. She shared and understood my vision of what the center could become. From her first days at Rancho

Rancho del Oso Nature and History Center, formerly our Casita; 1999

del Oso, until she retired from this job fourteen years later. Diane was the heart and engine of the success of the center.

Getting ready for the opening was hard work. Most of it was done by the family— Bob and Anne, Tore and Cheri (they had just been married; Tore was a fine addition to the family) and by Diane and the board of directors. Anne and Diane had beautifully mounted my shell collection; we had the photograph exhibit from the Octagon Museum; in our galley we had some of my ranch watercolors; the McCrary family loaned an exhibit of old timbering artifacts; there were taxidermied birds and animals in the living room, which was pleasantly furnished. It had a Mexican rug, which Chuck and I had bought at a market there, a carved wood and black Naugahyde sofa that Joe Branstetter, Rob's father-in-law, had given us, with a matching one I had found at a yard sale, and black Naugahyde chairs picked up at a second-hand store. There was an opening day party. The nice ranger's wife arranged refreshments. She had been told to expect about thirty people, but I told her there would be many more than that. About a hundred people showed up. We had a fine party.

Our first history programs, started in January 1987, were evening fireside talks with old-timers like Agnes McCrary, Bernice Taylor, and Catherine Steel, telling about bygone times in the area. The talks were well attended and appreciated. We had other programs about history and about nature. Some of them have been memorable:

A popular program is the annual Newt Night, a great children's program. We catch a bunch of newts for temporary exhibit. The children can handle them gently and admire their tiny fingers and shining green eyes. There is a short instructive program about newts and frogs and similar creatures, and then docents in newt costumes sing their newt songs. It is an evening of song and fun and learning.

The McCrary family with the D.A.R. National Conservation Award
for Ecologically Sound Lumbering

There are programs about snakes. One evening, a small boa, who was being passed around and admired, was let loose by a reluctant admirer and crawled down into the sofa to wind himself around the springs. No amount of urging and tugging would get him out. We had to take the back off the sofa in order to unwind him.

In the art room and hall we have shows of paintings and photography, landscapes and flowers, and other natural objects. The quality varies from mediocre to breathtaking. At first, my paintings filled any hiatus in scheduling, but soon we had no lack of exhibitors. It was a good way for local artist to show and sometimes to sell their work.

I participated and helped Diane in any way I could, being careful not to be possessive or critical even of disasters, as when maintenance crews unthinkingly disrupted the courtyard's underground tile drainage system, or when John Lisher's beautiful handcrafted paneled oak front door was stained pink, or the time that silvered exterior redwood siding was covered with brown paint. Diane persuaded the maintenance crew not to paint the courtyard walls. They were left a time-silvered background for the garden.

I served on the volunteer board of directors, filled in when a hostess was needed on weekend afternoons, coordinated the schedule of ranger station volunteers, gave occasional talks on ranch history, and prepared written material. Classes were encouraged to visit the center, and nature- or history-oriented groups were invited to hold their meetings there. Our Casita had changed its use, décor, and ambience to become the Rancho del Oso Nature and History Center, and I could visit it without my heart aching too much for what it had been. In its metamorphosis, it remained a central part of my life.

Peacocks

Peacocks had lived in the Stanford Arboretum and graced surrounding fields with their beauty for many years, until houses invaded their territory. Then they roosted on the roofs and, in mating season, squawked their raucous cries. Daddy rescued a few from extermination and brought them to the ranch, where they lived, appreciated and happy until the ranch became a state park and officials decided they were not appropriate. For the first time in more than seventy years, the ranch was without peacocks. I grieved for them.

I loved them for their beauty and independent spirits and the ambience of elegance they radiated with their shimmering displays. When not displaying, they strutted, dragging their green shining trains, which the kittens liked to ride on. They roamed the gardens and fields, catching grasshoppers and eating weeds. They roosted at night high up in pine trees, safe from prowling coyote and bobcats. But one agile, specially hungry bobcat created such a commotion that some of the peacocks flew up the mountain, all the way to Last Chance Road, where a new flock was started.

There was usually a peacock or two in the courtyard, admiring their reflections in the sliding glass doors of the Casita. They were a happy iridescent splendor displaying themselves for us inside the house. Or, perhaps they thought that there were peacocks inside. Peacocks are gloriously raimented turkeys and have no more sense than turkeys. They nested in fields, and when the chicks hatched, they made such a cheeping racket that they attracted predators from acres around. Very few chicks made it safely back to the Casita. An occasional peacock, like cockerels and turkey gobblers, was pugnacious and would make life miserable for dogs and children. These unfriendly birds we ate. Their flavor was indistinguishable from tender turkey.

One night, returning home late, I found three peacocks nesting on the back of the sofa in the living room. Someone must have left a door ajar. They had wrought chaos, not only from their digestive processes, but because they'd evidently had moments of panic. Furniture was turned over, bric-a-brac was demolished, and fireplace ashes were everywhere. I guided them out, and they flew up into their safe pine bough perches. As I regarded the living room chaos with despair, a strange cat emerged from under the couch and dashed into the back of the house. I looked for him, but he was invisible, hiding in some nook or cranny. Unable to cope, I went to bed, leaving the backdoor open for the cat's escape—or for any interested burglar's convenience.

West Branch, Iowa, 1950–1997

Our first visit to the village of West Branch, Iowa had been in the late 1950s, long before the Hoover Presidential Library was established. Chuck and I went because I needed to do some research for the biography I was writing about my grandmother, Hulda Minthorn Hoover. Grandmother Hulda had lived there with her husband, Jesse, and her three small children, Bert, Tad, and May. We found copies of old newspapers and searched them for references to Hoovers and the other people she had mentioned in her letters.

I loved the village; I was so at home there that I felt I might be the reincarnation of some early ancestor. I loved the country—wavy, rolling green prairie, tree-bordered streams, wildflowers, beautifully kept barns, and old green-shuttered white farmhouses, miles and miles of cornfields, and ponds. There were brief heavy rainstorms and steamy sunshine. No subdivisions, billboards, or smog. Iowa farmland, stretching to the horizon over rolling prairie, is beautiful, and the farms themselves are neat and attractive. Houses and barns, usually painted white, and colorful gardens make them picture perfect.

In 1964, we went back for a brief, sad visit for Uncle Bert's funeral. On the Army plane taking us home, I painted a watercolor from the sketch I had made while standing in the funeral procession winding up the hill and behind the birth cottage. By this time the Herbert Hoover Presidential Library was built. It and the cottage where Tad, Bert, and May were born had been incorporated into a national park. This, a personal museum of Herbert Hoover's life and accomplishments, complements the Hoover Institution—a research center at Stanford, devoted to the study of war, revolution and peace.

Funeral procession for President Herbert Hoover,
West Branch, Iowa, 1964
Watercolor by Hulda

In 1974, we went to West Branch for the celebration of the hundredth anniversary of Uncle Bert's birth. This time we took eleven-year-old Allison with us. It was also a fine opportunity to fill in some further research for my biography of Grandmother Hulda Minthorn Hoover. The information was not as hard to come by, or as scattered, as it had been the previous time I worked on it. It had been microfilmed from all local sources and gathered into the new Hoover Presidential Library archives. The library staff and the people of West Branch were hospitable and helpful. We felt that we had been blessed with many new friends.

Ten years went by before my next West Branch visit. In 1985 the Library Association asked me to give a talk about Aunt Lou for the annual birthday celebration of Uncle Bert. The association would pay my expenses. This seemed like a fine opportunity to complete the research for Grandmother Hulda's biography. But there was a problem. I was in the middle of the horrendous job of moving out of our Casita. I had been packing and sorting for weeks. However, a brief escape from this chore was tempting. Nineteen-year-old granddaughter Judy, Rob's daughter, said she'd like to go with me, a grand idea. She was good company, and she kept me from getting lost in airports.

I put together notes about Aunt Lou; I had no idea whether a talk about her accomplishments was wanted, or just some reminiscences. I made a list of some of the things she had done. She took care of wounded in China during the Boxer Rebellion, organized the American Women's Hospital in London, equipped a fleet of ambulances during World War I, did geological research for Uncle Bert, took care of Mrs. Harding when President Harding died, helped innumerable young people through college, and was national head of the Girl Scouts. She searched for and restored furniture to the White House that had been historically used there. I wanted to be sure to give an understanding of her courage, dignity, graciousness, and kindness, and her aura of beauty, although she was not beautiful except in character.

Judy and I both had fun in Iowa. The National Junior Olympics was being held in nearby Iowa City, so the place was full of teenagers. I rented a car, which Judy used after she had chauffeured me. The people of West Branch were dear and wonderful—friends we had made before and others who welcomed me. The staff coddled me. I was treated like a sainted dowager, fragile and valuable.

My talk was scheduled after the formal evening reception. It went well. I talked about Aunt Lou for about half an hour. The audience laughed a good deal and occasionally some cried. They clapped as if they wanted more. Cousin Allan was there. He saddened me. A year younger than me, at 78 he was a stooped old man, almost blind and deaf, but still with his teasing humor and quiet affection. Home again, Allan wrote me, "You no doubt are aware that the talk you gave at West Branch Library brought the house down . . . It made a memorable celebration."

It was 1997 before I returned to West Branch. This occasion was the re-dedication of the graves on the hill. Coby, cousin Allan's widow, and I made arrangements to go to it together. Her children, Allan, Andy, and Lou would be there. Anne and Bob Briggs decided to go. And there would be other Hoovers, some of them dear and all of them interesting. There would be my old friends, and the ones from the Library tour of the West whom we had entertained at the ranch ("High point of the trip," they wrote). As I had felt on my first visit so many years ago, going to West

Branch was like returning home. Perhaps I knew it better than some of the people who lived there. In the years I had been writing about Grandmother Hulda, I had, figuratively, lived there in the 1800s.

Coby always flies first class, which I consider a waste of money. But, this time, it turned out to be a very good idea. We hit a storm in Chicago and had a wait of four hours. In the first-class lounge it was quiet and comfortable, with good service and refreshments. But, by the time we arrived at the Inn in Iowa City, I was exhausted. There were flowers, candy, and notes from friends in my room. I ate a banana and fell into bed.

The next morning I guided Anne and Bob Briggs, who were there on their first visit, through the park and the library exhibits. The afternoon I spent with West Branch friends. At the reception and formal dinner, Senator Mark Hatfield, the speaker, thanked me for my research and had me autograph books. At dinner, a crucial button popped off the front of my dress. I said, "Oh dear me, does anyone have a safety pin?" No one had one. A few minutes later there was a tap on my shoulder. Coby's gentle, partially blind son Allan gave me a safety pin.

The rededication ceremony next day was impressive. Soldiers marching with flags, the Marine Band, Boy Scouts, wreaths and messages, speeches. As a frontpiece, the printed program had a reproduction of my watercolor of Uncle Bert's funeral procession. In the afternoon I spent time autographing pictures and books. The next morning we were up and off again. An uneventful trip back. I picked up my car at Coby's and got lost twice on the way home.

From Farmyard to Park Headquarters, 1978–2000

Rancho del Oso State Park had opened officially on July 15, 1978. There had been a story about it in the *Santa Cruz Sentinel* with pictures (taken on our property, not the park's). Scads of people came. They didn't know their way around and signs were inadequate, with the result that there was considerable milling around and confusion.

The California parks department set about establishing its Rancho del Oso park headquarters in the Farmhouse. Most of the decrepit farm buildings were demolished and the lower area reorganized into a horse camp for equestrians. The only demolition I really regretted was when the huge old barn came crashing down. Generations of barn owls had lived in it, tolerant of boys and girls who, for sixty years, had climbed up the wall ladder to inspect the nest and fluffy nestlings. Less agile bird watchers had been content to watch the adult owls who, when disturbed by the opening of the barn door, would fly in majestic silence into an adjacent Monterey pine tree. When the barn went down there had been three eggs in the nest. Also dispossessed were the cliff swallows who nested there every spring, barn swallows who nested in the rafters, black phoebes and Say's phoebes who nested under the eaves. Less regretted were mouse and woodrat residents. We had lost a community. The owls resettled in the Farmhouse attic.

The dusty rutted road from the front gate got paved. The resident ranger was moved from the Farmhouse to an elaborate mobile home. A smaller trailer for the ranger station was put where the milk house had been. The Farmhouse was then burned as a fire-fighting exercise. It had needed considerable repairs which, we were told, would cost more than a million dollars. Hard to believe.

When state budget cuts eliminated staffing for the ranger station, the Waddell Creek Association, which, along with California State Parks, managed the nature and history center, was asked to staff the park ranger station weekend afternoons with volunteers. This became my job. I enlisted a corps of about twenty men and women who found the job to be fun, although we did have problems, mostly due to our initial ignorance or to the idiocies of bureaucracy. Our job was to help the hikers, bikers, and horseback riders who came in. We answered questions, sold maps and publications and odds and ends, had hot drinks and cookies available, and furnished band-aids for small injuries. For major injuries, such as broken bones, we called 911 for help. It came quickly—not longer than ten or fifteen minutes. The response was always massive, often an ambulance, two fire engines, and perhaps a helicopter. The victim would be sent a massive bill. That motivated us to cope with as much as we could ourselves. Driving up the road to get a mobile injured hiker to a phone or to his car, treating stings and nettles with the anesthetic mugwort from the roadside, phoning a helpful friend or relative.

The job was interesting and rewarding, but it was time- and energy-consuming.

X Y Hiking, 1964–2000

The Hiking Group was part of my life for more than thirty years. It was a YWCA program until the Y connection with the national organization was broken. Then we became the X Y Hiking Group. We explored local trails, from Butano on the north to Elkhorn Slough on the south, enjoying our redwood forests, beaches, and backcountry roads. Occasionally we'd venture further afield, perhaps to Monterey, Point Lobos, or San Francisco's Golden Gate Park.

Two of my most inconvenient talents are getting lost and falling down. These can be real problems when hiking. To keep from getting lost, I made sure to keep the others in sight. I'd keep falls to a minimum by watching where I was going and injuries to a minimum by rolling in a fall to distribute weight harmlessly. That was not always possible.

On a hike in 1996, I tripped over a root and hit my face on a rock. Ointment and ice packs were soothing but did not prevent two black eyes and a magenta face from hairline to neck—severe social handicaps but not important. What I didn't know at the time was that I had also cracked four teeth, which broke off a year later.

Walking down our Walnut Avenue hill in April 1998 to the Women's Center to join the hiking group one morning, I tripped on the broken sidewalk and crashed, without time to turn and roll harmlessly. Not severe injuries but extremely painful. I rolled over and sat up and found myself involved with a hedge. Problem. How to get up. I was reluctant to kneel on my bloody knees to push up. The hedge offered no handholds. I sat there hurting and laughing at my predicament. A PG&E truck went by, backed up, and two men got out. Evidently they thought that a bloody old lady sitting in a hedge laughing was worth investigation. I was grateful when they pulled me upright.

We took turns planning and leading hikes. After I'd gotten us all lost a couple of times, my turns as leader were for ranch hikes only.

As the years went by, hills became steeper, miles got longer, my breath was shorter. I realized that I could no longer keep up on four- to six-mile weekly hikes. The thought of giving it up was painful, but I didn't want to stay and slow them down. Then I realized that the solution would be to do only part of the hike, half an hour and sit and rest, and then back to the lunch spot, to sketch, or write or just admire the scenery. When my hiking slowed down to a saunter, I decided to plant California poppy seeds in meadows and sunny trail sides as I went along. I made a tool small enough to fit into my backpack for disturbing the soil for a pinch of seeds in likely spots. As time went on, others fell back with me. It was a good excuse to favor a hurting leg or to saunter and watch the birds.

Each year we had a Christmas party at the ranch. We decorated the Christmas tree with nature's gifts. A dried starfish at the tree tip, shiny jingle shells, bright pebbles, tiny redwood cones. I made a dozen or so paper monarch butterflies.

Each summer there was an overnight campout at Hidden Redwoods. It was full of adventure for us, "recycled Girl Scouts": the night that Oso, Cheri's huge friendly dog came and campers thought he was a bear; the night a camper had a nightmare and sprang up, yelling "FIRE!"; the raccoon who stole chocolate kisses and spread foil wrappers up and down the road; rare marbled murrelets we listened for and never heard; the night some of the hikers got lost in the dark and were found by Cheri's children. The most scary incident was when I was driving our truck with thirteen hikers jammed into it, when two racing horsemen ran into us around a blind curve. What if the hikers had been walking, spread out on the road! One horse bounced off the left front fender unhurt and the other scrambled up the bank and got caught in barbed wire. I got wire cutters from nearby Green Cottage. The horse was unhurt but the rider was bloody. I bound him up with a towel from the truck—one of Jean's best towels, which he didn't deserve.

We walked the ranch trails. Sometimes we went to Berry Creek Falls, six and a half miles, on the way to Big Basin headquarters, often stopping on the way at quiet, out-of-the-way Slippery Falls, with its deep dark pool. After dark, we sat around the campfire, told stories, and sang.

We went on Emeritus Trail, which Daddy had built on a five-percent grade when he retired from teaching at Stanford. It goes from the Casa up the mountain Mummie named Grateful Mountain. Their graves are there with a pink granite obelisk. Louise's grave is nearby. Sometime I would like Chuck and me to have memorial plaques there, although my ashes, like his, will be scattered to the wind above the canyon. Emeritus Trail climbs up through oaks, out and up to skirt the dry mountainside which overlooks the valley to the ocean. Each New Years Day, Cheri and her family, and as many others as wish, climb the trail. I take flowers for the graves. Her husband, Tore, carries hot chocolate and sticky buns that Cheri has made. We blow huge soap bubbles which shine and dance and burst over the valley. I think how pleased Mummie and Daddy would have been to know of this happy custom.

Loma Prieta Earthquake, 1989

We frequently have earthquakes in Santa Cruz. In early August 1989, there was a sharp quake—about 5 on the Richter scale. Earthquakes cause a rush of adrenaline, preparing for possible disaster. What is coming next? But they do not make me feel afraid. Nothing can be done to prevent them, so worry and fear seem useless. Just keep emergency supplies on hand and hope to cope as well as possible when it becomes necessary.

On October 17, 1989, at 5:04 PM, there was a severe earthquake, 7.2 according to reports. Ed and Margaret Koch, Dr. Halley, Clarence Mowbray and I were having an early dinner in Capitola. Dishes and food flew into the air; people dived under the tables, except Clarence and me. Tubby Clarence was stuck and blocked my way under. I worried about the plate glass window next to us but was fascinated by the general turmoil. When the shaking finally paused for a while, people crawled out from under tables, and the restaurant owner came out and said the kitchen was a shambles and the restaurant was closed. We lurched out in the aftershocks. Parked cars were bouncing in the parking lot.

I made my way home through chaos. Traffic lights were out; there was broken glass and debris from buildings along the streets. I had not gone via the highway, being wary of damaged bridges. Young men, teens and twenties, took charge at the worst intersections. At Soquel and Forty-first Avenues there was a boy in shorts, and nothing else, carrying a surfboard. He was doing a fine job unsorting traffic. I avoided Santa Cruz downtown, which, it later turned out, had the worst damage because of all its brick buildings. They had been built after a firestorm demolished the wooden buildings of the town in 1894.

I arrived home at last. I found our chimney moved a foot off its base, cracks in the sidewalk and in some interior walls, floor covered with books and broken dishes. A bottle of champagne, fallen from the top of the refrigerator, sat intact amid broken pottery. There were continuing aftershocks which I had not felt while driving. They seemed like 3, 4, 5 on the scale. It was getting dark. I took pillows, a flashlight, and battery radio, and went out and settled down on the front porch, watching fire engines, ambulances, and excited people going past the house. Knowing that telephone lines would be jammed, I didn't try to phone anyone. Soon Rob arrived to check on me and our gas line. Then Scott, Carol, and the little girls arrived. They had been evacuated because of a broken gas line. They eventually went to bed in the bunkroom. Scott had been at a baseball game in San Francisco when the stadium began jumping around. Sixty thousand people evacuated quietly and made a terrific traffic jam. Allan arrived home about 9:30 PM. It took him four hours to make the forty-five minute trip from Sunnyvale. In Los Gatos, cement streets buckled in such big blocks he could not get through. Highway 17 was closed, but he found his way around by Highway 9.

Cheri and family came the next day, and Ted, too. Green Cottage was okay. Ted's cottage bathroom had fallen into the basement. Stores were closed. Sixty percent of downtown was wrecked. There was no way to get food, but we had a good canned stock and could feed the family adequately.

Tooke, in Penn Valley, finally got a line to phone us and find if we were safe. We gave him a list of people to reassure, including Mally and sister-in-law Peggy Crowell and cousins Pat Leavitt and Allan.

I drove around looking at residence areas. There was practically no damage except to chimneys. A few hillside homes slid down. Aftershocks continued. There were more than a thousand people in shelters, evacuated from hotels and danger spots. Myra and Gene Saylor, having had emergency service training, were supervising one. Emergency services were working effectively.

I noticed some big equipment with a crane and told Allan about it. He went and got it to come and take our chimney off the roof. It sat in the driveway intact. (A couple of days later a passerby asked for it to use as a barbecue! We were glad to get rid of it.) It took a long time, months, to get someone to fix our chimney. He came finally and put a large steel pipe down it for a flue and then poured concrete around it so then we didn't have to worry about mending cracks in the chimney. It worked fine.

Our damages were slight. There were cracks in plaster. Some of my favorite things were broken, including all the good dinner plates. However, Mummie's set of Crown Ducal George Washington plates and Chuck's mother's big rose Haviland platter, our most valuable china, were all hung on the wall, decorating the dining room and were unbroken.

Except for the fact that Santa Cruz downtown was destroyed and took years to recover, we got off lightly, although the quake epicenter was in nearby Nisene Marks State Park. San Francisco freeways and some sections of the City were badly damaged. Santa Cruz fatality count was low, only five deaths. In countries which do not have our strict, and much grumbled about, building safety codes, hundreds die in lesser quakes.

Reporters and TV men came from all over to take pictures. They said they were amazed at how people were helping each other, "It couldn't happen in New York." A photographer, pausing by the highway on our ranch boundary, just south of Wilson Gulch to take pictures of the scenery, found himself in the earthquake. He turned his camera to the crumbling cliffs with their dust clouds. His pictures are in the May 1990 issue of *National Geographic* magazine.

At the ranch, damage was slight; the worst was in the nature center courtyard, where a sidewalk had sunk about three inches, leaving a crack in the basement wall where rainwater could flow into the basement. The greatest effect in the valley was on the springs. For a few days their out-flow was very much above normal and then, for several weeks, there was little or no water. Eventually they were back to normal. A forest ranger, watching Berry Falls, saw such an increase in flow shortly before the earthquake that, frightened, he went back along the trail—where he was when the quake occurred.

"Hulda's World" and Other Enterprises, 1989–

In 1989, the biography of my grandmother, *Hulda's World: A Chronicle of Hulda Minthorn Hoover, 1844–1884,* was published. It was a great satisfaction to me that this fine woman's life had been extricated from the ephemeral stuff of memory and scattered records. For years I had researched her life in letters and records to add to the stories Daddy and Great-aunt Ann had told me. Now it was written down, published, and appreciated.

Like my shorter biography *Uncle Bert,* published twenty-five years before, it had been an absorbing joy to research and write.

While working on it, I had gone back to live in the 1800s. I went with the Quaker family on their long covered wagon trip from the Toronto wilderness to the pioneer Iowa village of West Branch. I had seen, with them, the shivering, hungry escaped slaves in their snowy camp in Canada; shared Hulda's frowned-upon love of pretty clothes; delighted with her vibrant use of talents as a "gifted girl"; felt her happiness with her gentle, fun-loving young husband; suffered with her terror of the choking croup death of her baby Bert and unbelieving joy when her brother, Dr. John Minthorn, breathed life back into him; traveled with her on trips, using her eloquent gift to preach personal integrity and God's love at nearby Quaker meetings. My heart went out to her valiant struggle as a young widowed mother and her despair over the future of her small children when she faced her own death. They, my father Tad, his younger brother Bert, and little sister May, were separated into foster care.

From the sublime to the ridiculous—my drive to create produced not only the serious stuff of this and other books, my paintings, and the talks I gave, but also silly things, like hundreds of pocket bears, small teddy bears, cut from flannelette, stuffed, and with embroidered faces. They were chewed by innumerable babies and they always looked out from the top of our little boys' Christmas stockings. They were donated to countless charitable bazaars. Stuffing them was the evening occupation of many a houseguest. Small, lovable, washable, each added a minute speck of happiness to the world. Not only teddy bears, but other things from time to time, green frog bean bags, doll clothes, utility patchwork quilts, rag dolls, and a big crocheted coverlet. I remember Daddy, sitting by the fire at his desk in the Casa library, concentrated on using a pencil to force stuffing into the long thin legs and arms of my rag dolls. There were potholders by the dozen. All were happy minutiae to please my mind and hands.

End of the Century, 1990s

The 1990s were full of activities, some important, some trivial, but fun. I volunteered at the nature and history center at whatever job I could do: helped with programs and exhibits; did a couple of watercolor workshops of ranch landscapes; coordinated the volunteer program at the ranger station; and served on the board of directors of the Waddell Creek Association.

As a money-raising project of Native Daughters, I wrote a short history of Santa Cruz County and also wrote for them a pamphlet *California Under Six Flags*. I did some TV programs on local history but did not watch them because I don't like the way I look in photographs, specially in the ones people say "look just like you."

Often, weekends were spent in a twenty-foot trailer Rob had found for me. It was well designed and comfortable. We parked it under trees at the edge of the Brown House field and attached Green Cottage water and electricity. Tooke painted it green so that it blended into the bushes and was practically invisible. It was a lovely vista point to watch deer and rabbits, bobcats and foxes, they seemed unaware of me. In late spring the meadow in front of the trailer was a glory of gold poppies. But when the meadow was ploughed up and fenced for farming, the animals were no longer there and no wildflowers bloomed. My enthusiasm for trailer weekends ended. However, the trailer was valuable as a guest house to replace, inadequately, the Casita and its guest facilities. Friends enjoyed it, and Cheri could use it as a guest room when she had need for it.

Our Walnut Avenue home has had its own collection of interesting wildlife: skunks lived in the basement; a raccoon occasionally annoyed the skunks; squirrels enjoyed Allan's bird feeders; finches and doves nested in the palm tree; jays called in the apple trees; mockingbirds sang from a telephone pole; fritillary butterflies visited the passion vine; swallowtails, monarchs, and cabbage whites danced in the garden; and there was the surprising purple and yellow parrot who sat on Allan's windowsill, screeching at dawn.

Allan cooked Sunday evening dinners, the only meal we shared; I did very little cooking. Sometimes I made odds and ends, jam from lovely tiny yellow plums which paved our driveway in autumn, fallen from a neighbor's tree until she cut it down, meringues for potlucks and bake sales, and persimmon cookies which kept well in the freezer. Looking for a persimmon source one day I found a tree in a vacant lot. The problem was that all the fruit had frozen solid in a recent cold snap and now were thawing into gooshy messes. One fell on my head. Splat.

Three times a week in Santa Cruz, I went dutifully to boring, nuisancy exercise class which kept my stiffening muscles functioning after I moved from the ranch, where hard work had been sufficient exercise. In odd hours I entertained myself by creating things of trivial importance. A pleasant occupation was making baskets, large and small, of natural materials, pine needles, willow, reeds, palm fiber, redwood twigs, wisteria stems, ivy, grass. They were decorative and useful. I taught Myra Saylor the craft and she made baskets much more beautiful than mine.

I traveled to Seattle by Amtrak to visit Mally a few times—train travel avoided the airplanes I detested. Amtrak was a comfortable overnight coach trip. Train food was fast-food type, so I usually took my own— peanut butter sandwiches and grapes. One night I awoke when a small Mexican child cuddled in my lap and went to sleep. In the morning she rejoined her mother's brood a few seats behind me.

There were three other trips in 1990. In February, a short trip with Mally, Ed and Margaret Koch, and Lupita up the Mississippi on the *Delta Queen*. Pre–Mardi Gras days in New Orleans and then up the river, tying to trees along the riverbank if we wanted to go exploring. Good service and fun. The captain and the crew loved their ship so much they made us love it, too. Lupita and I, in bunny costumes (I'd brought along two rabbit masks and two rabbit-colored tunics and we borrowed large carrots from the galley), won first prize at the costume ball, a bottle of champagne which we didn't want so we gave it to the room steward. This modest, uneventful trip was one of the most delightful I have ever been on.

In May, Tooke and I went to a Hoover family house party at Rapidan Camp in the Adirondacks. It was the vacation camp Uncle Bert had built while he was president, then gave it to Shenandoah National Park. The Hoover Library Association surprised me by having published, in a handsome pamphlet, a collection of Herbert Hoover's quotes I had gleaned from his writings. Tooke and Peggy Ann, who had last seen each other as very small children, enjoyed meeting again—Peggy Ann Brigham—delightful lady, Quaker, community leader, dowser.

Dowsing had been a talent prominent in ancestral Hoovers. Daddy said he had seen it done many times but still didn't believe it. Chuck and I, amazed, tried it and, with brass dowsing rods, solved the puzzle of the Farmhouse complicated pipeline locations. Our friends didn't believe us, so we gave them the brass rods and turned them loose in the field by the house where they, to their surprise, could follow the underground pipeline's meandering course as we had done. Explanation?

There is the Hoover Ranch Property Owners Association. It was formed by my children and Mindy's as a method of cooperation in managing the 900+ acres of the ranch still in family ownership. Rob was elected President; Ted Willis, Treasurer; Anne Briggs, Assistant Treasurer; and Bob Briggs, Secretary. The meetings have been interesting, efficient, and socially enjoyable.

In 1995, Thomas Leavitt, cousin Van Ness's grandson, came to stay with us in our little back bunkroom with the furnace and washing machine.

He attended Cabrillo College and wrote a book about computers and then made a fine career in the computer world. Profitable and fascinating but, to me, totally befuddling. His living arrangement graduated to more elegant quarters and our bunkroom became again a refuge for others needing temporary lodgings.

Cousin Van Ness died in 1992, cousin Herbert had died in 1964 and Louise in 1985, cousin Allan in 1993 and Mindy in 1995. That left me alone of the six Hoover cousins. So many memories, now unsharable.

Life Is Full of Mysteries

Einstein said, "The most beautiful things we can experience are mysterious. Even small mysteries are interesting." Life is full of them. Dreams?

What are dreams made of? Life? Where does it come from; where does it go? Love? What is it? And then there are the small everyday mysteries, like "What on earth happened to my keys?"

In my life, there have been four specially puzzling occurrences, mysteries for which I've never figured out explanations: the blue light, UFOs, voices, and a restored vision pattern.

The Blue Light. On February 19, 1945, in a letter to Chuck's mother, I wrote about it. "The most intriguing event of the week was a flame that came up the valley and went out in a puff of smoke on the terrace by the house. Had the invasion of the Pacific Coast that Tokyo radio announced happened?

"Peggy Crowell, Allan, and Rob were standing by the Casa front gate. Peggy glanced at Robbie and saw him with his mouth open and his eyes popping, so she looked for what he was seeing—a blue light coming above the road, traveling fairly slowly. In a straight line it cut across the corner of the field by the gate, went over the fence and went out in smoke above the pergola.

"Peg brought her flowers into the house, and when I came down to get dinner started a few minutes later, asked me if those things often happened down here. We told Chuck and Daddy and we all went out and looked around, but there wasn't anything to see. Daddy phoned the sheriff's office to report 'an unusual occurrence' such as we had been asked to do. (We are told there is submarine activity along the coast.) Soon an FBI agent called and interviewed Peg. He said he'd be down the next day, but he didn't come. I was looking forward to hearing him interview Robbie, because by that time Robbie's story involved blue sparks and a whistling noise."

Now, in 1999, Rob has no memory of this adventure when he was six, and Peggy Crowell, at eighty-six, doesn't remember it either. But Allan, who was ten, remembers it. He adds that it was at Icebox Corner, about an eighth of a mile away, when first seen, that it came slowly, that it was a very bright greenish-blue with a paler nimbus, and that we searched unsuccessfully for residue where it had vanished in a puff of smoke.

Perhaps Robbie's elaborations were not, after all, as imaginary as his purple monsters in the garden. Or were they?

UFOs? On March 21, 1977, at about 7:30, just after dark, I was driving home from Santa Cruz to the ranch. I saw UFOs. They were certainly flying objects and they were, and remained, unidentified. There were six unusual looking yellow lights, about the brightness of airplane lights at night, until I realized that they were too near to be an airplane, flying low over the sprout fields. They were in formation and could have been six separate objects or one large, somewhat diamond-shaped object. I was near Yellowbank, where the road was narrow, so I could not stop because of passing cars. I watched the lights as they came toward me and passed me, and then were reflected in my rear mirror. I wondered why other traffic had not stopped to look.

During the next couple of days, newspapers reported several sightings of these UFOs from here to Los Angeles.

Tooke said they were probably whales flying south with torches in their mouths.

Voices. Every once in a while one reads a news story about a psychopathic murderer whose crime was committed because "voices" told him to do it. It's hard to see why anyone would give credence to these "voices," but I understood the concern of the person hearing them.

For more than twenty years, "voices" in my head had been a nuisance to me. Allan suggested that I might be sensitive to radio waves or something, perhaps the same as caused the shudders I always felt when passing one perfectly ordinary-looking house downtown. Other people thought that I must be nuts. Probably right. I decided it was some kind of short circuit in my brain. Life is full of little mysteries.

The phenomenon was something like hearing a sentence or two of one side of a conversation on a crossed telephone line (which sometimes happened on our early ranch lines). Sometimes the voices came frequently and sometimes not for several weeks. It happened when my mind was coasting on neutral—perhaps when sewing or painting or washing dishes. At first I paid attention and tried to make some sense out of it. But because the voices never said anything interesting, I mostly ignored them. They were like harmless buzzing bees.

They came in varied tones and accents. For a while I noted them down to try to find a pattern. A teenage boy's voice, "If yuh want a flashlight I'll get it, but I'm not gonna start any more for yuh." An English woman's voice, "He said he would come this afternoon. It will be difficult." A young woman, "I will like to see the L series." A comforting male southern drawl, "Honey, it's goin' to be all right." Some others were "I tried to go back but didn't have time." "Don't forget to tell Annie about it": "What will this phase do?"

One day, not long ago, I realized that I had heard none for a long time.

Restored Vision Pattern. As I aged, I developed macular degeneration in both eyes, a nuisance, not a disaster. On squared paper that the oculist gave me for the purpose, I outlined the missing area from vision in each eye, small jagged holes in the middle of my focus. For instance, if I focussed on an ornament on the mantelpiece it vanished, or the tip of a tree disappeared. The most annoying thing was that, at a certain distance, people had no faces. Fortunately, I found that if I looked slightly to the side, everything turned up again. After months of periodically drawing outlines of lost vision, I saw that there was no change and stopped bothering.

It was another couple of years when I realized that people in the distance had faces again. I checked with the squares of paper. There was still a small blank space in my left eye's vision but there were no squares missing when I looked with my right eye, or both eyes at once. Because we only need one eye to see an object, my right eye was filling in the blank. I told the oculist about this happy development but he dismissed it with "That's impossible." Mystery.

Genealogy

McLean Clan. From the time Chuck and I were married, I had worked on McLean genealogy, talked to the older members of the family, asking them what they knew of previous generations. Not very much. It made me realize that Daddy's family interest was not universal.

My questions surprised the McLeans. However, they gave me clues, remembering what Uncle Angus had once told them, or that Aunt Fan had mentioned Prince Edward and a McLean. Clues, researched, let me trace Chuck's family back to their Highland clans: McLean, Macdonald, McKinnon, MacKenzie, McLeod, MacPherson, MacRae, until I lost them in unwritten clan histories and myths.

It was fascinating to learn that the Spanish Armada had been destroyed by our McLean witches making spells on Ben Mor. I was appalled to discover the savagery of Highland barbarians long after the rest of Scotland and the British Isles were civilized.

In contrast Chuck's maternal ancestors, the Robertson's, were Lowlanders, gentle and civilized with more traceable histories.

All this I wrote down in 1971 and brought up to date and expanded as additional information accumulated. The ninety-six-page, mimeographed (there were no computers or copiers then) "History and Gene-alogy of One Branch of Clan McLean," illustrated with photo-graphs, pleased Chuck's relatives. Several became interested in genealogy and continued to expand our knowledge of family forebears and descendants.

Hoover Family. Ever since I can remember, our family history has fasci-nated me. Who were my forebears? What were they like? Why did they en-dure the fearsome hardships of the voyage to the New World in the 1700s? What were they doing during the American Revolution? What was it like to be in the waves of covered wagons on their trek westward? How did the Civil War affect them? Who am I?

Daddy had worked on family history since he was a boy. Perhaps, being an orphan, a sense of family was magnified in him. He had asked his great-grandmother, Rebecca Hoover, who lived near the farm where he labored, about family stories. When Uncle Bert was elected president, a flood of letters came, giving and asking family connections. Daddy worked out a family tree that became part of his "Memoranda." By 1946, he was tired of coping with the continually increasing information and the letters he kept on receiving. So he handed them over to me. Uncle Bert, too, sent me the information and letters he received. What a mass of stuff.

All this belonged as public information for researchers and genealogy libraries. I worked very hard for years to get it into publishable form. In 1967, the first edition of my 485-page *Genealogy of the Herbert Hoover Family* was published by the Hoover Library at Stanford University.

It is a fact of life that, when compiling family trees, people who don't answer the letters asking for information complain when they are left out of the result. Other people, who didn't know that a family history was being compiled, come out of the woodwork when it's published. As new information came in, I added it to my copy of the 1967 publication. In the course of time, it became obvious that a new edition was needed. The Herbert Hoover Presidential Library Association, in West Branch, Iowa, agreed to do this. The 1997 edition was much improved over the 1967 one, but not as handsome a volume.

While researching the Hoover family genealogy, many family stories turned up. Some of the documented ones were included in the book, but most were not definite enough to be suited to this publication. Gathering them together in 1970 and showing our relationship to the development of our country was an interesting project. The result wasn't published, but copies were made and given to family members who were interested.

The Other Ranch Residents

In all the years we have been in the Waddell Valley, we have tried to keep it safe and comfortable for the other resident animals, birds, reptiles, and all wildlife. Our family, our friends, and, now, the park people find special pleasure in them and responsibility for them. We owe them our protection and concern. In spite of our efforts and sometime, sadly, because of them, there have been changes. There are residents now that were not here when we came, and some of the original inhabitants are gone.

For instance, we seldom see a rattlesnake, to my regret but not to most people's. They used to be on the trails and in fields and gardens. When one was seen, it was killed—not by me. If I saw one, I caught him in a butterfly net and moved him far away. Yes, they are poisonous, but they are timid, and we never heard of anyone in the area being bitten. The snakes at the ranch always tried to get away from people: they were not the vicious rattlesnakes of the desert. Badgers, too, are gone, poisoned at the same time the ground squirrels were eliminated. "An unplanned effect of planning." The number of steelhead and salmon are reduced, possibly the effect of fishing boats that crowd the bay when the fish are here. But a few still escape up the creek each winter to spawn.

Alders by Waddell Creek
Watercolor by Hulda

Waddell Beach
Watercolor by Hulda

Little white and spotted harbor seals still visit the low rocks of Buena Point, and California sea lions ride the waves. New since our early days are elephant seals. At that time they were believed to be extinct. Now thousands of them overrun Point Año Nueva. One occasionally comes to bask on Waddell Beach, a welcome guest as long as too many don't come with their stinky habits. Other newcomers, most unwelcome, are feral pigs, a mixture of wild boars imported as game animals and domestic pigs. Herds of them now plow up the meadows, root out and eat wild-flower bulbs and roots, and pollute the creek. There are also unwelcome raven intruders, destructive of other birds.

There are more mountain lions than there were in the years they were bounty-hunted. There are more people, too, resulting in more sightings, several a year when there used to be years between encounters. Mountain lions are among the shyest and most cautious of animals. People who catch a glimpse of one should consider themselves blessed.

The bobcat population seems to have remained about the same. We frequently see them in the meadows watching at gopher holes or looking for mice. Each bobcat has his own territory. I know of four, one around the nature center, one around the ranger station (he sometimes sits in the road or on the fence watching us), one around Dave Willis's house, and one by the Green Cottage, where his interest is the chicken yard.

Coyote and raccoon populations go in cycles. For a few years we hear coyote concerts at night, and then there may be month after month when one is neither heard nor seen. For years there will be raccoon tracks on every dusty road, and campers complain of their thefts. "Just be glad they are not bear-sized," I tell them. Then there are no tracks nor thefts for a number of years. We are told that the explanation is outbreaks of distemper.

Brush rabbits too are cyclic; when numerous, they seem to cause a red-tailed hawk population explosion, also. As we drive the ranch roads at dawn, there is a constant scurrying into the bushes. And then there come years when we see only one or two rabbits as we drive along.

Possums, skunks, squirrels, foxes (fortunately no invasive red foxes yet, as far as I can tell) are seen occasionally, as always. Chipmunks I see very seldom. Perhaps I am looking in the wrong places. Squirrels still scurry across the road and up into the trees.

Deer are plentiful everywhere, too plentiful. When food gets scarce in the woods, they invade the fields and gardens. Hunting is impractical because of the many people now living at the ranch. Although they are the staple food of mountain lions, there are not enough lions to solve the problem.

Turtles, frogs, bats, lizards, and garter snakes, are seen as always, not often in sight, but met if you are in their territory. I could find one if I looked for him. In addition, there are other friends, mice and voles, gophers, moles and weasels, none of these can be summoned at will. There are birds, lots and lots of birds, the Good Creator's delight for our eyes and ears.

Probably more than anything else that I miss, now that I am not living on the ranch, is contact with its other residents. But I take pleasure in knowing that they are there and that all is well, I hope.

Awards, 1990s

A puzzling development in the late 1990s, when I was in my eighties and nineties, was recognition I received from several sources—now, when I was not doing anything significant! I would have appreciated a bit of this encouragement in the years when I was trying to save the world, or at least improve Santa Cruz.

In 1995 *Who's Who of American Women* decided to list me again; I had been listed when I was on the board of supervisors in the 1950s. In 1999 they listed me in the more prestigious *Who's Who in America.* Puzzling.

In 1997, the Santa Cruz Chamber of Commerce named me "Woman of the Year." This was more than a little ironic, not only because I had not done anything of note recently, but because, when I was doing something important, the chamber was opposed to most of my projects. However, I realized that the current members probably have no memory of all this and that the University of California official who had nominated me knew mainly of my work helping to establish the university here and of promoting its scholarship program. The chamber of commerce awards dinner was impressive. My sons surprised me by being there, and Soroptimists had a table of members. University Chancellor Marcy Greenwood gave an embarrassingly laudatory introduction.

In 1998, Soroptimists named me their "Woman of Distinction," an honor I deeply appreciated because it was given by women who know me and it was not only for what I have done, but for the person I am.

In 1998, too, the Santa Cruz County Republican Central Committee honored me, sensibly saying it was for "long-time service." This was also ironic because the central committee has consistently opposed my election or appointment to office. The chairman of the central committee phoned me. "Hulda, are you planning to come to the central committee annual barbecue?" Well, no, I was not enamored of the current activities of the Republican Party, almost as distressing as those of the Democratic Party. She continued, "You have to be there because we are going to honor you for your years of service to the party and your community service." How nice! How crazy! All I had done recently was complain about the party platform putting abortion into politics where it has no place. "I feel honored," I said, "I'll be there."

There was a good barbecue dinner at the country club and then several candidates made long speeches which drew restrained applause. I was introduced in a speech which I enjoyed because it wasn't about me but a lot about the good things Uncle Bert had done for the world. They presented me with a plaque, framed suitably for hanging in what Mally calls my "Ego Alley" and a huge bouquet of four dozen roses. I made a brief speech saying that I always had been a Republican and probably always would be, but that I wished our present party leaders would act less like politicians and more like statesmen [cheers] and that they would have the vision and courage to lead our party back to our basic principles: less intrusive government, local control, and individual responsibility. The audience got to their feet and cheered, either for the speech or because it had been short and now they could go home. I hoped that the candidates present had listened to what I had said.

The *Santa Cruz Sentinel* listed me as one of the twenty-five individuals who had been most influential in Santa Cruz County in this century. This was startling; if I had made up such a list, I would not have been on it.

In these years, there was also a spate of feature articles and television programs about me. When I expressed puzzlement about why, Margaret Koch guessed that it was probably because in my nineties I was still alive and upright. At any rate, there were articles in the *Santa Cruz Sentinel, San Jose Mercury, Stanford Alumni Magazine,* and several weeklies, most of them with numerous errors. I had asked reporters for Heaven's sake to read to me what they write about me so that errors can be corrected. No luck.

7
Summing Up

Change, 1906–1999

"THE ONLY CONSTANT IN LIFE IS CHANGE." The world in these past ten decades has changed more than at any other period in human history, a trend which appears to be accelerating to a dizzying degree.

My early memories of London are of cobbled streets, gas streetlights, horse-drawn vehicles, thick London fog (we'd call it smog today), and soot from thousands of coal fires that were our only heat. Middle-class households included five or more servants but probably no telephone and certainly no car. By the time we went to Palo Alto in 1917, most families had telephones and cars, but few servants.

Take a moment to imagine what life was like then, lacking so many things we now take for granted:

In medicine there were no antibiotics or vaccine for polio, flu, or children's diseases. In households there were no washers, dryers, or refrigerators (there were iceboxes serviced by dripping icemen), electric stoves (and few gas stoves), microwaves, mixers, percolators, garbage disposals, vacuum cleaners, electric blankets. Ants, fleas, bedbugs, and mosquitoes led insecticide-free lives. Grocery stores carried no frozen food or bake mixes and had only a limited variety of canned goods. There was little style choice in ready-to-wear (a dressmaker came for a week's work now and then to make our dresses), no permanent press or synthetic fabrics, no nylon or panty hose, no blue jeans. There was no plastic except a little celluloid, mostly for combs. No plastic toys, no Barbie dolls—most of us had Kewpie doll families. There were no fast-food places and no carry-out food, no pizza or Coke, or Chinese food except in Chinatown. There was no radio or TV. There were windup phonographs. In an office there was no computer or copier, just manual typewriters and carbon paper. I remember struggling to make ten copies of a report with carbon and onion-skin paper. One heard of airplanes, but we never saw one and certainly never dreamed of scheduled flights.

Most women did not work. Taking care of a house, husband, children, servants, garden, and the cultural life of the family without labor-saving appliances was not considered "work." Spinsters usually lived with married relatives. If a woman had a job, it was in teaching, nursing, or office work. No woman left home without a hat and gloves. "A lady puts on her gloves *before* she leaves the house," said Mummie. Little girls wore dresses and little boys wore knee pants until they graduated to long trousers in their teens.

Alcohol was then as much of a problem as it is now, but there were no other drug problems among our young people and few drug-induced crimes of theft or passion.

Modern life happened so gradually I didn't notice the nature of change until I suddenly looked around and thought back to our lives a few years previously. Now it seems a hardship to be without a car, phone, television, and all the other taken-for-granted luxuries. Back then we had no idea of our pitiful deprived existence. Life had joy, meaning, and comfort. What more does one need?

Nothing has brought more change to the world than computers, the offspring of Bill Shockley's invention of the transistor. Television is an agency of accelerating change that is not sufficiently recognized. It is much more than an entertainment marvel; it affects our national character. As an educational medium, it brings us an awareness of the whole world's news; it brings nature into our living rooms (until the cast begin to eat each other and I turn it off); it gives us global travel and shows us the problems of our despoiled planet and suffering humanity. As a stimulative of imagination, there is technically astounding fantasy, such as the philosophically based adventures of the *Star Trek* series and the gentle *Bewitched*. As food for the soul, there is music, ballet, and drama.

But TV has a dreadful downside. Its time slots are overwhelmingly taken over by programs of explosive violence and irresponsible sexual activity. By the time a TV-watching child is in his teens, he has seen thousands of such scenes. He has been given the message that these are common and accepted solutions to life's problems. TV's violent message, combined with other media assaults, the easy availability of drugs and weapons, and the disarray of our historic code of sound character values can result in lifestyles too often gruesomely evident in the evening news. Our young people are growing up in a chaotic and dangerous world.

All this does not bode well for civilization. But there are even darker trends that menace the entire human race. One is the explosion of world population, using up irreplaceable resources and poisoning the planet. The other is our humanitarian reversal of nature's law, "survival of the fittest." We encourage the reproduction of people with flawed genes, presaging a population weakened in mind and body. Can we find the will and the ways to save the human race? Or will planet Earth, no longer despoiled by the presence of humans, gradually regain the health of its air and water and ecosystems when *Homo sapiens* no longer exists?

Perhaps the hardest change experienced as one grows older is the loss of those we love. There is no way to light the dark loneliness left when Chuck died. Dear Soozie cannot be replaced, nor beloved Miss Pickering, cousins Allan and Van Ness, Shep Quate, and other close friends. Their loss aches just as cruelly as aching bones and the loss of youthful energy and mental agility. But, enough of that!

One morning a reporter phoned and asked me what I considered the most important development in the century and what would be the most important in the coming century. Quite weighty questions to answer before breakfast! I thought a while and gave him answers which, amazingly, he quoted accurately in the *San Jose Mercury News* of January 22, 1999.

> "The most important development of the past hundred years has been the growth of freedom, acceptance and encouragement of women to use their capabilities in fields of their choice. This has happened only in the Western countries. The twenty-first century should bring about worldwide opportunities for education, income security and public acceptance that will make possible the utilization of women's largely untapped potential. Women comprise half the human race. Release of their abilities would accelerate the discovery of marvels in medicine, science, technology and other fields as yet undreamed of."

I didn't want to confuse the reporter with elaboration of this statement. However, it seems to me that, if women truly had partner status in humankind and a full role in major decisions, there would be tremendous changes caused by the combination of male and female approaches to problem-solving. There appears to be a male hormonal imperative to action and violence, just as there is a female hormonal imperative to nurturing and conciliation. If these characteristics were to work together, we might make great strides towards world peace, justice, and human survival.

Hereafter

I often think of the old joke: a pastor was visiting an elderly parishioner and asked "Mary, do you give thought to the hereafter?" "Oh yes, constantly." she replied, "When I go upstairs, or to my desk, or open the refrigerator door, I say to myself, 'I wonder what I'm here after.'"

Immortality, God, and the purpose of life are mysteries for which mankind has sought answers from before history. Some people say they know the answers. I envy them their faith.

Worship of trees and mountains appears to have been the earliest religion. The belief that storms were God's wrath and that sacrifices would appease them seems to have appeared a bit later. Into the Jewish worship of Jehovah, Jesus brought the message of a God of love. Christianity, in the Middle Ages and the Renaissance evolved into a pageantry of Heaven and Hell, the devil and angels, which inspired music and art and nourished the human soul for generations. But it does not satisfy our present era of logic and science, nor do the other world religions. It is hard to reconcile the concept of the Christian omnipotent, compassionate God with the reality of the Holocaust or natural disasters of flood, fire, and famine.

Reincarnation is a tempting idea, but what profit is it if memory is each time lost? Another explanation is that we are players in a cosmic struggle between the forces of Good and Evil, that, after life, the good that we have created increases the strength of the forces of good, and that the evil we have done strengthens the power of darkness. How do we create good or evil? By the development of our characters, for there is nothing else we can make that is not merely moving around already existing mass and energy. Is this the purpose of life—that we develop virtue? There is the flavor of logic to this idea, but not a smidgen of evidence.

Perhaps our purpose in life is a role in evolving the human race. Into what? Pierre Teilhard de Chardin, the Jesuit anthropologist, wrote (and was forbidden to publish) that man is evolving into a spiritual being. An encouraging thought, but slowly, slowly, slowly. Stephen Leacock, the humorist and economist from whom we took classes at McGill University, told us that the only improvement in the history of the human race that he had discerned is that cruelty is no longer an approved form of public entertainment. No more Christians thrown to lions in the Coliseum, or

242

gladiators fighting to the death, or public hangings as social events. However, every issue of a newspaper tells of instances of man's inhumanity to man. We still have a long, long way to go.

The only scenario which satisfies science and logic is that when the flame of life is out, it is snuffed with the finality of a vanished flame. But that does not satisfy our innate feeling that there must be something more. We instinctively protest such finality. We crave immortality, God, and a purpose for life. Is there no validity to this imperative craving of the human heart? Is there not evidence of an intelligent designer in the working of the universe, in its precision of beauty? What devised the mathematical glory of a shell, a flower, a crystal? Is there universal intelligence so much greater than human as to be unimaginable? What does a mayfly know of building a castle? What do I know of designing a universe? Questions. But no answers.

Evidently human intelligence is not capable of understanding these mysteries. As the poet Omar Khayyam wrote of his search for answers: ". . . and heard great argument . . . but evermore came out by the same door where in I went."

If there is an afterlife, it probably won't be very long before I'll know. In the meantime, as long as I'm alive, I want to live and enjoy the beauties and opportunities, fun and humor, of life.

The United States

In our travels, Chuck and I visited many countries: Mexico, Guatemala, Belize, Costa Rica, Panama, the Caribbean islands, Canada, England, Scotland, France, Holland, Belgium, Italy, Greece, Turkey, Egypt, Russia, Japan, India, Korea, China, Thailand, Indonesia, Malaya, Bali, Tahiti, Hawaii, the Philippines, Australia, New Zealand. We were in many magnificent places and a few horrible ones. It is an amazing and glorious world.

People, everywhere, are fascinating. We made friends as we went along. Human nature is basically the same worldwide. However, in some places there seemed to us to be a characteristic attitude, colored by circumstances. There was an aura of fear in Korea, self-approval in Canada, art expression in Japan, suspicion in China, danger in Thailand, gentle friendliness in Bali, hostility in Tahiti, truculence in Russia, pride in New Zealand, violence in Panama. However, as generalizations, these observations can be only partly true.

Travel brings one a treasure of memories, scenes, happenings, and people. It brings a better understanding of the history of civilization, an appreciation of the vastness of the world, the peoples, their accomplishments and problems. Perhaps the most surprising result is a greatly increased appreciation of our own country, the United States of America. Almost all the countries we visited had some of the same blessings we have, but we did not see any other country that had them all. None had a combination of our freedoms, opportunities, and standard of comfortable living.

Our America is far from perfect. There is much here to be deplored, as evident in the crime, tragedy, and corruption reported daily in our newspapers. But nowhere else in the world did we see all the blessings we enjoy: our right to stand up for what we believe and to say what we want to say, to vote as we wish, to enjoy opportunities open to everyone for education and career choices. Few countries show the public and private concern we do for those around us who are suffering from illness, poverty, or injustice.

Our government and justice system, flawed as they are, are shining examples compared to those in most of the world. Our public offices are not riddled with bribery as are those in many countries. Our education system, open to everyone, may not measure up to the best of the best, but it shines in comparison to most, as does our health care, housing, highway system and streets, telephone and postal systems, protections of our water supply, our farming methods, sewer and waste disposal. Perhaps most obvious of all to a world traveler are the cleanliness standards of our people and cities, roadsides, and public buildings in comparison with the grime in most countries.

It hurts me when I see our flag desecrated. I deplore the ignorant rage of participants in flag-burning and empty demonstrations against our government's imperfections. I could wish that the participants visit other parts of the world to find out the value of this country, but I would advise them to be careful while out there not to burn any flags or they may find themselves in abysmal prisons or the victims of court systems sometimes reminiscent of the Dark Ages. The best protest is still the ballot box. In spite of the inadequacy of one vote, it is not difficult, with knowledge and determination, to influence many, and perhaps a critical number, of votes. That is the way Democracy progresses.

Our form of government, a Democratic Republic, is inefficient and slow, but no better form has been invented. Our economic system, capitalism combined with socialism, is unwieldy and prone to abuse, but it has brought us a high standard of living, world trade dominance, and the invention of most of the world's technical marvels.

Actually, our government is a Bureaucracy. This has its good and bad points. On the downside it is costly and inefficient. Its proliferation of regulations is a burden on the public. Entrenchment of inept idiocy is exasperating to everyone. However, it has its advantages. It is dependable. It is, generally, protected against political pressures so that greedy or incompetent public officials cannot use it to gain power. Nor can they fundamentally change it. The other side of this coin is that an outstandingly capable elected official can do little to improve it.

My optimism falters a mite when I see the direction of so many government, social, and economic trends. In each of these arenas, the tenets of democracy are being violated: in government, by the proliferation of bureaucratic empire builders and the fact that elections are decided by multi-million dollar campaigns; in economics, by technology's effect of reducing the market for low-skilled labor, by huge conglomerates' control of world trade, and by the worldwide acceleration of inflation; in society, by the tensions between persons of different lifestyles and races, the willing dependence on tax subsidy by many who could be productive and self-reliant, by the epidemic of harmful drug use. In ethical values, I worry about the low standard of public entertainment and the public trivialization of the distinction between right and wrong, loyalty, truth, and honor.

Then I remember that blemishes and faults show up much more conspicuously than do virtues. Our government is full of competent, honorable, hard-working men and women doing the day-by-day jobs of running the country. Our economy and comfort-in-living standards rise decade by decade. There is a vast, unpublicized majority of us living upright lives, teaching our children good values and an understanding of their responsibilities.

I think of what Uncle Bert once said to me: "Truth, like cream, always rises to the top." So, although I see difficult times ahead, I have hope that the basic honesty, abilities, and strengths of our intelligent citizenry will find ways to solve the nation's most threatening problems so that it may maintain its blessings and pass a legacy of honorable strength to future generations.

Happiness

What are the foundation principles of a good life? Love and Integrity above all. How can one live by these principles? By following the guidance of enlightened conscience, or what the Quakers recognize as God's voice within you, "the Inner Light."

Love and Integrity. Simple words with infinite depth of meaning. "Integrity" encompasses a wide spectrum of virtues, including honesty, courage, fairness, grace, and intrinsic worth. "Love" has many facets, perhaps best expressed by the Greeks. They had four words for love. One was for romantic love and passion. Another was for the love between parent and child, brother and sister. Another was for the affection between friends. The last was for compassion and love of mankind.

Human nature is a tangle of virtues and flaws; talent, ambition, lethargy, generosity, and (quoting the king in *Anna and the King of Siam*) "etcetera, etcetera, etcetera." All we can do is try to meet life's challenges and opportunities as they come, with love and integrity, guided by the inner voice which tells us what is right and what is wrong.

Where does happiness come into this? Happiness is the reward. Flashes of happiness come as blessings to light our lives. Daddy described it as "gold threads in the fabric of life." In a Stanford philosophy course it was suggested that the best recipe for happiness is "A task, a plan, and freedom."

What advice would I give for having a good life? Have fun. Or as philosopher Joseph Campbell advised, "Follow your bliss." With love and integrity, as much as circumstances allow, do what brings you joy. Following my bliss has brought me great satisfaction: using my art talents, appreciating the blessings of friendship and family, accepting opportunities to help or make something better if I can. Our forefathers declared that "the pursuit of happiness" is a God given right. Finding it is up to each of us.

Some Things I Have Learned

I'd like to think that these words of hard-won wisdom would be taken seriously and the advice followed. They probably will not be. It's a time-wasting and painful fact that we each have to learn most of the lessons of life by making our own mistakes and suffering the consequences ourselves. I also learned that, even when I knew exactly what was the right and intelligent thing to do, I didn't always do it.

Advice. People usually don't want advice, even when they ask for it. If you give it, give it in small doses. Don't give it in huge dollops as I am about to do in this chapter.

First impressions. First impressions are made on the basis of appearance, speech, and manners. It would be a good idea to always look, talk, and act as the best you want to be. One can only make a first impression once. It may last forever. It could have a real effect on your future.

It is fortunate that the impression I made on a man who came out of the woods behind the chicken coop in the rain while I was feeding the chickens had no part in my future. It was a cold rainy day and I had wrapped an old shabby robe around the outside of my clothes. A saucepan was needed for gathering eggs, and because my hands were full of chicken scraps, I'd put the saucepan on my head. While I scolded the man for trespassing, he sidled around me apprehensively and fled down the road. He was not interested in conversation with a cross, shabby lady wearing a saucepan on her head.

Do it now. If you have a necessary chore to do, don't put it off. Do it in the first available time you can make for it. Then you won't have extra hours of worrying about it and it won't interfere with a more interesting project, as it did the time I put off a book report due Monday until Sunday afternoon. My procrastination cheated me out of a spontaneously planned picnic with special friends. *Do what needs to be done, when it needs to be done.*

Kindness. Be kind always. There is already too much pain in the world—don't add to it. Be kind to everyone, whether he deserves it or not. The curt, irritating sales clerk may be suffering from a stomachache. The driver who cuts in ahead of you may be hurrying to an injured child.

"Politeness is to do and say, the kindest thing in the kindest way." Those who have no manners waste their time battling obstacles that would move aside for courtesy.

Concern. In the Quaker discipline, if you feel concerned about a person or problem, you have a responsibility to act on it. If you believe that someone is unhappy, perhaps a simple kindness will help. Someone said, "I can't do everything, but I can do something, and what I can do, I must do." Often one can't cure an ill, but one can almost always help in some way.

Ethical standards. A society's moral sense changes, but there are basic principles, ethical standards, which never change. Base your character on a personal ethical code and cling to it through life's troubles, like to a raft in a storm. Embrace moral standards in all you do. These worldwide immutable principles are worded in various ways, but however expressed, they are:

Truth, which cuts through sophistry and expediency, always, eventually, prevails.

Integrity, honorable, courageous behavior in everything.

Love for family, friends, and humanity.

Beauty, appreciation of the radiance of form, sound, and spirit.

Kindness, to everyone, including yourself.

Reverence for the universal creative force.

Worry. Don't be a perpetual worrier. Work through it. Accept worry as a notice that something is wrong. Sit down and think the situation through. If there is something consistent with your ethical code that you can do to cure or ameliorate it, do it. If not, make a plan for future action if an opportunity comes. Having done that, put your worry firmly aside so it will not sap the energy you need for happier things.

Patience. Exercise patience. Time can be on your side. Time eases pain in body, soul, and human relationships. When opportunity comes, move in the right direction. Patience is not resignation. Resignation is giving up. Patience is positive, it is waiting for constructive change. Don't give up. Be patient.

Be a good loser and a gracious winner. Life goes on after both. There were times when I lost and times when I won in my campaigns for a position on the Santa Cruz County Board of Supervisors. There is seldom a political campaign without bitterness developing somewhere. To accomplish projects and also to heal friendships, it is important that rifts be bridged. Facilitate future cooperation. Accept loss gracefully, with praise for the winner; accept winning gracefully, with praise for the loser. We are not, thankfully, very often involved in political campaigns, but the necessity for grace as a winner or loser is the same in any situation.

Do more than is expected of you. "Walk the extra mile." This is double edged advice. In any job there is something that needs doing beyond your responsibility. Do it unless it would trespass on someone else's empire. A secret of career promotion is to have the ability to see needs and to be cheerfully willing to work beyond your commitment.

In our ranch years we found that most of our workers did as little as possible, but an occasional one was anxious to be really helpful. We showed appreciation with words and wages. Mrs. Cleaves was a shining example, although she was so dedicated to neatness that I sometimes felt that she was following me around with a mop and dustpan.

Rejection, or defeat. Surely these are among the hardest lessons of life. Meet them. Stand up straight and smile. Study them. Is there any way to soften them? Is there a way to avoid them in the future? What did they teach?

Remember that adversity builds character (how I disbelieved Mummie when she told me that!) and you may need this strength and knowledge to help avert a future disaster. It will certainly give you empathy in helping someone else who is dealing with a bad situation. I know of no remedy for the hurt of defeat. It must be endured until time fades it.

Bad luck; it comes to everyone from time to time. Pause and ponder if it was in any way your fault, and if so, whether you can change or soften it. Sometimes it is only a minor annoyance. Sometimes it is a disaster. Sometimes bad luck comes because you are not paying attention to what is going on—something I neglected to do when I had a small part in a play at Stanford. My brief appearance included a line for me to say as I entered and handed a little poodle to the lead. My entrance cue came, but where was the poodle? Happily romping around the stage: that's where he was!

Philosophical acceptance is the only positive reaction. Figure out if it can be avoided in the future. Salvage what you can: "If given a lemon, make lemonade." They say that if one door closes, another door opens. That was certainly true when storms made it impossible to harvest our cabbage crop. The sun came out and the cabbages went to seed, and we found a market for the seeds.

Service. "Service is the rent we pay for our space on earth," said Elizabeth, Queen Mother of England. Service to those who need help is both the easiest and hardest road to happiness. Easy because opportunities surround us, hard because it often involves hard work and sacrifice.

Family responsibility is our foremost job, and next come career requirements. These fill our lives, but sometimes we should fit in other uses for our skills, in volunteer service to expand our horizons with new knowledge and happiness. Those who ignore opportunities for volunteer service deny themselves rich experience.

In my volunteer work in the 1930s I had great satisfaction in being able to give women who were beaten down by the economics of the Great Depression, training and opportunities and hope. At the present time I find joy, as well as exhaustion and frustration, in working as a volunteer for the parks department. Working at our Rancho del Oso State Park, in the ranger station, and in the nature center, gives me an opportunity to encourage hikers, families, and children to discover the importance of the natural world, to fall under the spell of its beauties and mysteries.

Appreciation. Show that you recognize a job well done. There is magic in a word of praise. Seize each chance to use this magic. It lightens burdens, encourages talent, rewards tenacity, restores stamina, and makes a sacrifice worthwhile. Share credit lavishly with expressed praise for those who helped your accomplishments. Compliment people; it will make their day.

More than once in my life, understanding and praise have given me resolve to continue some vital task almost beyond my strength. I am forever grateful to those who made many of my enterprises possible by their encouragement.

Help generously, accept help graciously. When you discover that help is needed, give it generously, as though it were a privilege to give it. And, truly, it is a privilege to be able to do something important for someone.

Chuck said to respond to small annoying solicitations with enthusiasm. Buy tickets, chances, Girl Scout cookies, veteran poppies, cheerfully. They are for causes worth supporting and we should encourage the effort of those doing the work. When you give, give happily.

Accept help graciously. We all want to be self-sufficient and provide for our own needs, but if our own efforts are not sufficient, accept help with gratitude. Ask for help candidly when it is necessary. This is a matter of common sense, difficult though it may be.

Avoid casual sex. Sex without commitment can be a trap for women. At its best it is risky and demeaning. At its worst it permits a man to discard responsibility without penalty, leaving his partner (and perhaps children) without support and protections. A long term uncommitted relationship can rob a woman of the ability to protect and support herself.

Common sense tethers impulse to reality. Ask, what is the sensible thing to do? What are the logical results of alternatives? In our partnership, Chuck was the one most gifted with common sense. While I would dream impossibilities, Chuck would be working sensibly, weaving possibilities into acceptable actualities.

A sense of humor. So much of life is senseless or so absurd that it helps to see humor in it. Seek the joy of laughter. Even ironic twists of fate often contain bitter humor.

Things that some people laugh at puzzle and distress me. There is nothing funny about a pie in the face or a painful pratfall. Laughing at the embarrassment or pain of another is not humor; it is cruelty. However, laughing at one's own misfortune sometimes eases the pain. Why? Again to quote the King of Siam, "It is a puzzlement."

Guilt. This is certainly the most painful of human emotions. Of course, it can be pretty much avoided if one does not do anything known to be wrong. However, human nature being what it is . . . How can one cope? Think. Is there any way to cure or ameliorate and make amends for the harm done? If so, painful as it may be, do it. Determine to marshal your strength of character so that you will not so err again. Then, forgive yourself, as you would a friend. But recognize that there will be recurring flashes of painful remorse. Sin does not go unpunished.

Forgive. To forgive one who has done you a wrong is not to condone. It is to heal. If you harbor the bitterness of unforgiving it corrodes your heart but does not harm the one who did you ill. Continued bitterness within a family or friendship is an ugly destroying force. Forgiving, difficult as it sometimes is, is the wisest, kindest and, eventually, the most rewarding path to take. Keep an open heart and forgive easily.

Hope for the best: prepare for the worst. This was the slogan printed on my composition book when I was in the third grade. It made a permanent impression on me. Be optimistic: be prepared. Look ahead and prepare for possible problems. Planning may avoid, cope with, or mitigate them. Expect sunshine but be ready for rain. Fill your life with cheerfulness which will warm you and those around you, through both happy and difficult times.

Savor the world we live in. Enjoy the riches of human achievement: our cultural heritage in music, literature, and art; the vast store of knowledge—of the universe, of countries and cultures different from ours; of the history of human development with its pains and victories; the marvels of science and technology, developments in travel, communication, medicine, and all the sciences.

Watch with fascination the parade of human behavior you see around you. Learn from it. Treasure the boon of friendship and love. Savor the natural world: the wonders of creation so much more glorious than human accomplishment; the beauty of the Creator's earth and sky and seas.

Delight in the wealth of sensory experience. Memories are made of these. The reason I remember so vividly our childhood adventure when Mally and I were lost on the mountaintop in a ceanothus thicket is the intense sensory impact of all we experienced. There was the discomfort of scratchy branches, of twigs and dry leaves down my neck, of spider webs as we crawled through tunnels in the brush, and ants wandering up my legs. Then, when we found our way out of the maze and ate our squashed peanut butter sandwiches, spiced by hunger and relief, we sat among the pines. We breathed warm scented air and lay on soft woodland duff. We listened to the distant muted roar of the ocean, a tractor in the valley, birdsong and cicadas. When we ran and slid downhill on slippery pine needles, there was the view below of fields and the road home . . . All as vivid in my memory as a taped video.

And, finally:

Keep your hands and clothes clean except when gardening.

On a highway, stay three seconds behind the car in front of you.
  (One chimpanzee, two chimpanzees, three chimpanzees)

Expect the best of people. It is better to be disappointed occasionally
  than always suspicious.

The time to hurry is *before* you leave the house.

You can choose your friends but you are stuck for life with your
  relatives. You don't have to like them all, but things will be
  much easier if you are cheerfully polite to all of them.

Donate to worthy projects and to street musicians.

Wash the dishes before you go to bed.

Save a little money every month. It may save you.

Keep away from people on drugs.

Leave things better than you found them.

Enjoy chocolate but eat your vegetables.

Diminuendo

Agnes de Mille observed that age is a continuing diminuendo. How exasperatingly true!

I can no longer hear bats high in the evening sky, nor crickets and the voices of other small things in the woods. I can no longer see little brown birds clearly enough to identify them by an eye-ring or wing-bar. I can no longer taste freshness of grass stems or violet petals. I can no longer smell a rose. These are now only cherished memories.

My legs will not take me up mountain trails, nor go upstairs two steps at a time, nor even stride blithely down the street. I move carefully, somewhat like a careful drunk. My hands lack strength and precision. There is so much I can no longer do, jobs that need doing but that I dare not undertake. Pain and exhaustion are cruel brakes on ambition. I sometimes rail in a desperation of frustration.

Once, years ago when things were difficult for us, Chuck said, "We play the hand we are given as best we can." So I look at the hand I now play and see that is not so bad after all. Life is still so full of potential that there is no point in mourning opportunities lost to time.

My eyes still see unending beauty; breathtaking sunsets, exquisite blossoms, misty mountains, ballets, the smiles of friends. There is still a symphony of sound. The problem is, to listen for it through the world's discordant clatter. I can hear the sweet chaotic chorus of red-winged blackbirds, the descending trill of a wrentit, the call of quail. I hear singing, and the laughter of a child. There is music, the murmur of the ocean, the roar of a storm.

I walk in a redwood forest and am drenched in its fragrance. I relish the faint whiff of a skunk on the evening breeze. There is the smell of a good meal cooking. There is the taste of raspberry jam, a ripe apple, and chocolate. The tartness of lemon, spice of a green bay leaf, vinegar of redwood sorrel—still a world full of flavors. There is the feel of rough bark, of sand and seaweed, the warm vibrating softness of a kitten, the coolness of spring water, the satin of a baby's skin, the smooth welcoming of bed at the end of day.

Yes, strength and energy must be dealt out carefully and wisely now. However, there is still an unending number of things that need doing that I can do. Things like making something a little easier or more fun for someone, or volunteering to help when help is needed. There are things to do that are pure fun like painting and writing, watching children at play, or idling away time with friends.

Thinking back, perhaps the problems and cacophony of youth were sometimes a bit too much. There is a pleasing gentle quality in the diminuendo of age.

The Family of Chuck and Hulda McLean

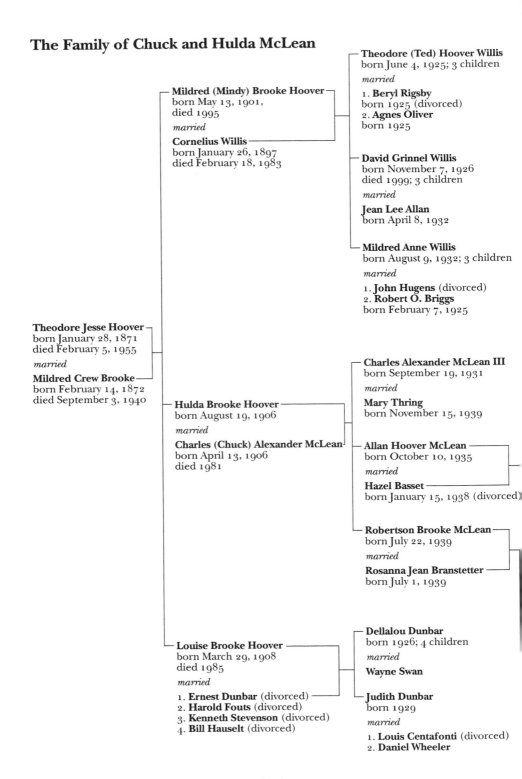

Theodore Jesse Hoover
born January 28, 1871
died February 5, 1955
married
Mildred Crew Brooke
born February 14, 1872
died September 3, 1940

Mildred (Mindy) Brooke Hoover
born May 13, 1901,
died 1995
married
Cornelius Willis
born January 26, 1897
died February 18, 1983

Theodore (Ted) Hoover Willis
born June 4, 1925; 3 children
married
1. **Beryl Rigsby**
born 1925 (divorced)
2. **Agnes Oliver**
born 1925

David Grinnel Willis
born November 7, 1926
died 1999; 3 children
married
Jean Lee Allan
born April 8, 1932

Mildred Anne Willis
born August 9, 1932; 3 children
married
1. **John Hugens** (divorced)
2. **Robert O. Briggs**
born February 7, 1925

Hulda Brooke Hoover
born August 19, 1906
married
Charles (Chuck) Alexander McLean
born April 13, 1906
died 1981

Charles Alexander McLean III
born September 19, 1931
married
Mary Thring
born November 15, 1939

Allan Hoover McLean
born October 10, 1935
married
Hazel Basset
born January 15, 1938 (divorced)

Robertson Brooke McLean
born July 22, 1939
married
Rosanna Jean Branstetter
born July 1, 1939

Louise Brooke Hoover
born March 29, 1908
died 1985
married
1. **Ernest Dunbar** (divorced)
2. **Harold Fouts** (divorced)
3. **Kenneth Stevenson** (divorced)
4. **Bill Hauselt** (divorced)

Dellalou Dunbar
born 1926; 4 children
married
Wayne Swan

Judith Dunbar
born 1929
married
1. **Louis Centafonti** (divorced)
2. **Daniel Wheeler**

254

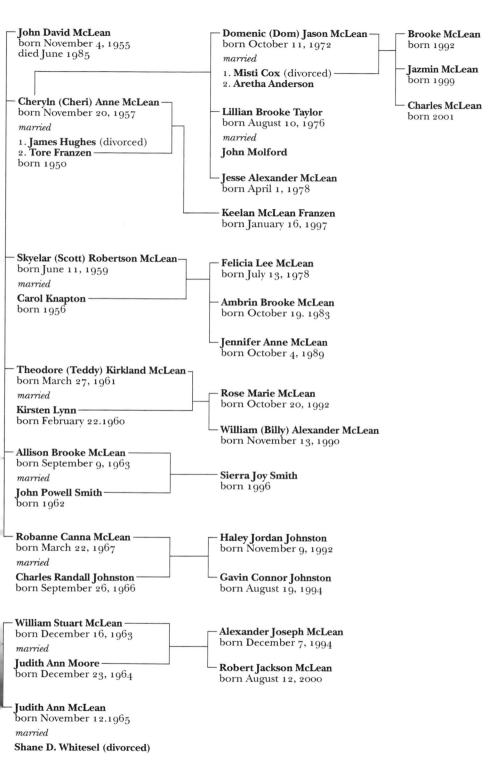

John David McLean
born November 4, 1955
died June 1985

Cheryln (Cheri) Anne McLean
born November 20, 1957
married
1. **James Hughes** (divorced)
2. **Tore Franzen**
born 1950

Domenic (Dom) Jason McLean
born October 11, 1972
married
1. **Misti Cox** (divorced)
2. **Aretha Anderson**

Brooke McLean
born 1992

Jazmin McLean
born 1999

Charles McLean
born 2001

Lillian Brooke Taylor
born August 10, 1976
married
John Molford

Jesse Alexander McLean
born April 1, 1978

Keelan McLean Franzen
born January 16, 1997

Skyelar (Scott) Robertson McLean
born June 11, 1959
married
Carol Knapton
born 1956

Felicia Lee McLean
born July 13, 1978

Ambrin Brooke McLean
born October 19. 1983

Jennifer Anne McLean
born October 4, 1989

Theodore (Teddy) Kirkland McLean
born March 27, 1961
married
Kirsten Lynn
born February 22.1960

Rose Marie McLean
born October 20, 1992

William (Billy) Alexander McLean
born November 13, 1990

Allison Brooke McLean
born September 9, 1963
married
John Powell Smith
born 1962

Sierra Joy Smith
born 1996

Robanne Canna McLean
born March 22, 1967
married
Charles Randall Johnston
born September 26, 1966

Haley Jordan Johnston
born November 9, 1992

Gavin Connor Johnston
born August 19, 1994

William Stuart McLean
born December 16, 1963
married
Judith Ann Moore
born December 23, 1964

Alexander Joseph McLean
born December 7, 1994

Robert Jackson McLean
born August 12, 2000

Judith Ann McLean
born November 12.1965
married
Shane D. Whitesel (divorced)

255